The Route 66 St. Louis Cookbook

The Mother Lode of Recipes
from the Mother Road

Wetzel's Café   Eureka, Missouri

To Sally,
Enjoy!
Norma Maret Bolin

Published by St. Louis Transitions
PO Box 191401
St. Louis, MO 63119
www.route66stlouis.com
© 2009 Norma Maret Bolin

All rights reserved. No part of this book may be reproduced in any form or by any electronic or mechanical means, including information storage or retrieval systems, without permission in writing from the publisher, except by a reviewer who may quote brief passages in review. Published 2009

Printed in the USA by A&J Printing, Nixa, Missouri
Graphic artist for book layout and cover: Joshua Hill, Slingshot Creative, Rogersville Missouri

The Route 66 St. Louis Cookbook: The Mother Lode of Recipes from the Mother Road
ISBN: 978-0-9823239-0-8
Library of Congress Control Number: 2009900828

The restaurant recipes contained herein represent a collection from many different sources, spanning many decades. While many of the recipes were professionally tested at some point along the way, others have just been passed along in their original hand written instructions or explained over the telephone. Some have never been shared before and were reduced to writing for the first time. Accordingly, there are some inconsistencies in recipe styles. The author and publisher have made every effort to ensure the accuracy of the recipes, to reconcile differences, and to pass along notes to help in the preparation and cannot be held responsible for any errors or the actual results of the recipes. This cookbook is sold without any warranty, express or implied.

Dedication

To my mother, an excellent cook and avid recipe clipper, who showed her love daily through her cooking and taught me to bake at a young age, and to my father who served the public at his grocery store for 60 years (seven long days a week), and there taught me the value of hard work.

Acknowledgments

A heartfelt thank you to all of those people who played a part in passing on vintage recipes and to the many generous restaurants and organizations that shared recipes for this cookbook. A special thank you to Janet Gillow, who first suggested I turn the recipes I had received from families into a separate cookbook, local cookbook collector Virginia Horrell, who shared some recipes, George S. Lux and Gene Kitson, who generously shared their matchcover collections, and Russell Kruetzman, who allowed me to use menus and accompanying text from his 1976 book *Gateway Gourmet*.

Foreword

Get ready to loosen your belt as you take a ride on Route 66 in search of good eats in *The Route 66 St. Louis Cookbook: The Mother Lode of Recipes from the Mother Road.* This culinary compendium of Norma Bolin's Route 66 classic restaurant recipes would, if you are on a diet, be best set aside, as the tantalizing treasures in these pages will quickly lure you into the kitchen. But, if you're ready to hit the road to some dining destinations of the past and present, grab a knife, fork and spoon, then ready yourself for an adventure in gastronomy. Proceed with caution though or you might end up like actor Sidney Greenstreet in the golden age of radio show "The New Adventures of Nero Wolfe," in which he was described as "The Gargantuan Gourmet."

In perusing these pages related to St. Louis, the biggest city between Chicago and L.A. on 66, you'd reasonably assume Norma must be a St. Louis native and has likely gone to each and every one of the more than one hundred places listed herein, but not so; she's a Texas transplant who came here in 1986 and discovered the magic of America's "Main Street." We can all tip our respective hat to Norma for her Herculean task of rounding up these recipes and highlighting history regarding their place of origin. This was no small undertaking, but it's merely a sample of her monumental book on Route 66 that she's created for near future publication. The book to be: *Route 66 St. Louis: From the Bridges to the Diamonds,* will take readers to many current as well as long ago locations of the St. Louis area's significant segment of "The Mother Road," so named by John Steinbeck in his 1939 Great Depression novel, *The Grapes of Wrath.*

If the late food connoisseur Duncan Hines were still grazing the land from restaurant to restaurant, he would most certainly give his legendary "Recommended by Duncan Hines" imprimatur to this unique collection of dishes that were at one time or another all available on or near that magical Route 66. I've dined at 72 of the 80 eateries east of 270 noted in these pages and based on the recipes provided I could come up with many a memorable meal, but here's what I've decided on for one day's dining of breakfast, lunch and dinner. I've also included a year in which you might have enjoyed these treats. This would be a day of wonderful meal memories...and it's all spelled out in the book!

Breakfast:

Harvey Girl Special-Little Thin Orange Pancakes
The Fred Harvey Restaurant at Union Station, 1948

Tropical Fruit Salad
Scruggs-Vandervoort-Barney Tea Room downtown, 1952

Lunch:

Special Salad
The Pasta House Co., 1974

Chicken Pot Pie
Forum Cafeteria. 7th Street, 1958

Chess Pie
St. Louis Art Museum Restaurant, 1959
(My mother, Mayme Elz, who managed the restaurant for many years created this recipe with a cook named Rena McClennan.)

Dinner:

Hellenic Salad
Tenderloin Room, 1962

Petto Di Pollo All'Agro Dolce (sweet and sour chicken)
Kemoll's, 1967

Austrian Cabbage
House of Maret, 1971

Cheddar Cheese and Chive Biscuits
Bevo Mill, 1966

Angel Food Cake
Hotel Beers, 1888

Late Night:

Johnny Rabbitt Chocolate Covered Cherry Concrete
Ted Drewes Frozen Custard, 2007

Author Norma Bolin's dedication, perseverance and intense research has given us a true treasure in this exceptional book as she connects us with the meanderings of Route 66 both through tried and true recipes as well as historical sketches of many of the people and places that gave Route 66 its character as the most legendary highway of America. A most interesting note is that Norma has not only devoted years to her two Route 66 book projects, but has done all of it on her own with her own money. No foundation, publisher, institution, group or individual helped in her work. She is shepherding these projects to completion because of her belief that the story of Route 66, its businesses, its people…and its recipes, deserve documentation for future generations. I feel the same, and after reading *The Route 66 St. Louis Cookbook*, I'm confident you'll agree as well. But don't just read it. Use the book to create delightful dishes and memories of Route 66.

Ron (Johnny Rabbitt) Elz
Host of Route 66 on KMOX

Preface

While writing *Route 66 St. Louis: From the Bridges to the Diamonds*, I requested and received numerous recipes from the families I interviewed. At the time, I wasn't sure if I would be able to use them but hoped to include them as an appendix. When I completed the book I had about 20 recipes, not enough to make into a separate cookbook, so I went back and contacted all of the families that were interviewed for the book. I also researched specifically the restaurants that were part of the Route 66 years and that were in downtown St. Louis and on all paths of Highway 66 including the Original route, the Historic route, and the two Chain of Rocks routes. The research came together and the restaurants I contacted were all very cooperative so I was able to produce this *Route 66 St. Louis Cookbook* as a companion to the original book.

Restaurants that are part of *Route 66 St. Louis: From the Bridges to the Diamonds* are covered in depth there so I avoided duplication and this cookbook only has the highlights for those places. More detailed information is given here for the places that are not covered in *Route 66 St. Louis: From the Bridges to the Diamonds*. Much of the research here is from newspaper and magazine archives, rather than family interviews, but many of the restaurants that are still in business proofread their sections to help ensure accuracy.

In keeping with my goal of preserving information before it is lost forever, I thought it appropriate to include a separate section on the other long-established institutions that served the dining public for years in St. Louis. The end result, which you now hold in your hands, is a collection of many treasured favorites from a mix of establishments that range from taverns and diners to high-end restaurants. The matchcover collections of George S. Lux and the late Gene Kitson are featured in both books. Russell Kruetzman's kindness in allowing me to reprint vintage menus (and the accompanying text where room allowed) from his 1976 *Gateway Gourmet* book is no less than icing on the cake. They are included solely for historic/nostalgic purposes so don't expect to find Filet Mignon at Tony's for $9.50 today.

As you may have guessed, this cookbook, which started out as an appendix and ended as its own unique collection of recipes and stories, is being published first with the hope of generating funds to publish *Route 66 St. Louis: From the Bridges to the Diamonds*, my much larger collection of Route 66 St. Louis stories that I wholeheartedly feel deserve to be shared and passed on to future generations. With that goal in mind, I thank you from the bottom of my heart for purchasing this cookbook and hope you enjoy its recipes and its stories.

Contents

Introduction. 1

Downtown 3

President Casino on the Admiral 5
   Potato Chowder

Lt. Robert E. Lee Steamboat 5
   Jack Daniels Pecan Pie

Al's Restaurant 6
   Creamy Lobster Bisque

St. Louis Union Station. 7
   Harvey Girl Special-Little Thin Orange Pancakes

Pet Milk 7
   Pumpkin Pie

Ralston Purina 8
   Chex Mix

Miss Hulling's Cafeteria 9
   Raw Spinach Salad, Autumn Glow Cake,
   and *German Potato Salad*

Pope's Cafeteria. 11
   Nut Torte and *Chop Suey*

Forum Cafeteria 12
   Baked Macaroni and Cheese, Chicken Pot
   Pie, and *Forum's/Hank's Favorite Apple Pie*

Famous-Barr 15
   French Onion Soup

Stix, Baer & Fuller 16
   Stix-Style Alligator Rolls and
   Made-From-Scratch Pancakes

Scruggs, Vandervoort & Barney 17
   Tropical Fruit Salad

Roberts Mayfair Hotel 18
   Mayfair Room's Mayfair Dressing

Tony's 19
   Capellini with Grilled Scallops

Kemoll's 21
   Petto Di Pollo All'Agro Dolce

Original Route 66 Alignment 23

Angel Food Cake and the Hotel Beers 25

Woolworth's 25
   No-Bake Lemon Cheesecake

Gaslight Square and the
Three Fountains Restaurant. 26
   Chicken a la Three Fountains

Tenderloin Room at the Chase Park Plaza
(Hack Ulrich and the Tenderloin Room) 28
   Hellenic Salad and *Dressing*

St. Louis Art Museum. 30
   Chess Pie and *Vegetable Nut Torte*

Blueberry Hill. 31
   Red Beans and Rice

Fitz's Root Beer 32
   Cajun Gumbo

Cicero's 33
   Cheese-Baked Pasta Alamara

Medart's and the Cheshire Inn 34
   Recreated Burger Relish, Pepper Steak with Savory Rice,
   and *Steak Butter*

The Parkmoor 36
   Chickburger

Schlafly Bottleworks 37
   Sticky Toffee Pudding

Monarch Restaurant and Wine Bar 38
   Chocolate Grand Marnier Crème Carmel

Engelhard's Tavern 39

Buckingham's 39
   Chicken Soup

Hacienda Mexican Restaurant 40
   Mole de Gallina

Charcoal House 41
   Batter Fried Lobster

Big Chief 42
   Big Chief Dakota Grill's Wild Mushroom Merlot Sauce

Purina Farm 43
   Gingerbread, Mashed Potato Pancakes,
   and *Shredded Ralston*

Historic Route 66 Alignment (to 270). . 45

Eleven Eleven Mississippi 47
   Gooey Butter Cake

Soulard's Restaurant. 48
   Pumpkin Cheesecake

Anheuser-Busch Brewery 49
   Creamy Lager and Jalapeño Soup

Hodak's 50
   Southwestern Black Bean and Chicken Soup

Bevo Mill 50
   Sauerbraten, Seafood Salad, and
   Cheddar Cheese & Chives Biscuits

Lemmons 52
   Lemon Meringue Pie

Steak 'n Shake 53
   Unofficial Steak 'n Shake-Style Chili

Contents continued

Southtown Famous-Barr 54
  Bakery Blueberry Muffins
White Castle 55
  Turkey Stuffing
66 Café, Stan Musial & Biggie's,
and the Flaming Pit 56
Pietro's 58
  Meatball Soup, Spinach Balls, and *Chicken Pietro*
Pagliacci's Pizzeria 60
  Brasciole a la Joe Parente
Garavelli's 61
  Boston Scrod and *Sirloin Steak Tips and Noodles*
Ted Drewes Frozen Custard 63
  Johnny Rabbitt Concrete and *Hawaiian Delight Concrete*
Johnny Gitto's 64
  Primavera Pasta
Shop 'n Save 65
  Deli's Greek Salad
Velvet Freeze Ice Cream 66
  Strawberry Shortcake Sundae
Dierbergs Markets 67
  Grilled Bratwurst with Onion Sauerkraut Relish and
  French Almond Cake
Tippin's Restaurant and Pie Pantry 68
  Banana Cream Pie
Lubeley's Bakery 69
  Florentine Lace Cookies
Grone Cafeteria 70
  Stir-Fry Chicken and *Orange Fluff Cake*
Malone's Neighborhood Grill
and Pub (and Romine's) 71
  Malone's Potato Soup
Grant's Farm and White Haven 72
  Grant's Farm and *Tower Grove Chowder*
Katz Drug and Howard Johnson's 73
Dillard's Garden Room 74
  Frozen Fruit Salad, Chicken Salad, and *Navy Bean Soup*
Sappington Barn Restaurant and Tea Room 75
  Vegetable Salad
Schnucks 75
  St. Louis Salad and *Springtime Quiche*
McDonald's and Chuck-A-Burger 76
Rich & Charlie's 77
  Chicken Vesuvio
The Pasta House Co. 78
  Special Salad

Sesame Chinese Restaurant 78
  Szechwan Eggplant
Nelson's Café and Viking Restaurant 79
Helen Fitzgerald's Irish Pub 79
  Cajun Grilled Shark Chunks
House of Maret 80
  Austrian Cabbage

Chain of Rocks Alignments 81

City 66 "Connector" Path 81

Lombardo's 83
  Black Russian Pie and *Famous Green Noodles*
Bissell Mansion Restaurant and Dinner Theatre 84
  Zucchini Bread
Crown Candy Kitchen 84
  Chocolate Banana Malt
Vess Soda 85
  Watermelon Popsicles
Brooks Tangy Catsup 86
  Super Chili

Path Around St. Louis/Bypass Route 87

Yacovelli's 89
  Shrimp Ponchartrain
Henry VIII Inn and Lodge 90
  Shrimp Scampi Sauce
Kreis' Restaurant 91
  Lamb Shanks with Rice Pilaf
Don Breckenridge, Highway 66, and
St. Louis-Breckenridge Inn 92
  Shrimp De Jonghe
Schneithorst's 93
  Rouladen and *Potato Pancakes*
Sunset 44 Bistro 95
  Pork Tenderloin with Cranberry Ginger Chutney
Spencer's Grill 96
  St. Louis Slinger
Citizen Kane's Steakhouse 97
  New Orleans-Style Barbecue Shrimp
  and *Boardinghouse Potatoes*
Manor Grove (formerly the Old Folks Home) 98
  Baked Eggplant and Mushrooms
Green Parrot Inn 99
  Waldorf-Astoria Fabulous $100 Chocolate Cake
Howard Johnson's/Layton's 100
  Karen's Meatloaf

Contents continued

**Continuation of Historic Route,
west of I-270 to Villa Ridge** 101

Cracker Barrel. 103
   Country Cornbread Dressing
Fenton, Times Beach, Rock City, and Eureka 103
White Squirrel Tavern 106
   Doughnuts and *Spanish Spaghetti Bake*
Sites Station Café 107
   Sites Chili
Haymarket Restaurant 108
   Minnesota Wild Rice Bisque
Red Cedar Inn 109
   Carrots Delight and *(Honeymoon) French Dressing*
Henry Shaw Gardenway, Jensen Point,
and Shaw Nature Reserve 110
   Lend A Hand poem
Parrett's III
   Cinnamon Coffee Cake
Cottrell's Restaurant. III
   Cottrell's Famous Cheesecake
George's Apple Orchard and Market 112
   Bavarian Apple Torte
The Diamonds 113
   Bread Pudding, Diamond Style
Key's Twin Bridge Café. 114
   Concord Grape Pie

Additional St. Louis Institutions 115

Busch's Grove 117
   Bellevue Dressing and *Wild Rice Supreme*
Pelican's Restaurant 118
Lemp Mansion Restaurant and Inn. 119
   Cheddar-Sour Cream Potato Casserole
Other Historic Houses in St. Louis 119
Al Baker's. 120
   Veal Talleyrand and *Sicilian Red Snapper*
Café Balaban. 122
   Sweet Potato Gratin
The Edge 123
   Pollo con Aragosta (Chicken with Lobster)
Ed's White Front 123
   Ed's White Front Famous Hamburgers
Goody Goody Diner 124
Wright City Big Boy's 125
   Coleslaw

Ruggeri's 125
   Erminia Salad with Shrimp and *Ruggeri's Ravioli Sauce*
Missouri Baking Company 127
   Deep Butter Cake
Pratzel's Bakery. 128
   Kamish Bread
Rosciglione Bakery 129
   Strufoli
Noah's Ark Restaurant 130
   Clam Chowder and *Brownies*
Straub's Grocery Store 132
   Mustard Potato Salad

Definitely Worth Driving to in Missouri . . 133

Blue Owl Restaurant and Bakery 135
   German Chocolate Pie and *Gooey Butter Cookies*
Lewis Café 136
   Blackberry Crumb Pie
Missouri's Natural Caves. 136
Meramec Caverns 137
   Georgia Pecan Muffins
Cuba, Missouri (Route 66 Mural City) 137
Route 66 Fudge Shop 138
   Hard Candy
Missouri Wine Country 138
St. James Winery 138
   Summertime Punch
Rolla, Missouri 139
Zeno's Motel and Steak House 139
   Seafood Lasagna with Asparagus and Lobster Sauce
A Slice of Pie 140
   Coconut Buttermilk Custard Pie
Springfield, Missouri 140
Alberta's Hotel 141
   Barbecued Ribs and *Cranberry Salad*
Lambert's Café 141
   Fried Potatoes and Onions
Southwest Tip of Missouri. 142
Ott's Famous Dressings. 142
   Ott's Catfish Fillets
Bradbury-Bishop Deli. 143
   Miner's Steak Sandwich
Granny Shaffer's 143
   Breakfast Strata and *Black Walnut Fudge Pie*

Contents continued

Definitely Worth Driving to in Illinois . . 145

Pere Marquette Lodge 147
 Stuffed Mushrooms Supreme
Ariston Café 147
 Hawaiian Wedding Cake, Rice Pudding,
 and *Cabbage Soup*
Springfield, Illinois 149
Pease's Candy 149
 Vanilla Caramels
Dixie Truckers Home 150
 Dixie Chili
Funk's Grove Famous Maple Sirup 151
 Maple Sirup Bars
White Fence Farm Restaurant 151
 Creamy Coleslaw Dressing
Dell Rhea's Chicken Basket 152
 Sautéed Chicken Livers
Lou Mitchell's Restaurant & Bakery 152
 French Toast

Some St. Louis Favorite Foods 153

Mississippi (Riverfront) Mud Pie 153
Mississippi (River) Mud Cake 153
(Mound City) Mounds Bar Cake 154
(Old and New) Cathedral Window Cookies 154
St. Louis Gooey Butter Cake 154
Toasted Ravioli 155
St. Louis Crab Rangoon 155
Texas Sheet Cake 155
Rye Bread with Dill Dip 156
Friday Fish Fry Beer-Battered Fish 156
Potato Candy 156

Some Family Favorites 157

Easy Fruit Cobbler 157
Mama Tina's Butter Pecan Cookies 157
Old-Fashioned Sugar Cookies (Cut-out) 157
Mom's Corn Fritters 158
Mom's Candied Sweet Potatoes 158
Mom's Homemade Flour Tortillas 158

Route 66 Party 159

How to Throw a Route 66 Party 159

Route 66 Drive-By Scavenger Hunt #1 . 163
Historic Route (Tucker/Gravois/Watson) to 270 area

Route 66 Drive-By Scavenger Hunt #2 . 166
Historic Route Times Beach to Twin Bridges

Photo Credits 169
Selected Bibliography 170
Additional Resources 171
About the Author 172
Order Form 173

Introduction

St. Louis has connections to many foods that were popularized at the St. Louis World's Fair in 1904. (Debate continues as to which were actually invented here.) Among these are the ice cream cone, the hamburger, the hot dog, and iced tea. Dr Pepper was introduced nationally at the Fair as well. These are all legendary American food and drink items today. Of course, St. Louis has long been known as a beer city with many beer companies located here through the years. Coffee and tea makers were also located here including C.F. Blanke. Some of the other drinks that followed are Whistle and Vess, 7-Up, and IBC root beer. The Rio Theatre was built on Riverview Boulevard next door to Lombardo's with Stuart Tomber as its first manager. In 1940, Tomber founded Rio Syrup inside the theater building and took the name for the company from the theater. The Rio Theatre no longer stands but the name lives on in Rio Syrup, still in the Tomber family, and now in all 50 states.

St. Louis is also known for some unique foods. These include toasted ravioli, barbecued pork steaks, gooey butter cake and a St Louis-style pizza, which is thin, made with Provel cheese, and cut into squares rather than wedges. Mostaccioli is a popular pasta and crab Rangoon is found at all St. Louis Chinese restaurants with St. Paul sandwiches at some Chinese carryout places. At one time, brain sandwiches and turtle soup could be found easily around St. Louis. Street vendors still sell pretzels in a bag on St. Louis streets but only two pretzel companies remain today with vendors now few and far between. Gus's Pretzel Shop, owned by Gus Koebbe, is in its third generation dating from 1920 or so when Frank Ramsperger started the business. Giegerich Pretzel Co. is in its fourth generation dating to 1855 when August Giegerich arrived here from Germany with a pretzel recipe and opened a pretzel shop.

Route 66 meandered through much of St. Louis with many restaurants coming and going along the way. Vintage postcards describe St. Louis as the "City of a Thousand Sights" and with St. Louis being the largest city on Route 66 between Chicago and Santa Monica, there were lots of attractions for travelers. There were also plenty of restaurants, diners, and bakeries that travelers could choose from. Just as the road fell to progress but still lives on, the food that comforted and satisfied also lives on. While many of the recipes have been lost along the way, some were also lovingly preserved by chefs, staff, families, and avid recipe clippers and cookbook collectors. This collection further preserves those beloved recipes and also salutes those places where countless folks ate with families and friends or stopped in for a rest and a bite. An in-depth story (or additional information) on some of the restaurants/places can be found in the upcoming *Route 66 St. Louis: From the Bridges to the Diamonds*. These are denoted with a diamond shape.

Featured here are some of the most popular restaurants that were on Route 66 with most of them in the St. Louis area. The owners and families shared the recipes for some of their most popular dishes. There are also some recipes from St. Louis area institutions and bakeries. Many recipes are from places that are now long gone but because the restaurants shared a recipe somewhere along the way, with the local newspapers or with groups trying to raise funds with a cookbook, these vintage recipes can be passed on to the next generation to try. Some businesses came in as Route 66 towns were being bypassed by the interstate or in more recent years. These places also play a role in the Route 66 story as the old road continues to evolve and new people discover the highway and its people. Even more special are those places that have stood the test (and tastes) of time and continue to satisfy, delivering wonderful food to our dining table.

The recipes (about 170) are presented by their location on Route 66, starting with the downtown area restaurants, cafeterias and historic department stores. (You can tell if the place is still in business because it will have the address, phone number and, if available, the web address for you to find them.) Next is the Original alignment, which took many paths to get to Forest Park then followed Manchester Road through Maplewood, Brentwood, Rock Hill, Kirkwood, and on west. This is followed by the Historic alignment down Gravois, Chippewa, and Watson Road, to the busy Lindbergh Boulevard area. The two Chain of Rocks Bridge paths are covered next, leading through downtown and connecting up with the Gravois route (the City 66 "Connector") or going around St. Louis (the Bypass route) and meeting up with the Historic route at the cloverleaf bridge at the intersection of Watson Road and Lindbergh Blvd. We then pick up the Historic route west of 270 and follow it west to Eureka, Pacific, and Villa Ridge, ending at the Diamonds. These alignments are followed by some St. Louis institutions that were not on Route 66 but were there in that time period and a few places that are definitely worth driving to in Missouri and Illinois (some farther than others). This is followed by some St. Louis favorite foods and some personal recipes. Lastly, and just for fun, is the Route 66 Party section, which includes details on how to throw a Route 66 party and two Drive-By Scavenger Hunts to get you exploring the famous highway.

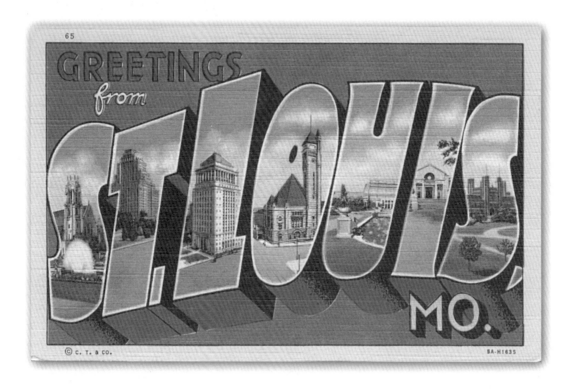

Downtown St. Louis

President Casino on the Admiral

Lt. Robert E. Lee Steamboat

Al's Restaurant

St. Louis Union Station

Pet Milk

Ralston Purina

Miss Hulling's Cafeteria

Pope's Cafeteria

Forum Cafeteria

Famous-Barr

Stix, Baer & Fuller

Scruggs, Vandervoort & Barney

Roberts Mayfair Hotel

Tony's

Kemoll's

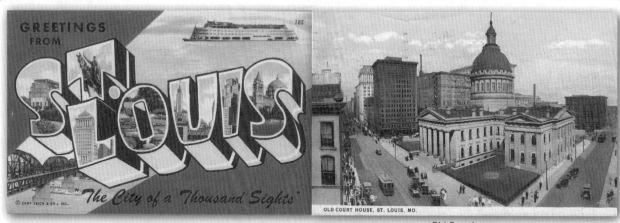

Old Courthouse

Jefferson Hotel

Purina complex 1954

Union Station, showing plaza & fountains

1966 aerial view of downtown St. Louis

President Casino on the Admiral

1000 N. Leonor K. Sullivan Blvd.
(currently docked at Laclede's Landing)
314-622-IIII or 1-800-772-3647
www. presidentcasino.com

The Admiral began her life in 1907 as a workhorse called the S.S. Albatross. After three decades of ferrying railroad cars, she got a well-deserved renovation into a five-deck Art Deco entertainment venue called the Admiral. She cruised the Mississippi River until 1979 when the Coast Guard discovered extensive hull damage. She has been docked on the riverfront since, under various owners. Today, she serves as a gambling casino owned by Pinnacle Entertainment.

President Casino's Potato Chowder
This recipe was shared in 2001 by lead cook Dwight Douglas for the <u>St. Louis Post-Dispatch</u> Special Request column.

3 potatoes, peeled	
1¼ cups diced onion	
3 cups plus 2 Tbsp water, divided	
2 tsp chicken base	
¼ tsp ground black pepper	
1¼ cups heavy cream	
2 Tbsp bacon bits	
1½ Tbsp cornstarch	

Cut potatoes into ½ inch cubes (about 3 cups). Add potatoes and onion to 3 cups water in a large saucepan; bring to a boil. Cook until potatoes are fork-tender, about 15 minutes. Stir in chicken base, pepper, cream and bacon bits; simmer 10 minutes. Stir cornstarch into 2 tablespoons water. Gradually stir into chowder; cook until thickened. Adjust seasonings to taste and garnish with sliced green onions, shredded Cheddar cheese or extra bacon bits. Yield: 6 (1-cup) servings.

Lt. Robert E. Lee Steamboat

The Lt. Robert E. Lee was one of several modern day steamboat replicas that had restaurants on the Mississippi riverfront. She opened for business in February, 1970. At one point, she featured six dining rooms on four levels including the seafood restaurant, Lt. Robert E. Lee, and the 275-seat Sternwheeler. After a brief stint in nearby Kimmswick, the Lee was auctioned off in December, 2008 for $200,000 to Andrew and Steve Petroff from Collinsville, Illinois who hope to keep it in the area.

Lt. Robert E. Lee's Jack Daniels Pecan Pie
This recipe was part of an October 28, 1990 <u>St. Louis Post-Dispatch</u> feature story on the Lee.

1½ cups granulated sugar
⅔ cup all-purpose flour
3 eggs
¾ cup (1½ sticks) butter
¼ cup bourbon or sour mash whiskey
1 (12-ounce) package semi-sweet chocolate morsels
3⅓ to 3½ cups pecan pieces
1 (10-inch) pie shell, unbaked

For Topping:
6 Tbsp whipping cream
1 Tbsp granulated sugar

In mixing bowl, combine sugar and flour; blend well with electric mixer. Add eggs; blend with mixer until well mixed. In small saucepan, melt butter completely. Stir melted butter into egg mixture. Add bourbon, chocolate morsels and pecans. Stir gently but thoroughly. Pour mixture into unbaked pie shell. Bake in a preheated 350-degree oven 30 minutes, or until set. Do not overbake. Let pie cool to room temperature.

Beat whipping cream and sugar with electric mixer until stiff. Top pie with sweetened whipped cream just before serving. Yield: 6 to 8 servings.

Al's Restaurant

1200 N. First Street (at Biddle)

314-421-6399

www.alsrestaurant.net

The building that today houses a bustling steakhouse was once part of a thriving warehouse district near the St. Louis riverfront. It was built as a sugar cane warehouse in the 1870s and became Julius Vogel's Sugar House Exchange Saloon in 1905. In 1925, Albert Borroni, a soda truck driver, and his wife Louise (Gina) bought the building and opened a small eatery. They often made egg sandwiches for workers en route to riverfront jobs. The following year was a big one with the Borronis having their son Albert Jr. (Al) and shifting the eatery into a full-service cafeteria. In the 1930s, the restaurant began offering dinner, with the five or six entrees recited verbally to customers. Al (whose name was changed to Barroni) grew up in the business and took over when his father died. In 1968, a fire at an industrial rag building next door caused that building to collapse onto Al's building. Al took the opportunity to remodel the building and reinvent the business as an upscale steakhouse.

Al's dedication and hard work, along with that of his wife Ann, grew the business and it achieved a reputation for excellence. Sadly, Al passed away in 2005. Now the third and fourth generations of this family-owned restaurant (daughter Pam Barroni Neal and her husband Gary Neal and their daughters Nicolin and Megan) along with a long-standing loyal staff, carry on over 80 years of a dining legacy. It continues its tradition of a fresh menu tableside presentation, generous portions, award-winning steaks and word of mouth advertising. It also includes an award-winning bar.

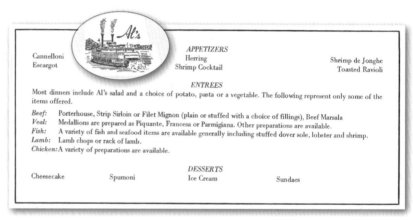

Al's Creamy Lobster Bisque
Recipe shared by Al's Restaurant

- 6 cups water
- 1 (8-ounce) frozen lobster tail (in shell)
- ½ cup (1 stick) plus 2 Tbsp butter, divided
- 1 medium onion, chopped
- ¼ tsp minced fresh garlic
- ¼ cup diced celery
- 2 bay leaves
- 2 cups heavy cream
- ¼ tsp salt or to taste
- 1 dash ground red (cayenne) pepper
- 1 dash ground white pepper
- 1½ Tbsp lobster base
- 1 cup all-purpose flour
- 6 Tbsp cream sherry

Bring water to a boil in a stockpot; add lobster tail and boil 20 minutes. Meanwhile, melt 2 tablespoons butter in a medium skillet. Add onion, garlic, celery and bay leaves; sauté until vegetables soften. Set aside. Remove cooked lobster tail; set aside to cool. Add cream and sautéed vegetables to stock pot; bring to a boil, then cook 10 minutes. Stir in salt, ground peppers and lobster base. In a small skillet, melt remaining 1/2 cup butter; whisk in flour to make a roux. Add enough roux to simmering soup mixture to achieve desired thickness. Simmer 20 minutes; strain soup through a colander into a second pot. Remove lobster tail from shell; chop meat into small chunks. Stir lobster and sherry into bisque; simmer 5 minutes. Serve hot. Yield: 6 cups.

St. Louis Union Station

1820 Market Street 314-421-6655;
Station Grille 314-802-3462
www.stlouisunionstation.com

Fred Harvey operated the food service for Union Station including the Fred Harvey restaurant and coffee shop. Fred Harvey opened his very first restaurant in St. Louis. After a few bad starts, he built an empire based on high standards of excellence and made a lasting mark on the food service industry. The Fred Harvey Restaurant is today the Station Grille.

Harvey Girl Special-Little Thin Orange Pancakes

The orange pancakes were a local favorite.
Shared by St. Louis Union Station

¼ cup diced orange sections and juice (½ orange)
1 cup pancake mix
1 tsp grated orange peel (½ orange)
1 cup orange juice

Combine all ingredients. Bake small pancakes on hot griddle, using 1 tablespoon batter per pancake. Serve with maple syrup, honey or jelly. Yield: 36 (2¾-inch diameter) pancakes.

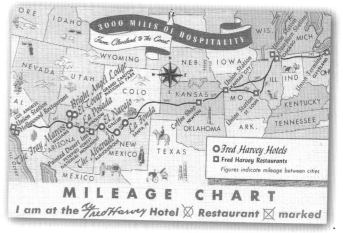

Pet Milk

Pet Milk, an evaporated milk, was started by John Meyenberg, a Swiss immigrant, in 1885 in nearby Highland, Illinois as the Helvetia Milk Condensing Company's Highland Evaporated Cream brand. The company gained market share in the South and West, which lacked refrigeration. It nearly went out of business due to shelf spoilage but was saved by Louis Latzer who rectified the problem, which was due to bacteria. The milk was sold under several brand names including Our Pet, which later became Pet. In 1922, Helvetia became Pet Milk Co. with world headquarters in downtown St. Louis. In 1933, Pet home economist Erma Proetz created radio personality Mary Lee Taylor who shared recipes and household hints with homemakers. The first recipe she shared was this pumpkin pie recipe, which became a favorite across the country. IC Industries (later Whitman Corp.) bought Pet in 1978 then spun it off in 1991. It was then purchased in 1995 by Pillsbury (a subsidiary of British Grand Metropolitan Plc). In 2004, J. M. Smucker, a multi-generational family business based out of Ohio, bought Pillsbury (and Pet). Smucker's founder started out selling apple butter from a horse-drawn wagon and the company has grown tremendously. Besides Pet and Pillsbury, it also owns several other American classics including Jif, Crisco, and Eagle and Carnation canned milks. The 15-story Pet headquarters building at 400 South Fourth Street, built in 1969 and touted as the only example in Missouri of the New Brutalism architectural style, was developed by Balke Brown Associates into a 118-luxury apartment complex known as Pointe 400.

Pet Milk Pumpkin Pie

This recipe from the cookbook, *A Celebration of Cooking in America, Timeless Recipes from the Kitchen of Pet* (1984), which celebrated the 100 year anniversary of Pet, says that the recipe is 75 years old, putting its origins at 1909/1910. *Reprinted with permission from J. M. Smucker Co. (Pet is a registered trademark of the J.M. Smucker Company.)*

- 1 cup firmly packed brown sugar
- 2 Tbsp all-purpose flour
- 2¼ tsp pumpkin pie spice
- ½ tsp salt
- 1 egg
- 1 can (16 ounces) solid-pack pumpkin
- 1 tall can (12 fluid ounces) Pet evaporated milk
- 1 deep dish pie crust shell
- • whipped cream or topping, optional

Preheat oven and cookie sheet to 375 degrees F. In large bowl, mix brown sugar, flour, pumpkin pie spice, and salt. Stir in egg. Beat in pumpkin and evaporated milk until smooth. Pour into pie crust. Bake on preheated cookie sheet 50 to 55 minutes or until knife inserted one inch from edge comes out clean. Serve warm or cold, topped with whip cream if desired. Note: in place of pumpkin spice, you may use 1¼ tsp ground cinnamon, ½ tsp ground nutmeg, ½ tsp ground ginger and ¼ tsp cloves.

Ralston Purina

Ralston Purina was located at the foot of the Municipal "Free" Bridge (later renamed MacArthur Bridge) and was part of both the Original (1926 to 1933) and the Historic (August 1933 to January 1977) routes. This recipe was developed by the Checkerboard Kitchens and has been popular for over 50 years. The original recipe as shown in a 1952 *Life Magazine* ad combined 7 cups Wheat Chex (created 1937) and 2 cups Rice Chex (created 1950) with 1 tablespoon Worcestershire sauce, ½ cup melted butter, ½ cup nuts, ¼ teaspoon salt and ¼ teaspoon garlic salt and was baked at 300 for 30 minutes, stirring every 10 minutes then cooled. The recipe began

appearing on Ralston Purina cereal boxes in 1955. A local 1964 recipe added Corn Chex and was baked at 250 for 45 minutes. Along the way, homemakers added pretzel sticks and Cheetos. Packaged Chex snack mixes were introduced in 1985. In 1994, Ralston Purina spun off Ralcorp (the human foods division) as a separate company and Ralcorp sold the Chex cereals and Chex Mix to General Mills in 1996. In 2001, Ralston Purina became Nestlé Purina PetCare Company. The snack mix continues to be popular today. A sweet version is the Muddy Buddies, which uses powdered sugar, chocolate chips and peanut butter.

Ralston Purina Chex Mix

This is the Chex Party Mix recipe from more recent years as found on the Chex website www.chex.com. Reprinted with the permission of General Mills, Inc.

- 6 Tbsp butter or margarine
- 2 Tbsp Worcestershire sauce
- 1½ tsp seasoned salt
- ¾ tsp garlic powder
- ½ tsp onion powder
- 3 cups Corn Chex
- 3 cups Rice Chex
- 3 cups Wheat Chex (or use 9 cups of whichever Chex cereal you prefer)
- 1 cup mixed nuts

- 1 cup bite-size pretzels
- 1 cup garlic-flavor bite-sized bagel chips or regular-sized bagel chips, broken into 1-inch pieces

Heat oven to 250 degrees F. In ungreased large roasting pan, melt butter in oven. Stir in seasonings. Gradually stir in remaining ingredients until evenly coated. Bake 1 hour, stirring every 15 minutes. Spread on paper towels to cool. Store in airtight container. Makes 24 (½ cup) servings.

This St. Louis institution was at 11th and Locust for over 60 years and closed in October 1993. The story of its beginnings as told in the 1969 *Miss Hulling's Favorite Recipes* cookbook is that Florence Hulling left her [Mascoutah,] Illinois farm life and headed for St. Louis where she secured a job as a waitress with the Child's restaurant chain. She worked her way up to head of the cafeteria department and saved up $600. When a downtown hotel's restaurant failed due to the Depression, she put all of that $600 toward the first month's rent and took over the operation in 1930. Florence Hulling said she went into business "on $600 and a prayer." (Other accounts say that her faithful customers pitched in the $600 to get her started.) Her husband Stephen R. Apted was first a devoted customer who became her business manager. The 1107 Locust location grew to a complex of five restaurants. Miss Hulling's also had locations at 725 Olive, 4th and Washington, the Cheshire Inn at 7036 Clayton Avenue, Deaconess Hospital, St. Mary's Hospital, a location in Fairview Heights, Illinois, and there was also a Miss Hulling's Creamery at Clayton and Skinker. Florence Hulling Apted shared her recipes in several cookbooks. Customers often brought favorite recipes in for them to try and they incorporated many of them into their menu offerings. The award-winning Miss Hulling's Cafeteria was recommended by Duncan Hines who wrote that sanitation was the watchword at the establishment and that even the back alley was sprayed down with DDT for cleanliness.

Miss Beulah McNulty, restaurant manager for Miss Hulling's, reported that the three most requested recipes were the Raw Spinach Salad, the Autumn Glow (carrot) Cake and the German Potato Salad. She shared the recipes below (which had never been published before) with the *St. Louis Globe-Democrat* for the restaurant's 42nd Anniversary in 1970. It appears that Anniversary dates were based on the 1928 year that Miss Florence Hulling came to St. Louis. (Note: The exact date these recipes appeared is unknown-they are from an undated clipping shared by local cookbook collector Virginia Horrell.)

Miss Hulling's Raw Spinach Salad

- 1 quart chopped spinach
- ¼ cup onions, chopped fine
- ½ cup celery, chopped fine
- 1½ tsp cider vinegar
- ½ tsp Tabasco
- ½ tsp salt
- 3 hard boiled eggs, grated or chopped fine
- 1 cup grated sharp Cheddar cheese
- 1 cup heavy mayonnaise

Be sure washed spinach is as dry as possible before chopping. Mix spinach, onions, celery, eggs and cheese. Blend Tabasco and salt with vinegar. Add to spinach mixture. Fold in mayonnaise, just before serving. Serve on lettuce leaf with ½ tsp horseradish on the side. Garnish with grated egg and cheese if desired. Yield: 6 to 8 servings.

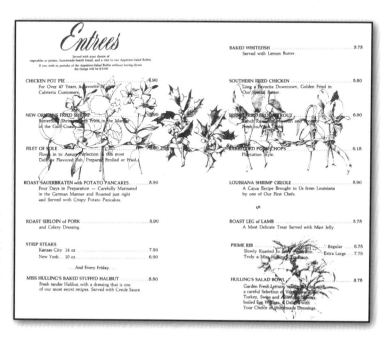

Miss Hulling's Autumn Glow Cake with Cream Cheese Icing

1½ cups salad oil
 5 whole eggs
 1 cup sugar
2⅔ cups cake flour (unsifted)
 2 tsp baking powder
 2 tsp baking soda
 ½ tsp salt
 1 lb carrots (ground in food chopper)
 ½ cup chopped pecans

Cream Cheese Icing:

½ lb cream cheese
¼ cup butter or margarine
 1 lb sifted powdered sugar
 1 tsp vanilla

This cake is very easily mixed by hand or in a mixer. Blend oil, eggs and sugar on low speed until well mixed. Sift flour with baking powder, soda and salt and mix on low speed until well blended. Fold carrots and pecans in by hand. Spread into two 9-inch or three 7-inch greased and floured pans. Note: can also bake in one large pan. Bake at 370 degrees for 35 to 40 minutes or until done. Invert on a cake rack to cool. When cool, split the layers and ice each piece and the top and sides with the following icing.

Cream all ingredients together until smooth.

Miss Hulling's German Potato Salad

1½ quarts, sliced boiled red potatoes
 3 Tbsp chopped onion
 3 Tbsp chopped pimento
 1 grated hard cooked egg
 2 Tbsp chopped parsley
 4 strips bacon, fried crisp and dried
 2 tsp cider vinegar
 6 Tbsp seasoned vinegar

Potato Salad Dressing:

¼ cup flour
¼ cup sugar
 1 Tbsp salt
 • dash of white pepper
 6 Tbsp bacon fat
 ½ cup cider vinegar
1½ cups hot water

Use small red potatoes. Peel and steam or boil until tender. Slice thin while still warm. Add remaining ingredients and let marinate for 30 minutes. Add dressing (see recipe below), mix carefully, and serve hot or warm. Note: you will need about 2 lbs of potatoes for this recipe. Yield: about 2 quarts of salad.

Bring water, vinegar and bacon fat to a boil. Mix dry ingredients; add to boiling mixture, stirring vigorously, and cook until clear.

Pope's Cafeteria was a St. Louis institution for more than 60 years. Harry Allen Pope and his wife Luella Wardwell Pope moved to St. Louis in 1912 from Massachusetts. The Popes started out as a contract catering company in 1916 when Harry was employed by International Shoe Co. and proposed a system of pre-ordered hot meals for his staff to eat. He converted his wife's New England recipes to commercial formulas and within ten years was serving up 15,000 meals a day while also keeping his job as personnel manager. In 1933, Harry Allen Pope was offered the old Y.W.C.A. building at 3538 Washington and he set up his sons, Harry H. Pope and Edwin K. Pope, in business. This was followed in 1936 by his purchase of the old Child's Restaurant at 804 Washington for which he finally left International Shoe and went into the family's restaurant business full time. (The City Museum is housed in International Shoe's former warehouse building.) The Popes expanded and in 1957 opened a cafeteria in Northland Shopping Center. By 1973 there were ten Pope's Cafeterias in St. Louis and the family owned other restaurants as well. The sons worked in the family business for over 50 years until they sold in the late 1980s. The company continued into the 1990s. Sadly, part of the Pope's legacy includes an October 1980 early morning robbery at the Des Peres location when four Pope's Cafeteria employees were herded into the office and shot. Many have great memories of the Pope's Cafeteria food including this prize-winning Nut Torte.

Pope's Cafeteria Nut Torte

This recipe originally appeared as a feature story in the St. Louis Post-Dispatch and was shared on January 21, 1962 by its creator Mildred Hoppe, director of food production for Pope's Cafeterias, shortly after the recipe won awards in an exposition. The original recipe made four tortes and is different from later versions (shown here), which appeared in the Pope's Cafeteria cookbook published in 1979 and was shared by readers for the June 10, 1996 St. Louis Post-Dispatch.

- shortening, for greasing pans
- 2 Tbsp vinegar
- 1 tsp salt
- ¾ cup (about 5 large) egg whites, at room temperature
- ⅛ tsp cream of tartar
- ½ cup packed brown sugar
- ½ cup granulated sugar
- ½ tsp vanilla
- ¼ tsp almond extract
- ½ cup plus 2 Tbsp graham cracker crumbs
- ½ cup chopped pecans
- 1 large banana
- 2 cups whipped topping or 1 cup heavy cream whipped with 2 Tbsp powdered sugar
- maraschino cherries, for garnish
- toasted almonds or pecan pieces, for garnish

Preheat oven to 400 degrees. Grease an 8-by-2-inch round pan. Combine vinegar and salt; use to rinse large bowl of electric mixer to dissolve any trace of grease. Rinse well with water and dry. Place egg whites and cream of tartar in bowl. Beat on high speed until egg whites form soft peaks. Use a wire balloon-type beater if you have one. Sift together brown sugar and granulated sugar. With a hand sifter, gradually sprinkle sugar over egg whites, adding about a tablespoon at a time and beating at high speed for at least a minute after each addition. When all the sugar has been added, continue to beat for at least 5 minutes or until egg whites are glossy and stand in stiff peaks. Tip the bowl; if whites start to slide, you haven't beaten them enough. Add vanilla and almond extract; mix thoroughly. Remove bowl from mixer. Combine graham cracker crumbs and pecans; mix thoroughly. Sprinkle a third over the egg whites and fold in gently. Gradually add remaining crumb mix, folding in gently after each addition. Pour into prepared pan and place in oven. Immediately reduce oven temperature to 350 degrees; bake for 35 minutes or until top of torte is firm to the touch but still light in color. Remove from oven; let cool in pan. Remove from pan and place on serving platter. Slice banana; place slices on torte. Decorate top and sides of torte with topping; sprinkle with cherries and almonds. Refrigerate until ready to serve. (If decorated with whipped cream, cake will not store very long). Yield: 8 servings.

Pope's Cafeteria Chop Suey

Recipe from the Pope's Cafeteria cookbook <u>No Experience Necessary</u> and March 17, 2001 <u>St. Louis Post-Dispatch</u> Recipe Exchange column

- 1½ pounds pork butt, well trimmed and cut into strips ½-inch wide, ¼-inch thick and 3 inches long
- 2 Tbsp vegetable oil
- 1 large onion, peeled and sliced
- 4 cups sliced celery (pieces should be about ¼-inch thick)
- 2 cups cold water
- 2 Tbsp cornstarch
- ½ tsp monosodium glutamate, optional
- ¼ cup soy sauce
- 1 (16-ounce) can bean sprouts, well drained, or ½ pound fresh bean sprouts
- 1 (6-ounce) can sliced bamboo shoots, well drained
- 6 cups hot cooked rice
- Chinese noodles, optional

Sauté strips of pork in oil over very low heat, using a large skillet, for about 30 minutes, or until tender. Cover skillet after the first few minutes. Add onion and celery; cook until vegetables are done but still crisp. Combine cold water, cornstarch, monosodium glutamate and soy sauce. Mix thoroughly. Add to meat; cook until thick and clear. If using fresh bean sprouts, blanch by pouring hot water over them, then drain. Add bean sprouts and bamboo shoots to skillet; heat through. Serve immediately over heaping mounds of fluffy rice, adding Chinese noodles for crunch. Yield: 6 servings. Note: To make chicken chow mein, substitute chicken for the pork and cooked noodles for the rice.

Forum Cafeteria

The Forum Cafeteria chain had locations around the country and locally included downtown and Crestwood Plaza on Highway 66. Corporate chef Oliver H. "Ollie" Sommer shared several recipes over the years. Hank Davenport joined the Forum in Kansas City at age 16 where he started off in the bake shop then worked his way up to baking everything they made. At age 23 he left the Forum to serve in Vietnam and then returned to the Forum, this time in St. Louis, serving as the head pastry chef from April 1968 to January 1969. He routinely made 36 apple pies each day. He left the Forum for good for a job with the Olivette Police Department but took the apple pie recipe with him. He served on the Olivette police force for 37 years, retiring as police chief in 2006. He has continued making this apple pie through the years, which is always well received. In 2004, he entered it into a local contest and won first place. He shares his prize-winning apple pie and pie crust recipe here. The Forum continues to be remembered fondly by many.

Forum Cafeteria Baked Macaroni and Cheese
This recipe was shared by Ollie Sommer and printed in the August 26, 2000 St. Louis Post-Dispatch.

12 ounces uncooked elbow macaroni
• salt
4 cups skim milk
6½ Tbsp margarine
½ cup all-purpose flour
• ground white pepper
4 drops yellow food coloring
1½ Tbsp granulated sugar
1½ cups grated Longhorn Cheddar cheese, divided
½ tsp paprika

Cook macaroni in salted water according to package directions until done but still firm to the bite. Drain; rinse with cold water until macaroni is cold and firm. Drain well. Preheat oven to 350 degrees. In a saucepan or in the microwave, heat milk until bubbles form around the edges. Set aside. Melt margarine in a large pot. Gradually sprinkle in flour; cook, stirring constantly, until smooth. Stir in 2 teaspoons salt, pepper to taste, food coloring, sugar and hot milk. Cook, stirring, until well-mixed and creamy. Stir in 3/4 cup cheese; mix well until melted. Stir macaroni into sauce. Transfer to ovenproof casserole. Sprinkle with remaining 3/4 cup cheese and paprika. Bake 30 minutes or until heated through. Yield: About 9 (1-cup) servings.

Forum Cafeteria Chicken Pot Pie
Shared by Ollie Sommer and printed in the January 6, 1997 St. Louis Post-Dispatch

• pie dough
1 egg
1 Tbsp water

Preheat oven to 425 degrees. First, make and bake the crust: Roll out pie dough to 1/8-inch thick. If you are serving the pot pies in individual casseroles, cut the dough into four pieces, each the size and shape of the top of the casserole dish. If you are serving the pot pie in one large casserole, cut one piece of dough. Place dough on cookie sheets; prick with fork to prevent blistering or puffing. Beat egg with water; brush on top of dough. Bake 15 minutes or until golden. Set aside.

⅓ cup vegetable oil (see note)
½ cup all-purpose flour
3½ cups chicken stock or low-sodium canned broth
3 drops yellow food coloring
1 tsp salt (or less, to taste)
1 pinch ground white pepper
2 cups diced cooked potatoes
¼ cup frozen peas
2½ cups cooked chicken, cut into ¾-inch-wide strips

While crust bakes, prepare the filling: In a small pan, combine oil and flour to make a roux. Cook over low heat, stirring constantly, until flour turns a light golden brown, 10 to 15 minutes. While roux is cooking, bring stock to a boil in large saucepan. Stir in food coloring, salt and pepper. Slowly add hot roux to boiling stock. (Be careful; stock will sputter and boil furiously.) With a whisk, stir until smooth to make a gravy. Stir in potatoes, peas and chicken; heat through. Divide among four individual casseroles or pour into large casserole. Top with baked pastry crust and serve. Yield: 4 servings. Note: The original recipe called for chicken fat.

Forum's/Hank's Favorite Apple Pie
Shared by Hank Davenport

Pastry for 9-inch double-crust pie:

2	cups all-purpose flour
¼	tsp salt
10⅔	Tbsp cold unsalted butter (or 1 stick and 2⅔ Tbsp)
1	Tbsp plus 1 tsp granulated sugar
1	extra large egg, separated
1	extra large egg (for brushing top crust)

Apple pie filling:

6	large Jonathan apples
1	Tbsp freshly squeezed lemon juice
1	Tbsp plus 1½ tsp cornstarch
⅓	cup packed light brown sugar
⅓	cup granulated sugar, plus more for sprinkling
1	tsp ground cinnamon (preferably Ceylon)
¼	tsp freshly grated nutmeg
1½	Tbsp cold unsalted butter, cut into small pieces

Prepare a 9-inch pie crust pan by greasing it with butter and lightly coating it with flour. Tap off excess flour then refrigerate for about an hour. Set oven rack to 4 inches from the bottom. Preheat oven to 425 degrees. Using a food processor, pulse flour and salt to mix. Cut butter into tablespoon size chunks and add to food processor. Pulse on and off until butter is combined with flour mixture. Do not over mix. It should resemble a crumbly cornmeal. Add 1 tablespoon and 1 teaspoon sugar to the mixture and pulse 1 to 2 seconds to blend in. Transfer mixture from food processor to large mixing bowl. Mix 1 cold egg yolk and 3 Tbsp of ice cold water (or more as needed). Knead in bowl until pie crust starts to form a ball. Stop and divide into 2 portions, 1 larger than the other. (The larger is for the bottom crust.) Cover both portions with plastic film and pat down. Refrigerate for 20 minutes. Prepare pie filling.

Peel, core and slice apples. (You should have 4 cups.) Toss with lemon juice. Combine cornstarch, sugars, cinnamon and nutmeg in a large bowl. Blend well. Add apples; toss to combine. Set aside.

Remove prepared pie plate and larger pastry portion from refrigerator. Roll out dough on lightly-floured cutting board. Sprinkle more flour if it sticks. Press into edges of prepared pie plate, ensuring there is no air in between crust and pie plate. Beat egg white until frothy. Brush over bottom of pie crust. Spoon filling into crust, mounding fruit in the center. Dot filling with the one and a half tablespoons cold butter. Now remove top crust from refrigerator and roll out on cutting board. Brush some egg white along the rim of the bottom crust then place top crust over filling; press and flute edges to tightly seal. Trim any overhanging edges. Using a sharp paring knife, cut several vents in top crust for steam. Beat whole egg until frothy. Brush lightly over top crust including edges, covering well. Sprinkle lightly with granulated sugar. Bake for 10 minutes and then reduce oven temperature to 350 degrees. Bake 45 minutes longer or until pastry is golden and filling is bubbling. If pie browns too quickly, cover top loosely with aluminum foil. Yield: 8 servings. Hank's notes: can use frozen pie crust if necessary; for a more tart pie, use Granny Smith apples.

Famous-Barr — now Macy's
601 Olive 314-444-3116
www.macys.com

Famous-Barr Department Store, created in 1911 but with roots to the 1870s, had restaurants and bakeries at several locations in the St. Louis area including downtown, Southtown at Kingshighway and Chippewa (66) and Crestwood Plaza (previously the Scruggs, Vandervoort, & Barney store) also on Highway 66. Famous had a loyal customer base and many made special trips on the streetcars to shop, see the Christmas windows, and to eat at the tea room. In 2005, the Famous-Barr chain became part of another American icon, Macy's.

Famous-Barr's French Onion Soup

This soup is a local favorite, which was served in the restaurant of the Famous-Barr stores and can still be found at the downtown Macy's store. *This recipe was developed for Famous-Barr by Chef Manfred Zetti who generously shared it with St. Louis Post-Dispatch readers, originally published on April 26, 1972. It has since appeared in many local cookbooks and has been modified slightly.*

5	lbs unpeeled onions or 3 lbs peeled
½	cup (1 stick) butter or margarine
1½	tsp freshly ground black pepper
2	Tbsp paprika
1	bay leaf
3	quarts or 7 (16-ounce) cans beef broth, divided (recommend Swanson)
1	cup white wine, optional
¾	cup all-purpose or instant flour (such as Wondra)
•	caramel coloring or Kitchen Bouquet, optional
2	tsp salt, or to taste
•	Sourdough or French baguettes, optional
½	lb Swiss or Gruyere cheese, optional

Peel onions and slice ⅛ inch thick, preferably in a food processor. Melt butter in a large (6-quart or larger) stockpot. Add onions; cook, uncovered, over low heat for 1½ hours, stirring occasionally. Stir in pepper, paprika and bay leaf; sauté over low heat 10 minutes more, stirring frequently. Pour in 6 cans broth and wine. Increase heat and bring to a boil. Stir together remaining 1 can broth and flour. Stir into boiling soup. Reduce heat to low and simmer very slowly for 2 hours. Adjust color to a rich brown with caramel coloring. Season with salt. Refrigerate overnight. To serve, heat soup in microwave or on stove top. If desired, pour into ovenproof crocks or bowls. Top with a slice of bread and a sprinkling of grated cheese. Heat under the broiler until cheese melts and bubbles, about 5 minutes. Leftover soup can be frozen. Yield: about 4 quarts soup or 16 servings.

The Famous-Barr (right), and Scruggs, Vandervoort & Barney downtown department stores

Stix, Baer & Fuller Department Store, founded in 1892, had tea rooms at several locations including downtown and Crestwood Plaza on Highway 66. Duncan Hines recommended the Stix, Baer and Fuller Tea Room and in 1952 told male readers, "Just because this happens to be a department store tea room you men needn't shy clear of it. Anyhow, if you are fussy, there is a room for men only." The chain sold to Dillard's in 1984. The Dillard's Crestwood store closed in October 2007.

Stix-Style Alligator Rolls

Stix served its salads with these rolls, which are remembered fondly by many customers. The hard-cracked top is made from rice flour. This recipe is not from Stix but produces similar rolls. *Adapted from the 1984 Food Editors' Hometown Favorites cookbook, contributed by then-St. Louis Post-Dispatch Food Editor Barbara Gibbs Ostmann*

For rolls:

- 3¾ cups unbleached all-purpose flour, or more, as needed, divided
- 2 cups lukewarm water, divided
- 1 Tbsp active dry yeast
- 1½ tsp salt
- • yellow cornmeal

For crunchy topping:

- 2 Tbsp active dry yeast
- 1 cup lukewarm water
- 4 tsp granulated sugar, divided
- 2 Tbsp safflower or corn oil
- 1⅔ cups rice flour (see note)
- 1½ tsp salt

For rolls: Measure 2 ½ cups flour into large mixing bowl. Make a well in center of flour and pour in ⅓ cup lukewarm water. Sprinkle yeast over water, stir to dissolve. Cover with a tea towel and let stand until yeast is foamy. Gradually add remaining 1⅔ cups water, beating in flour until well blended. Beat vigorously about 3 minutes, until air bubbles form. Cover batter with tea towel and let rest at least 30 minutes or as long as 8 hours.

Sprinkle salt over batter; stir in. Gradually beat in remaining 1¼ cups flour (or more as needed) to make a stiff dough. Turn out onto lightly floured board and knead at least 10 minutes, or until smooth and pliable but still soft, adding additional flour only as needed. Form into a smooth ball, place in a lightly floured bowl and sprinkle top lightly with flour. Cover with plastic wrap and a lightly dampened terry towel. Let stand at room temperature 1 ½ to 2 hours, or until double in bulk.

Punch dough down, knead briefly about 1 minute, cover with tea towel and let rest 10 minutes. Divide into 16 equal portions (about 2 ounces each). Form into smooth balls; cover with tea towel and let rise 1 hour. With palm of hand, flatten each ball slightly, fold in long edges as if forming a loaf, and shape into ovals; reshape into smooth balls. Arrange on a greased baking sheet that has been sprinkled with cornmeal. Cover with tea towel and let rise 45 minutes, or until almost double in size. (At this point, rolls are ready to bake.)

For topping: About 20 minutes before rolls are ready to bake, sprinkle yeast over water, stir in 1 teaspoon sugar and let stand until foamy. Stir in remaining 3 teaspoons sugar, oil, rice flour and salt. Beat well; set aside.

Place a shallow pan on the bottom shelf of oven and preheat oven to 375 degrees. Just before baking, beat topping mixture, and dip each ball of dough in mixture to coat upper one-third of each ball. Place each roll, dipped-side up, on baking sheet. (Beat topping several times during process to make sure it remains well mixed.) Pour ½ cup water into heated pan in oven. Place baking sheet of rolls on rack above pan. Bake in the preheated 375 degree oven 20 minutes or until golden, removing pan of water after first 10 minutes. Transfer rolls from baking pan to wire rack. Serve warm. Note: Don't buy sweet rice flour-it's not the baker's kind. The appropriate rice flour is sold in Asian markets and natural-foods stores. Yield: 16 rolls.

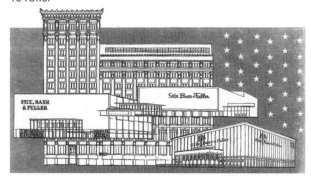

Stix Made-From-Scratch Pancakes

This recipe was in the cookbook that the department store gave to brides registered for its Bridal Registry.

- 1 cup sifted all-purpose flour
- 1 Tbsp baking powder
- 2 Tbsp granulated sugar
- ½ tsp salt
- 1 egg
- 1 cup milk (see note)
- 2 Tbsp vegetable oil or melted fat
- • margarine, syrup or cinnamon sugar, for topping

Sift together flour, baking powder, sugar and salt. Beat egg; stir in milk and oil. Add egg mixture to dry mixture; beat until smooth. Drop by tablespoons onto hot ungreased griddle. Cook until bubbles appear over surface, then flip and cook other side. Top with margarine, syrup or cinnamon sugar. Yield: 10 pancakes. Note: adjust milk to suit your taste for thickness of pancakes.

Scruggs, Vandervoort & Barney

This department store was started in 1850 by Richard M. Scruggs. Charles E. Barney and William L. Vandervoort joined as partners about 1870. The firm prospered downtown for decades and had a solid reputation for fine quality goods, service and courtesy, and integrity. In 1907, it relocated to the Syndicate Trust building at 10th and Olive, later joining with the Century Building. (Both historic buildings faced demolition in recent years; the Syndicate Trust building narrowly survived and the Century Building was razed amid many protests.)

Scruggs, Vandervoort & Barney later opened a store in Clayton and was part of the first regional mall in St. Louis when the Zorensky brothers opened Crestwood Plaza in 1957 on Highway 66 with two competing department stores, Vandervoort's (later Famous-Barr and more recently Macy's) and Sears. The company closed in the late 1960s. The Vandervoort's Tea Room was recommended by Duncan Hines who pointed out their butter baked chicken with clear chicken gravy, colorful salads, delectable caramel rolls and fresh fruit pies.

Scruggs, Vandervoort & Barney Tea Room Tropical Fruit Salad

Recipe from the 1954 <u>Symphony of Cooking</u>, courtesy Saint Louis Symphony Volunteer Association

- ½ fresh pineapple
- 1 large lettuce cup
- 3 orange slices
- ½ banana, sliced
- 6 grapefruit sections
- 2 dates
- 2 prunes stuffed with cream cheese
- • cream cheese, softened
- • mint and strawberry or parsley and maraschino cherry

Wash pineapple; leave green top on. Cut lengthwise in halves, through green top. Cut out core and discard. Cut fruit from half, leaving a shell of rind. Dice into large pieces. Place pineapple shell in large lettuce cup. Fill shell with pieces of pineapple, sliced banana and grapefruit sections. Place orange slices on right side of shell near edge of lettuce cup. Place stuffed prunes on left side of shell. Place dates at bottom of pineapple. With a pastry tube put a border of the softened cream cheese on cut edge of pineapple shell. Garnish with mint and strawberry, or parsley and maraschino cherry. Yield: 1 salad.

Roberts Mayfair Hotel
806 St. Charles St.
314-421-2500 or 800-996-3426
www.wyndham.com

The Mayfair Hotel's story begins with Charles Heiss. He started out as a busboy at the Victoria Hotel in Heidelburg, Germany then moved up to management at the Tudor Hotel in London and the Statler hotel chain in Detroit then St. Louis. He left the Statler to fulfill his dream of owning a first-class hotel, the Mayfair, which he opened in the mid 1920s. It was designed by famed architect Preston J. Bradshaw. Bradshaw also designed the Chase, the Hotel Coronado and the Lennox Hotel (also started by Heiss), all of which still survive today along with the Mayfair Hotel. Charles was joined in the family business by his son C. Gordon Heiss who owned the Mayfair and the Lennox until the late 1960s. Gordon went on to own the Clayton Inn, the St. Louis and Chicago Nantucket Cove restaurants and the Nantucket Lobster Trap chain.

The Mayfair has had many memorable guests through the years but the most famous story seems to be the stay in the 1950s of Cary Grant and a female companion in room 1802. The debonair Grant is said to have left a trail of chocolates from his parlor suite through the bedroom, ending on the pillow. The female companion's identity appears to have remained a mystery. (Apparently, there were tight-lipped employees at other places besides the Coral Court.) Regardless, the story goes that the manager liked the idea and began placing chocolates on all guest pillows, starting a trend that spread industry-wide. The Mayfair Hotel was also famous for its Mayfair Dressing, developed by Gordon Heiss and served at the Mayfair Room and at the Lennox.

Mayfair Room's Mayfair Dressing
Various recipe versions have appeared but this one was shared on July 25, 2007 by Charles Heiss' granddaughter, Nicki Dwyer, who personally responded to a St. Louis Post-Dispatch reader's request for the recipe.

½ large onion, peeled and diced
1 rib celery, diced
1 clove garlic, peeled and crushed
2 (2-ounce cans) flat anchovy fillets
3 eggs (see note)
2 Tbsp prepared mustard
¼ cup water
2 cups safflower oil
1 tsp cracked black pepper
1 tsp monosodium glutamate (Accent), optional

Combine all ingredients in a blender. Pulse on low speed until mixture is completely homogenized. Increase speed to high; blend for 1 minute. (Or use a food processor, pulsing until homogenized and then processing until well combined.) Yield: about 1 quart. Note: If you are worried about the risk of salmonella from the raw eggs, use Davidson's pasteurized eggs, which are sold in most local supermarkets.

18

This upscale restaurant, which is often a special-occasion choice had humble beginnings and has been in the same family for decades. The restaurant was started in 1946 by Tony Bommarito as Tony's Spaghetti House, located in a four-story building at 826 North Broadway, part of the old Produce Row area and across from the downtown Greyhound bus station. Two years later, Tony passed away and his teenaged sons, Vince and Tony, took over. Under Vince's watchful eye, the restaurant evolved from a checkered-tablecloth spaghetti house to a steakhouse to the area's highest-rated restaurant, often the only 4 or 5-star restaurant in all of Missouri. In 1992, the building was needed as part of the football stadium complex and Tony's relocated to its current location in the Equitable Building at Market and Broadway. In the process, the tradition of the dining room captain ascending the stairs backwards as he escorted patrons was lost but wheelchair access was gained.

During a 1994 local lecture series, Vince told the story of turning a customer away. "Once that hockey player from Los Angeles, Mr. Gretzky, showed up with some friends in beat-up jeans. They wouldn't wear the jackets we offered, so we said no." Vince's sons, James, Anthony and Vince Jr. have joined him in the business and Tony's continues as a St. Louis institution. The Bommaritos also own and provide the food service for the lower key Anthony's Bar, which is right across the lobby, serving up some of the same offerings, including the soup, desserts and wines.

Tony's Capellini with Grilled Scallops
Recipe shared by the Bommarito family

- 12 large sea scallops
- 1½ tsp chopped garlic, divided (or more, to taste)
- 2 Tbsp olive oil
- 1 lb capellini (a thin pasta similar to angel hair)
- ½ cup (1 stick) butter
- • salt and pepper to taste

Toss scallops with ½ teaspoon garlic and olive oil; marinate for at least 5 minutes. Grill scallops over a charcoal fire until done or broil about 4 minutes on each side (about 4 inches from heat source). Meanwhile, add pasta to boiling water in a large saucepan. Cook pasta until almost done, about 4 minutes. Drain pasta, reserving about 1 cup of the cooking water. Return pasta to pan with 1 cup cooking water. Return pan to burner; add butter, remaining garlic, salt and pepper to taste. Continue cooking until pasta is done. The butter and water mixture should be thickened and absorbed by the pasta in 3 to 4 minutes. Place pasta on a platter. Arrange grilled scallops around the pasta. Serve immediately. Yield: 4 servings as a main course and 6 servings as an appetizer. Notes: can add a couple of drops of vegetable oil to boiling water to keep pasta from sticking; scallops weighed between ½ to ¾ lb and were 1 ¾ inches in diameter.

Tony's

Tony's has a nation-wide reputation for excellence that would be the envy of any businessman. Unequaled in food and service, Tony's has won all major restaurant awards including the Holiday Magazine Award and the Mobil Five-Star Award. Tony's offers a dining experience long to be remembered and can be compared with the finest restaurants anywhere in the world.

Cannelloni Cappricio   3.25
Shrimp de Jonghe   3.00
Escargots   3.50
Soup   1.50

Beluga Caviar   9.50
Italian Antipasto   3.50
Prosciutto Con Melone   3.00
Shrimp Cocktail   3.00
Tartare of Tenderloin   4.00

Pastas

Tagliatelle Con Pesce   8.50
Tagliatelle with Fresh Clam Sauce   6.75
Tagliatelle with Marinara Sauce   6.50
Fettuccine Romano   6.50
Cannelloni Cappricio   6.50
Cavatelli with Broccoli   6.50

Seafood

Fresh Trout Almadine   8.75
Turbot, Poached, Veloute Sauce   8.75
Dover Sole   8.75
Lobster Albanello   8.95
Lobster Tails   11.50

Steaks

Sirloin Steak, 16 oz.   10.50
Filet Mignon   9.50
Sirloin Steak 12 oz.   8.95
Lamb Chops   10.75
Chateaubriand Bouquetiere   21.00
Roasted Rack of Lamb, Bouquetiere   21.00

Entrees

Tournedos of Beef, Bordelaise   8.95
Scallopini of Beef Tenderloin   8.95
Boneless Breast of Chicken Alla Crema, Rissotta   8.00
Boneless Breast of Chicken, Fresh Fruit, Wild Rice   8.00
Boneless Breast of Chicken Capri   8.00
Veal Marsala   8.95
Veal Piemontese   8.95
Veal Piquante   8.95
Veal Cutlets alla Parmigiano   8.95

Salads

Tony's Salad   1.75
Sliced Tomatoes, Red Onions, Anchovies   1.75
Bibb Lettuce, Artichoke Hearts and Hearts of Palm Salad   2.00
Fresh Spinach Avocado, Crumbled Roquefort   1.75

Tony's

This restaurant began at 4201 North Grand Boulevard, nine blocks from Sportsman's Park. Kemoll's Italian Restaurant was started in 1927 by Doris (affectionately called Dora) and her husband James Kemoll (known as Joe). Their original names were Vincenzo Camuglia (changed by immigration officials to Kemoll) and Gaetana Danna. The restaurant was an ice cream and candy shop that sold sandwiches but evolved into a restaurant using Sicilian recipes from Dora's mother, Grace Danna. Joe and Dora had two daughters, JoAnn (later Berger), and Mary Grace (later Cusumano) who was born in 1927 in an apartment above the restaurant. The girls began working in the restaurant at an early age, working alongside their parents. Mary Grace married Frank Cusumano who joined the Kemoll family at the restaurant in 1952. Under Dora and Frank's leadership, the restaurant continued to expand and prosper with an emphasis on Italian food and the Kemoll women doing much of the work in the kitchen. By the 1960s, the restaurant was hosting International Gourmet Nights in its four dining rooms, the Florentine, Rosetelle and Caesar rooms and the Gallery. Dora continued to live in the building until her death in 1987. Her husband Joe died in 1988.

After decades at the Grand location with multi-generational employees assisting in the operation, Kemoll's, now owned by Frank and Mary Grace's son Mark Cusumano, relocated to the One Metropolitan Square building, opening on June 13, 1990. Within a couple of weeks of the move and just months after Mark had sold the landmark restaurant building, it burned down under what the fire chief called suspicious circumstances. It was a big blow to the Kemoll family. As an aside, Dora also passed on the food gene to JoAnn's daughters, Kate Berger and Julie Hale, who owned the Pan Dora Bakery (named for their grandmother) for a while. Kemoll's continues today as an elegant restaurant in the heart of downtown and, counting Grace Danna's original Sicilian recipes, is in its fifth generation.

Kemoll's Petto Di Pollo All'Agro Dolce

When this recipe was originally shared in 2003 with *St. Louis Post-Dispatch* readers in response to a special request, JoAnn copied the recipe from one that was in Dora's handwriting. It's Kemoll's version of sweet and sour chicken. *Recipe shared by Mark Cusumano*

- 2 skinless, boneless chicken breast halves
- about 1/4 cup all-purpose flour
- ¼ cup clarified butter
- ¼ cup plus 2 Tbsp wine vinegar
- ¼ cup plus 2 Tbsp water
- 2 tsp capers, drained
- 2 Tbsp golden raisins
- ¼ cup plus 1 Tbsp granulated sugar
- 2 Tbsp chopped whole almonds, toasted

Pound chicken to an even thickness of about ⅜ inch; dip in flour and shake off excess. Heat a skillet over medium-high heat. Add butter and chicken; brown both sides of chicken, turning only once. Remove chicken, set aside and keep warm. Add vinegar, water, capers, raisins and sugar to the skillet; place over high heat and stir to combine. Cook for a minute or two, until sauce is slightly reduced and thickened. Stir in almonds. Return chicken to the skillet; cook until chicken is done, about 3 minutes. Place chicken on serving plates and pour sauce over. Yield: 2 servings.

Kemoll's

pasta asciutta

CANNELLONI ALLA TOSCANA
The dish that impressed Mrs. Kemoll on her trip to Italy
A very delectable treat of homemade noodle dough stuffed with chicken and veal filling, topped with mushroom, tomato and wine sauce and Mozzarella cheese ... 5.20

CANNELLONI ALLA CREMA 5.20

MANICOTTI
A perfect dish prepared as the above with a delicious Riccotta cheese filling . 5.20

MANICOTTI ALLA CREMA 5.20

LINGUINI con VONGOLE
A favorite of ours served exclusively at Kemoll's. Flat noodles flavored with a delicious fresh chopped clam sauce and topped with fresh clams in the shell ... 5.50
With Fettucini 5.75

SPAGHETTI ALLA CARBONARA
Prepared at your table. An old favorite in Italy now at Kemoll's. Prociutto, eggs and cheese tossed with spaghetti — a dish you will long remember ... 5.50

LASAGNE or MOSTACCIOLI al FORNO
Layers of noodles, meat filling, Riccotta and Mozzarella cheese. Topped with our delicious sauce and baked in a casserole ... 4.75

SHELLRONI WITH BROCCOLLI 4.75

SPAGHETTI or MOSTACCIOLI
with Meat Balls ... 4.00
with Sauteed Fresh Mushrooms ... 4.50
with Sweet Butter ... 4.00
with Roast Top Round of Beef ... 5.25
with Our Delicious Homemade Pork Sausage ... 5.00

CAVATELLI con MELANZANA (Egg Plant) 4.75

SPAGHETTI
ALLA MARINARA with or without anchovies 4.75

SPAGHETTI alla CARUSO ... 5.00
with chicken livers

HOMEMADE RAVIOLI ... 4.50
with Sauteed Fresh Mushrooms ... 5.00

OUR DELICIOUS HOMEMADE GREEN NOODLES OR FETTUCINI — All' Alfredo-
Tossed with pure sweet butter, cream and fresh grated Parmesan cheese ... 5.00
with Meat Balls or Meat Sauce ... 5.50
with Sauteed Fresh Mushrooms ... 5.50
(Prepared at your table)

PAGLIA E FIENO
White and Green Fettucini with peas, prosciutto and cream, tossed at your table ... 5.50

pesce

FROM THE LAKES AND THE SEVEN SEAS

Fried Squid, Lemon 5.50

Fried Scallops, Tartar Sauce 5.50

Chicken Fried Colossal Shrimp, Tartar Sauce ... 6.50

Poached Fillet of Sole, Hostaria 6.00

Fried Filet of Sole, Tartar Sauce ... 5.50

Fresh Poached Fillet of Scrod in Vermouth 6.45

Assorted Seafood Platter, Shrimp, Sole, Lobster Tail, Scallops, etc. 8.20

Broiled Tiny Danish or African Lobster Tails 8.75

Fresh Hake- A dish from Spain ... 5.75
Dipped in Butter and Crumbs and Baked in Casserole

daily features

Half Chicken, Skillet Fried or Broiled ... 4.50

Broiled Home Made Italian Pork Sausage ... 4.75

Pesce and Daily Features include:

Kemoll's Italian Salad - Hot Cheese Rolls
Baked Potato or Italian Spaghetti

BISTECCHE ... *aged to perfection*

from our Genuine charcoal broiler

Broiled Choice 12 oz. Strip Steak	6.95
Choice Strip Steak, Full Pound Size (16 oz.)	7.50
Choice Filet Mignon, King Size	7.50
Queen Size	6.75
20 oz. Beef T-Bone Steak	7.95
20 oz. T-Bone Steak alla Sicilliana (A Choice Steak Breaded in the True Sicilian Style)	8.25
Lobster Tail and Fillet Mignon	8.25

Steaks Include:
French Fried Potatoes, Oven Baked Potato or Spaghetti
Fresh Mushroom Sauce   Our Italian Salad Bowl
Our Now Famous Hot Cheese Bread

Service charge for splitting orders.   **we do not use tenderizers**

kemoll's pranzo festivo

aperitivi

Assorted Italian Antipasto	Sliced Egg with Anchovies	Fresh Shrimp Cocktail	Marinated Herring
Fruit Cocktail	Prosciutto con Melone (in season)	Tomato Juice	

minestra

Minestra del Giorno

		A la Carte Baked Potatoes or Spaghetti Salad and Cheese Rolls	Complete Dinner
bistecche	**FILLET CLETO** (Sliced Fillet of Tenderloin Sauteed to Perfection)	7.20	9.70
	ROLLED BRACIOLE, with Buttered Green Noodles (Beef Steak Rolled with Prosciutto and Italian Meat Filling)	6.20	8.70
	BREADED BEEF STEAK ITALIAN (Breaded with Our Own Delicious Italian Bread Crumbs)	6.00	8.50
	ITALIAN PEPPER STEAK (Sliced Beef Tenderloin Sauteed, Wine, Green Pepper, Fresh Mushrooms)	7.20	9.70
	FILLET ALLA GRANDUCA (In a wine sauce with aspargus spears)	7.75	10.25
pollo	**BROILED HALF CHICKEN OREGANATO** (Basted with Olive Oil, Lemon Juice, Oregano, Touch of Garlic, Parsley)	6.00	8.50
	HALF CHICKEN ALLA CACCIATORA (Sauteed in Butter, Fresh Tomato, Mushrooms, Green Pepper, Marsala Wine)	6.00	8.50
	CHICKEN ALLA ROMANA (Disjointed Chicken Sauteed in Butter, Special Spices, Wine, Garlic)	6.00	8.50

INTRODUCING KEMOLL'S NEWEST CREATIONS FROM ITALY

petto di pollo	**PETTO di POLLO ALLA CACCIATORA** (Sauteed in Butter, Fresh Tomato, Mushrooms, Green Pepper, Marsala Wine)	6.00	8.50
	PETTO DI POLLO GRAN SASSO FROM ABRUZZI Boneless breast of chicken sauteed in imported olive oil in a picanti sauce made of fresh tomatoes and spices	6.00	8.50
	PETTO DI POLLO CONTI, FROM TURIN Boneless breast of chicken with slivers of procuitto and cream sauteed in butter	6.00	8.50
	PETTO DI POLLO FEDELINARO, FROM ROME Boneless breast of chicken sauteed and topped with prociutto, mozzarello and wine	6.00	8.50
	PETTO DI POLLO CONCA D'ORO FROM PALERMO Boneless breast of chicken dipped in egg and Kemolls own special Italian Bread crumbs, lightly sauteed in imported olive oil and butter	6.00	8.50
	PETTO DI POLLO PAULUCCIO, FROM NAPLES Boneless breast of chicken sauteed in a picanti sauce with capers	6.00	8.50

vitello	**VEAL SPIEDINI ALLA GRIGLIA** (Small Slices of Veal, Rolled Around Seasoned Prosciutto filling on Skewer)	6.75	9.25
	VEAL CUTLET PARMIGIANA (Breaded Veal Cutlet, Topped with Tomato Sauce, Mozzarella Cheese)	6.75	9.25
	VEAL SCALOPPINA, with Fresh Mushrooms (Sliced Veal Steak, Sauteed in Butter, Marsala Wine)	6.75	9.25
	VEAL SALTIMBOCCA ALLA ROMANA (Sliced Prosciutto Between Two Veal Cutlets, Delicately Seasoned with Aromatic Spices, Sauted in Butter and Wine)	7.70	10.20
	VEAL PICCANTI (A Lemon Flavored Veal Favorite Sauteed in Sweet Butter)	6.75	9.25
	VEAL ALLA BOLOGNESE (Sauteed in Butter, Parmesan Cheese with Fresh Mushrooms)	6.75	9.25
pesce	**ZUPPA DI PESCE** (The Italian Version of Bouillabaisse)	7.20	9.70
	BROILED FILET OF MACKEREL, Lemon Parsley (Italian Style)	6.20	8.70
	HALIBUT GAETANA — Broiled with a Delicious Topping Created by Mrs. Kemoll	6.20	8.70
	COLOSSAL SHRIMP split and stuffed with our special Italian filling. Served with Italian baked tomato	7.50	10.00

Spaghetti or Potatoes Served with Above Meat Orders
Except on Orders with Pasta

insalate

Italian Salad   Hot Cheese Bread

dolci

Our Own Italian Cannoli, Pignolata or Ice Cream Pie
Spumoni   Sherbet   Gelati   Ice Cream   Italian Cookies   Crostolli
Imported Provolone

Service charge for splitting orders.

Original Route 66 Alignment

Angel Food Cake and the Hotel Beers

Woolworth's

Gaslight Square and the Three
    Fountains Restaurant

Tenderloin Room at the Chase Park Plaza
    (Hack Ulrich and the Tenderloin Room)

St. Louis Art Museum

Blueberry Hill

Fitz's Root Beer

Cicero's

Medart's and the Cheshire Inn

The Parkmoor

Schlafly Bottleworks

Monarch Restaurant and Wine Bar

Engelhard's Tavern

Buckingham's

Hacienda Mexican Restaurant

Charcoal House

Big Chief

Purina Farm

Hotels on the Original Alignment   The Arena   1926 Forest Park Highlands ad

Bartold's Grove in Maplewood, MO   Nine Mile House in Rock Hill, MO   Eleven Mile House in Kirkwood, MO

Carl's Drive-In in Brentwood, MO   Fairfax House in Rock Hill, MO   Motor Inn in Labadie, MO

Angel Food Cake and the Hotel Beers

According to *The New Symphony of Cooking Cookbook* (1964 edition at page 101), angel food cake has early ties to St. Louis. While I was unable to locate and have not reviewed the original documentation, I pass on the story. According to the excerpt, angel food cake "was the invention of a St. Louis lady" then was "taken up by the Hotel Beers, the first to offer it for sale." The Hotel Beers was located at the corner of Grand and Olive, in Midtown near Lindell Boulevard and St. Louis University. An 1888 Hotel Beers catalog touted the new discovery as "not surpassed by anything known to the confectioner's art." (Apparently, this 1870s/1880s era is consistent with the timing for recipes on the East Coast first using the term "angel" for cakes made with a dozen or so egg whites. This mystery St. Louis baker may have been the first to introduce the cake to St. Louis.) Regardless, George S. Beers embraced the cake as an original and he so advertised in the catalog. The Hotel Beers also claimed that the cake could be shipped "to any part of the globe and arrive fresh as the day it was baked" by a special packing process, which removed the air. The hotel backed up this claim by shipping the cake to a confectioner's journal in London, England who said of the cake that "no more appropriate name could have been received, for it fairly melts in one's mouth" and predicted success for the manufacturer. While the exact origin of angel food cake is unknown it definitely had early commercial beginnings here in St. Louis and continues to be popular today. The 136-room Hotel Beers burned down in 1931 and the site later became a Woolworth's store.

Woolworth's

Many have wonderful memories of the food and desserts served up at the Woolworth (also called Woolworth's) lunch counters. The pioneer five and dime store was founded in 1879 in Lancaster, Pennsylvania by Frank Woolworth. Soon, the stores could be found across the country, in downtown areas and in the suburbs. The Woolworth's lunch counter, famous for its sandwiches, banana splits and pies, also became famous for its role in the Civil Rights Movement with blacks across the country protesting the whites-only counters. The last six Woolworth's stores in St. Louis closed in 1993 and January 1994. After being shuttered for some time, the Woolworth's Midtown building was purchased by Big Brothers and Big Sisters, with plans to renovate it and incorporate Woolworth's (and its lunch counters) role in St. Louis' own desegregation. The more famous Woolworth's lunch counter at Greensboro, North Carolina is part of the Smithsonian Institution.

Woolworth's No-Bake Lemon Cheesecake
This recipe was obtained from a Woolworth's store by Jean Lindstrom of St. Peters, Missouri and shared with St. Louis Post-Dispatch readers on June 19, 1999.

3 (3-ounce) packages lemon-flavored gelatin
½ cup (1 stick) butter
½ lb plain graham crackers
1 Tbsp plus 2 cups granulated sugar, divided
2 (8-ounce) packages cream cheese
2 tsp vanilla
¼ cup lemon juice
3 cups whipping cream

In a saucepan, combine gelatin with 3 cups water. Bring to a boil; cook, stirring for 2 minutes to dissolve gelatin. Remove from heat; let cool to room temperature. (If you cool in freezer, do not let it set as it must stay in liquid form.) Melt butter. Finely crush graham crackers. Combine butter, crumbs and one tablespoon sugar. Pat evenly into bottom of a 10-inch by 15-inch pan. Refrigerate while you proceed with filling. Beat cream cheese with remaining 2 cups sugar. Add vanilla and lemon juice. In another bowl, whip cream until stiff peaks appear. Fold in cream cheese mixture. Pour in gelatin in a small stream, mixing well. Pour mixture onto crust. Refrigerate at least 4 hours or until set. Cut into squares and serve. Yield: 20 servings. Note: You can vary the gelatin flavor or add a fresh fruit topping.

Gaslight Square and the Three Fountains Restaurant

Gaslight Square represents a bygone era that flourished in St. Louis' Central West End, near the intersection of Boyle Avenue and Olive Street, just north of the Original alignment's path on Lindell. In 1953, before the area developed, Richard Mutrux took a chance and bought the Musical Arts Building, a music/dance studio, and there opened the Gaslight Bar. The success of the bar sparked more development in the area and in 1958, Fran and Jay Landesman opened the Crystal Palace where many famous entertainers appeared including Barbra Streisand, Lenny Bruce, Woody Allen, George Carlin, the Smothers Brothers, Phyllis Diller and comedian turned activist Dick Gregory. Although it encompassed less than a two-block area, it grew into an entertainment district that lined both sides of Olive Street, paying homage to the riverboat age and lit up with over 100 gas lights, a tribute to the days when St. Louis streets were illuminated by gas lanterns. Gaslight Square, complete with talent and beatniks, was in a special league where patrons strolled from one end to another, carrying their drink along. They could stop anywhere along the way as there were no cover charges. The place was filled with the excitement of the unexpected. It was akin to the French Quarter and Greenwich Village but with a St. Louis flair. Gaslight Square became the cultural center of St. Louis where antique stores, coffee houses, sidewalk cafes, art galleries, Kosher delis and nightclubs all happily welcomed "moneyed Bohemians" and artsy types from around the country.

Around 1960, Mutrux and his brother Paul (who played flamenco guitar) joined together to open the upscale Three Fountains restaurant, also in the Musical Arts Building. The restaurant included brass chandeliers from the World's Fair, a wrought-iron balcony from an old Grand Avenue bridge, mahogany panels from the Merchant's Exchange Building, stained glass windows from an old St. Louis home and three brass fountains. The Mutrux brothers took in a partner, Weston Colbrunn, and featured the Mutrux family's French recipes. The restaurant had a 5-star rating and was considered the fanciest restaurant in the hottest district. The Three Fountains won awards and was written up in *Gourmet* and other magazines. Then, poof, it closed in 1968. Hippies and flower children with less money became abundant and transients settled in the area. Crime became more common, which scared customers away. O'Connell's Pub opened in 1962 and was the last restaurant to move from the area in 1972. Because it took much of its former self with it to the new location on Shaw Avenue, it stands today as a link to the past. Gaslight Square fell into gradual disrepair, a victim of crime and suburban flight, and is but a memory today. No serious development plan with preservation of the remaining buildings ever surfaced and, due to continued neglect, the buildings became derelict and could not be salvaged. Most of what was once the magical Gaslight Square was redeveloped into the Gaslight Square housing area.

Chicken a la Three Fountains (Poulet Sauté Trois Fountaines)

This recipe was a Three Fountains house specialty. It is a reminder of a unique period in St. Louis' cultural history and a link to the Mutrux family who saw promise in the area and helped build the all too short-lived Gaslight Square. *Recipe from "Clowning Around" with Cookery, a 1965 cookbook by the Salvation Army Women's Auxiliary of St. Louis*

- 1 whole chicken
- 4 strips bacon
- 1 stick butter
- 1 tsp paprika
- 1 Tbsp rosemary leaves
- 1 cup sliced mushrooms
- ½ cup dry white wine
- 1 cup brown gravy
- 1 Tbsp chopped parsley
- • salt and white pepper to taste

Clean the chicken, cut into quarters. Remove wing-end, backbone and heavy thigh bone. Shape each quarter into firm portion and wrap with strip of bacon. Hold with a toothpick. Melt butter in small baking pan and lay chicken pieces side by side. Sprinkle with salt, pepper, paprika, rosemary, sliced mushrooms. Bake at 400 degrees for 15 minutes. From time to time, baste with melted butter from bottom of baking pan. When golden brown, add dry white wine and continue to bake for 5 minutes. Add the brown gravy and bake for 10 minutes more. Remove chicken to plate and keep it warm. Add chopped parsley to the sauce in baking pan and let simmer over low flame until sauce is reduced. Pour sauce over chicken and serve with Pommes croquettes, broccoli, Hollandaise sauce and broiled tomatoes. Yield: 2 servings.

The Three Fountains

4306 Olive Street, at Boyle
Attendant Parking
JEfferson 1-4464

Cuisine par Excellence

PRE-THEATRE DINNER 6:00 P.M.

Tenderloin Room at the Chase Park Plaza

212-232 N. Kingshighway Blvd.
314-361-0900 • www.tenderloinroom.com;
Chase Park Plaza 1-877-587-2427 • www.chaseparkplaza.com

Hack Ulrich and the Tenderloin Room

The Chase Hotel, opened September 29, 1922, was built by Chase Ulman and the Park Plaza Hotel, next door, was built by Sam Koplar in 1929. During the Depression, both hotels fell on hard times. Koplar lost control of the Park Plaza project and construction stalled but by the early 1930s it was completed, opened, and reacquired by Koplar. Sam Koplar managed the Chase and other hotels to support himself. By 1947 he had enough Chase stock to take control of it as well.

In 1961, the two hotels were physically combined into one complex with the Tenderloin Room (opened March 28, 1962) serving as a connector between the two. The Chase served as the center of St. Louis nightlife for decades and closely intertwined with the hotel was Henry "Hack" Ulrich who worked there for 50 years, from 1936 to 1986. He began as a busboy and left briefly to pursue a baseball career in the minor leagues. There he earned the name Hack after a teammate heard him say he wanted to hit like Hack Wilson, a Chicago Cubs slugger. Hack also served in World War II but then returned to the Chase in 1946 and stayed put. He served as Maitre'd then manager of the Starlight Room and the Chase Club. He oversaw 40 New Year's Eve celebrations at the hotel, many in the hotel's heyday when big stars like Nat King Cole, Dean Martin, Perry Como, the Andrews Sisters, Tommy Dorsey, and Billie Holliday entertained the thick crowds. Hack met his wife Eleanor who started out as a cigarette girl at the Chase in 1950 and they worked side by side for 35 years.

In 1961, the Chase Club closed and he moved over to the helm of the new Tenderloin Room. Hack was a master at seating people, managing the place smoothly, and keeping customers happy. It was said that if a man came twice to the Tenderloin Room, Hack knew his name, and that of his children, banker and barber as well. Hack was known to deliver the Tenderloin's famous steaks to hospital rooms, gladly putting on a show for August A. "Gussie" Busch Jr. and Harry Carey. He admitted getting into trouble for it when criminal lawyer Morris Shenker wasn't yet recovered enough for that type of food and

a doctor at Jewish Hospital chewed him out for it. Shenker, a Russian-Jewish immigrant who never forgot his humble beginnings and went on to be a celebrity of sorts, was married to Sam Koplar's daughter Lillian and the couple practiced law together. Shenker was the attorney for some local criminal elements as well as the Highway 66 Business Association. The Ace Cab Company owned by Joe Costello and likely involved in the laundering of the Bobby Greenlease ransom money was a client as well.

In 1963, Hack observed Tom Karagiannis waiting tables in the Khorrasan and Starlight Rooms and recruited him for the Tenderloin Room. Several generations of Karagiannises would work at the Tenderloin Room under Hack. On Christmas Eve 1968, a fire destroyed the restaurant but Harold Koplar rebuilt it and reopened it in 1970. In 1981, the Koplar family sold both hotels. The new owner redeveloped the Park Plaza into apartments, opening in 1988, but closed the Chase Hotel in September 1989. Only the Tenderloin Room stayed open. There were many heavy hearts in St. Louis and parts beyond, particularly those of the long-tenured employees. Jack Milster who spent 38 years as a bellman was in disbelief, having served under several generations of Koplars. Longtime doorman Charlie Woodley recalled Bob Hope's stay as his favorite hotel memory and Pearl Zanella who retired at age 82 as a kitchen worker said that throughout her employment she felt the Chase was her home. Unfortunately, an auction of the hotel's contents followed and people forgot about the lone Tenderloin Room. It closed in August 1991 with Hack (who had retired in 1986) remarking that it was a sin to close such a beautiful room.

Fortunately, the story does not end there. Kingsdell LLP bought the historic Chase and restored it to its former glory. The Chase today serves as a luxury hotel with five restaurants: Café Eau, Eau Bistro, Chaser's Lounge, Marquee Café and the Tenderloin Room. Hack's long-time employee, Tom Karagiannis and his family took over the Tenderloin Room's operation in 1992, continuing most of the traditions and menu offerings, closing it only briefly to renovate it in 1999. The Karagiannis family continues to operate the Tenderloin Room today. The Tenderloin Room has long been known for its Pepperloin steak served with a mustard sauce, its

cheesecake, and its (U.S. Senate) navy bean soup. Hack Ulrich passed away in 2002 but he passed the Tenderloin Room's torch to the Karagiannis family.

Tenderloin Room's Hellenic Salad and Dressing

The Tenderloin Room originally shared this recipe in 1989 just before the Chase Hotel closed. Shared by the Tenderloin Room and the Karagiannis family

Hellenic Salad:

- 1½ cups torn iceberg lettuce
- 1½ cups torn Romaine lettuce
- ¼ cup shredded red cabbage
- 6 slices peeled cucumber
- 4 Tbsp crumbled Feta cheese
- 1 (¼-inch) slice green bell pepper, diced (scant 2 Tbsp diced)
- 1 (1/4-inch) slice red bell pepper, diced (scant 2 Tbsp diced)
- 6 red onion rings
- 2 tomato wedges
- 1 tsp dry leaf oregano
- 4 Greek kalamata olives
- 3 anchovy fillets, cut in small pieces
- • Hellenic dressing (see recipe), to taste

Combine lettuces, cabbage, cucumber, cheese, bell peppers, onion rings, tomato wedges, oregano, olives and anchovies in serving bowl. Add enough Hellenic dressing to moisten greens. Yield: 1 main-dish salad or 2 dinner salads.

Hellenic Dressing:

- ½ cup apple cider vinegar
- 2 cups vegetable oil
- 2 Tbsp diced red onion
- 2 Tbsp diced white onion
- 2 Tbsp diced seeded cucumber
- 2 Tbsp lemon juice
- 1 Tbsp diced green bell pepper
- 1 Tbsp diced red bell pepper
- 1 Tbsp capers
- 1 Tbsp diced dill pickle
- 1 tsp salt
- 1 tsp black pepper

Combine vinegar, oil, onions, cucumber, lemon juice, bell peppers, capers, dill pickle, salt and pepper in medium bowl or in jar with a tight-fitting lid. Refrigerate for 3 hours to let flavors mingle before using. Stir or shake to mix before using. Store remaining dressing in refrigerator for later use. Yield: about 2¾ cups dressing.

St. Louis Art Museum

One Fine Arts Drive (Forest Park)
314-721-0072
www.slam.org

Forest Park is considered the Crown Jewel of St. Louis. The Original alignment took several paths in the early years but all ended at Forest Park before eventually getting over to Manchester Road. Forest Park has a lot to offer with much of it free or nominally priced. While exploring there, stop for a bite at the History Museum's Meriwether's restaurant, the clubhouse at the golf course, the Boathouse restaurant or the restaurants at the zoo. Or you can do like many St. Louisans have done for decades and eat at the Art Museum's restaurant, today called Puck's.

St. Louis Art Museum's Chess Pie

This recipe has appeared in several vintage cookbooks including <u>The New Saint Louis Symphony of Cooking</u> *(1964) where it was shared by Mayme Elz. Courtesy Saint Louis Symphony Volunteer Association*

- 1 unbaked 9-inch pastry crust
- ½ cup butter
- 1½ cups sugar
- 1 Tbsp cornmeal
- 3 eggs
- 5 Tbsp milk
- 1 tsp vinegar
- 1 tsp vanilla

While mixing pie, melt butter in oven (see note). Beat sugar, cornmeal and eggs. Stir in milk, vinegar and vanilla. Stir in melted butter. Pour into crust. Bake at 400 degrees for 35 to 40 minutes, or until firm. Note: today, it is easier to melt the butter in the microwave.

St. Louis Art Museum's Vegetable Nut Torte

The note for this recipe says it is a very moist cake that keeps beautifully. *Submitted by Betty Collins for the St. Louis Art Museum's 1977 cookbook,* <u>The Artist in the Kitchen</u>

- 2 cups flour
- 1½ tsp baking soda
- 2 tsp baking powder
- 1½ tsp salt
- 2 tsp cinnamon
- 2 cups sugar
- 4 eggs
- 1½ cups oil
- 1½ cups grated carrots
- ½ cup finely diced celery
- 1 8-oz can crushed pineapple (drained)
- ½ cup chopped pecans

Icing:
- ½ cup butter
- ½ tsp almond extract
- 1 8-oz package cream cheese, softened
- 1 lb powdered sugar

Cream butter; add almond extract, cream cheese and powdered sugar. Beat until creamy. Spread icing between layers and on top of cake.

Sift flour with baking soda, baking powder, salt, cinnamon, and sugar. Beat eggs; add oil, carrots, celery, pineapple and nuts. Add flour mixture. Grease and flour three 8-inch round cake pans. Bake at 350 degrees for 35 minutes. Cool then frost with icing. Yield: 8 to 10 servings.

The bustling University City Loop is located just north of the Original alignment's path into Forest Park. Blueberry Hill is an award-winning food and entertainment establishment where you can definitely get a thrill. Legend Chuck Berry still performs here regularly.

Blueberry Hill Red Beans and Rice
Shared by owner Joe Edwards

      2 cups chopped onion
      1 green bell pepper (cut into 1-inch pieces)
      ½ rib celery with leaves, chopped
      1 cup chopped tomato
      1 Tbsp plus 1 tsp minced garlic
      3 (15-16 ounce) cans kidney beans, drained
      1 cup water
      1 bay leaf
      1 Tbsp dried basil
      2 tsp dried thyme
      1 tsp salt
      1 tsp ground black pepper
   1½ tsp Tabasco sauce or to taste
   • hot, cooked seasoned brown or white rice

Combine onion, green pepper, celery, tomato, garlic, beans, water, bay leaf, basil, thyme, salt, pepper and Tabasco sauce in a large pot. Bring to a boil then reduce heat to a simmer. Cook about 30 minutes or until vegetables are tender, stirring occasionally. Remove bay leaf; serve bean mixture over hot seasoned rice. Yield: 4 to 6 servings.

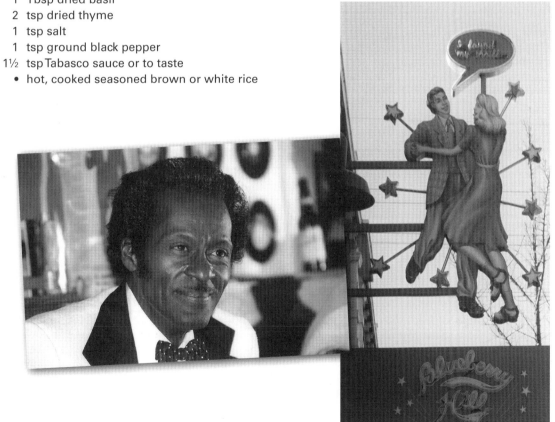

Fitz's is a popular restaurant with a root beer bottling operation on site. It is housed in a 1928 bank building.

Fitz's Cajun Gumbo
Shared by owner Bob Gunthner

¼ each red pepper and green pepper, diced
7 carrots, medium diced
1 stalk celery, medium diced
2 medium onions, diced
1 Tbsp each of thyme, oregano, coarse black
    pepper, Kosher salt, basil, granulated garlic
    and cayenne pepper
2 oz seafood stock
3 medium tomatoes, diced
4 oz clam juice
16 oz can clams, drained and chopped
1 Tbsp Worcestershire sauce
½ cup flour
½ cup butter
1½ lbs small shrimp, peeled
10 oz bay scallops, chopped
6 oz Tasso ham, medium diced
6 oz Andouille sausage
4½ cups water

Add oil to skillet and heat. Add flour to oil and make into a roux. Cook roux to a deep, dark brown color. Add all diced sausage, ham and vegetables except tomatoes. Let it cook for 10 minutes, stirring repeatedly. Add tomatoes, clam juice, water and seafood base, and all spices and cook for 5 minutes, stirring repeatedly. Bring to a quick boil and add shrimp, scallops, and clams. Reduce heat and cook for the final 15 minutes, stirring continuously. Gumbo is ready once all seafood products are cooked thoroughly. May be garnished with white rice and scallions. Yield: 4 servings with leftovers.

Cicero's

6691 Delmar Blvd. (University City)
314-862-0009
www.ciceros-stl.com

Cicero's is one of the pioneer establishments of the Loop, opening in 1977. Besides great food and entertainment, it also has a beer school and serves a large variety of beers.

Cicero's Cheese-Baked Pasta Alamara
Shared by owner Shawn Jacobs

8	ounces small or medium shell noodles
1	Tbsp minced garlic
¼	tsp seasoned salt
6	Tbsp (3/4 stick) butter, softened
4	cups Half-and-Half
⅔	cup condensed cream of shrimp soup
2	cups surimi (imitation crab), cut into ¾-inch pieces, or lump crab meat
2	cups sliced mushrooms
24	medium cooked shrimp, peeled and deveined
1	cup plus 2 Tbsp grated Parmesan or Romano cheese or a blend, divided
•	salt
•	ground black pepper
1	to 1 ½ cups marinara sauce
1	cup (4 ounces) grated Mozzarella cheese
1	cup (4 ounces) shredded Provel cheese
2	Tbsp dried parsley

Cook noodles according to package directions; drain well and set aside. In a small bowl, work garlic and seasoned salt into softened butter. Transfer to a deep skillet or large pot; melt garlic butter over medium heat. Add noodles, Half-and-Half, condensed soup, crab and mushrooms. Cook, stirring occasionally, until heated through, about 10 minutes. Stir in shrimp. Gradually add 1 cup Parmesan; stir to a uniformly creamy consistency. Add salt and pepper to taste. Remove from heat; divide among 4 individual broiler-safe casserole dishes (such as 8-by-4-inch au gratin dishes) or transfer to a 9-by-13-inch baking dish. Pour marinara sauce over the top; cover with Mozzarella and Provel cheese, dividing evenly if using individual dishes. Place under the broiler and cook until cheese is golden brown. Garnish with remaining 2 tablespoons Parmesan and parsley. Yield: 4 servings.

The St. Louis Walk of Fame

Medart's and the Cheshire Inn

Located just west of Forest Park and the Hi-Pointe Amoco was a hamburger restaurant with curb service called Medart's. It was owned by William S. Medart who did well during the Depression selling hamburger buns. The restaurant was one of the country's early drive-ins, along with the nearby Parkmoor. Medart also owned a second location on South Kingshighway, near Chippewa/Highway 66. Medart's was popular for many years. In the late 1940s, William Ernst bought the Medart's Kingshighway location and there opened The Fireplace. It operated for some years and then in 1960 Ernst changed the concept and the name to Uncle Bill's Pancake House. It was one of St. Louis' first pancake houses. The Clayton Road Medart's became the more upscale Medart's Rose and Crown (still with curb service) and in 1963, Stephen Apted, son of Florence Hulling Apted, bought the place and turned it into the Cheshire Inn. Four years later he added the Cheshire Lodge. The Cheshire Inn operated from 1964 to 2006 and was leased out by Apted in the later years. Medart's was known for its hamburgers with special sauce, which can be found today at John's Town Hall in the Dorchester Apartment Building, 665 South Skinker Blvd., 314-725-3555. (They have the official recipe, which is different from the one below.) Continuing the Hulling-Apted family tradition, the Cheshire Inn was known for many delicious items.

Medart's Recreated Burger Relish (unofficial version)
Recipe from the June 30, 2001 St. Louis Post-Dispatch Recipe Exchange column

William Fogarty Jr. wrote in to the Recipe Exchange column saying Medart's Burger Relish recipe had been published in the St. Louis Post-Dispatch years ago but he had then modified it to suit his memory of the flavor. He also gave strict instructions for assembling the burger, which included using flat bakery buns and using thin, large (not lean) hamburger patties, and cooking both on a griddle, not a grill. Serve with shredded lettuce and a slice of onion.

1 cup sweet pickle relish, drained
2 tsp horseradish
1½ tsp prepared mustard
2½ Tbsp chili sauce
2 Tbsp mayonnaise
¼ tsp Worcestershire sauce
2 Tbsp finely chopped onion
3 drops Tabasco sauce
1 Tbsp French dressing (optional)
1 pinch salt

Combine all ingredients. Yield: about 1 cup. Note: Another option is to use 2 tablespoons horseradish, 1 ½ tablespoons prepared mustard and 6 drops of Tabasco instead of the above amounts.

Medart's Rose and Crown

Cheshire Inn and Lodge

Cheshire Inn Pepper Steak with Savory Rice
Recipe from <u>Pierre's Secrets</u> De Smet Jesuit High School Mothers' Club 1980 cookbook

1⅓ lbs lean beef (cut in 1-inch cubes)
1 onion, chopped
1 Tbsp shortening
¼ tsp garlic powder
1 tsp salt
1½ tsp whole black pepper
1½ cups mushrooms, sliced
4 green peppers (cut in inch squares)
2 cups beef stock or bouillon
½ cup tomato paste
½ cup Burgundy wine

Sauté beef and onions slowly in a heavy skillet until onions are clear and meat has lost its red color. Add remaining ingredients except wine. Bring to a full boil; cover and simmer until flavors are blended and meat is tender. Thicken gravy with 2 tablespoons flour mixed with 2 tablespoons water. Add wine. Serve piping hot with savory rice (see recipe).

Savory Rice:

1 small onion, chopped
1 small green pepper, chopped
3 Tbsp salad oil
1½ cups rice, uncooked
3 to 4 cups strong chicken stock
2 Tbsp pimento, chopped

Sauté onions and peppers in oil until onions are clear but not brown. Add rice and sauté until coated with oil. Add chicken stock; cover and simmer until rice is done. Do not overcook. If rice is too dry, add more stock. Salt and pepper to taste and add pimento last for color. Helpful hint: Chicken bouillon cubes and water may be used to replace chicken stock. Yield: 6 to 8 servings.

Cheshire Inn Steak Butter
Recipe contributed by reader Ruth Zueifel to the <u>St. Louis Post-Dispatch Recipe Exchange</u> column. Zueifel said her husband had received the recipe from the lady who made the steak butter at the Inn.

2 Tbsp prepared horseradish
½ cup grated onion
2 cups (4 sticks) butter or margarine, softened
2 Tbsp chopped parsley
2 Tbsp Worcestershire sauce
¼ Tbsp Tabasco sauce

Stir ingredients together until smooth. Serve with steak. Yield: about 20 servings.

Looking for Informality?

THE GREAT HALL

OPENS AT 7 A. M. FOR BREAKFAST   LUNCHEON   DINNERS FROM $1.75

Whatever you are looking for, you will find it at

medart's

THE ROSE AND CROWN   CURB SERVICE   THE OLDE CHESHIRE
Southwest Corner of Forest Park   STerling 1-1226

The Parkmoor was a beloved St. Louis restaurant chain whose beginnings were in a tray for curbside eating. When St. Louis rejected the drive-in concept that Lou McGinley was promoting for his curbside trays, he showed them that it could succeed by opening St. Louis' first drive-in restaurant at Clayton and Big Bend, near Forest Park and the Original 66 route. The Clayton location served as the first and the last in the chain, operating from July 15, 1930 to October 15, 1999. There were also two locations on Chippewa (Historic route) and one location on Lindbergh Blvd. and Manchester Road (Bypass route).

Parkmoor Chickburger (developed by founder Lou McGinley in the 1930s)
Recipe from <u>Honk For Service</u> by Lou Ellen McGinley and also recreated by employee Bob Park for the July 12, 1999 <u>St. Louis Post-Dispatch</u> Special Request column

- 1 lb finely chopped broiled or baked chicken or turkey, boned
- 2 Tbsp barbecue spice or to taste (such as Farmer Brothers)
- 5 Tbsp granulated sugar
- 1 Tbsp celery salt
- ¾ tsp ground black pepper
- 10 to 12 ounces chicken broth

Preheat oven to 350 degrees. Finely chop chicken or turkey. Combine barbecue spice, sugar, celery salt, and pepper. Toss chicken with dry spice mixture in a 9-inch by 13-inch pan. Cover mixture with chicken broth. Bake uncovered for 35 to 40 minutes or until crust forms on top. Mixture should be moist when removed from the oven. If it is too dry, add a little more chicken broth. Serve on toasted bun with tartar sauce, lettuce and tomato. Yield: 5 or 6 servings.

Parkmoor 60th Anniversary 1930–1990
ST. LOUIS, MISSOURI
CLAYTON ROAD AT BIG BEND
FIRST DRIVE-IN IN ST. LOUIS—NOW A FULL SERVICE FAMILY RESTAURANT

Schlafly Bottleworks

7260 Southwest Avenue (Maplewood)

314- 241-2337

www.schlafly.com

Tom Schlafly and Dan Kopman started the Saint Louis Brewery, Inc. in 1989 with hopes of producing a microwbrewed beer. They hired a brewmaster, Dave Miller, who had helped get Missouri's laws changed to allow microbreweries to exist and later expanded on that so that microbreweries could sell to other bars and restaurants. They opened the Tap Room in late 1991, housed in a historic building they bought for $137,000. Initially, they only sold their beer at the Tap Room, then Blueberry Hill became their first draft account in 1993 and they kept expanding from there. In 1996, due to customer demand, they began bottling the beer, using a brewery in Minnesota. As demand continued, Schlafly bought an old grocery store building in Maplewood and converted it into the bottling operation for Schlafly beer, opening in 2003. At the time, Maplewood was struggling so Schlafly was seen as a risk taker. With Schlafly Bottleworks as the anchor, other businesses followed suit and Maplewood has experienced a revival. The Schlafly Bottleworks complex includes a restaurant, bar, and farmer's market and it is host to various community events. Schlafly Bottleworks also has its own garden on site.

Schlafly Sticky Toffee Pudding

Schlafly's signature dessert is found at both the Tap Room and the Schlafly Bottleworks Restaurant.
Shared by Schlafly Bottleworks

- 1 lb dates, chopped in food processor
- 2 cups hot water
- 2 tsp baking soda
- 5 oz butter, unsalted
- 1 lb sugar
- 5 eggs, large
- 1 lb all-purpose flour
- 2 tsp baking powder
- pinch salt
- 2 tsp vanilla
- Caramel sauce (see recipe below)
- fresh whipped cream (for garnish)

Preheat conventional oven to 350 degrees. Grease a 9-inch by 13-inch pan with butter and coat lightly with flour; shake out excess flour. Combine dates with hot water in a saucepan and bring to a boil. Remove from heat and add baking soda. Set aside to cool. In a mixing bowl, cream butter and sugar on high speed for 3 minutes. With mixer on low speed, add eggs one at a time until fully incorporated. Add flour, baking powder and salt. When fully mixed, add the dates and their liquid as well as the vanilla. Place batter into greased pan and bake in preheated oven until a skewer inserted comes out clean (30 to 45 minutes). Cool on a baking rack before removing from the pan.

For Sauce:

- 1 lb dark brown sugar
- 1 lb butter
- 1 tsp vanilla extract
- 1 cup heavy cream

Stir together first three ingredients on low heat until blended and brown sugar has melted. Whisk heavy cream into brown sugar and butter mixture. When ready to serve, spoon warm caramel over individual servings of Sticky Toffee Pudding and top with a dollop of freshly whipped cream.

Although there is no featured recipe here, don't miss Tiffany's Original Diner (7402 Manchester Road in Maplewood), Carl's Drive-In (9033 Manchester Road in Brentwood) and the Trainwreck Saloon, originally the historic Nine Mile House, still in the same building at 9243 Manchester Road in Rock Hill.

Monarch Restaurant and Wine Bar is in the old Katz Drug building. It became Bobby's Creole restaurant in 1997 and Monarch in 2003. This upscale restaurant has received a lot of attention due to it is great food and wine as well as hip atmosphere.

Monarch's Chocolate Grand Marnier Crème Carmel

This recipe is the one most requested by customers. *Shared by Executive Chef Brian S. Hale*

For the Custard:

- 16 oz heavy cream
- 6 egg yolks
- 4 oz sugar
- 4 oz semi-sweet chocolate
- ½ oz Grand Marnier
- 1 vanilla bean split lengthwise

Combine yolks and sugar in a stainless steel bowl and mix well. Cut vanilla bean lengthwise and put into a pot with the cream. Heat cream to a boil and remove from heat. Scrape seeds from vanilla bean into cream and reserve. Melt chocolate in a double boiler and add into cream mixture along with the Grand Marnier. Slowly temper cream into egg mixture while constantly stirring until it is all incorporated.

For the Carmel:

- 1 cup sugar
- 1 Tbsp water

For the Garnish:

- 6 mint leaves
- 12 raspberries

Put 1 cup of sugar into a pan with 1 tablespoon of water and cook until all sugar is dissolved and golden in color. Remember to constantly stir mixture while cooking to avoid burning. Spoon carmel into six 6-ounce ramekins and let cool for 5 minutes. Pour custard mixture into carmel-filled ramekins and bake at 310 degrees, in a water bath, for about 2 hours or until custard is firm. Center will jiggle like Jell-O. Let cool to room temperature, then refrigerate for at least 6 hours, preferably overnight. To serve: run a knife around the rim of the crème carmels. Tap out onto desired plate and garnish with fresh raspberries and mint. Yield: 6 servings.

◆ Engelhard's Tavern – in operation today as the Sports Attic Bar and Grill
8212 Manchester Road (Brentwood)
314-963-7829
www.sportsatticbar.com

This restaurant at 8212 Manchester Road in Brentwood had early beginnings, predating Route 66. The tiny lunch room, owned by a man named Tony Heller, was purchased by Fred Engelhard in 1926 who had left his downtown St. Louis saloon and relocated to the country. Fred expanded the building after Prohibition was repealed and it stayed in the Engelhard family, owned by Fred's youngest daughter Mary and her husband Van, until 1974. The tavern served up standard fare and the only family recipe that was preserved was one for wild rabbit (Hasenpfeffer), which was served free to tavern customers. The place became Ruby's Brentwood Inn and is currently the Sports Attic Bar and Grill.

◆ Buckingham's

Buckingham's, another famous Brentwood spot, was known for its delicious fried chicken and was recommended by Duncan Hines. It was a destination restaurant for decades. The building still stands today, renumbered to 8949 Manchester Road.

Buckingham's Chicken Soup
From the 1954 <u>Symphony of Cooking</u> cookbook, courtesy Saint Louis Symphony Volunteer Association

1	4-lb chicken
5	cups water
1	small onion
1	stalk celery
1	carrot
2	Tbsp chicken fat
1½	Tbsp flour
•	salt and pepper to taste

Disjoint chicken, place in kettle. Cover with water; add onion, celery and carrot. Cook until tender, cool in liquid. Remove chicken and leave stock in cold place until chilled. Skim off fat. About 4 cups of stock should remain. Strain and reheat. Blend 2 tablespoons chicken fat with 1½ tablespoons flour. Add 1 cup hot stock to flour paste. Stir constantly to avoid lumps. Simmer to thicken. Season with salt and pepper to taste. Yield: 4 servings.

This restaurant is housed in a historic building, which was originally the residence of a steamboat captain. The place is purportedly haunted. It has also been several restaurants, including Chalet de Normandie, Parente's, and Oliver's, some of which were part of a supposed "add-on" curse. Shortly after adding on to the building, the restaurant would go out of business. Hacienda, owned by the Rodriguez family, finally broke the curse and apparently made peace with any ghosts as the business has been thriving since 1977.

Hacienda Mexican Restaurant Mole de Gallina
Recipe shared by Hacienda Restaurant

4	oz chicken mole paste
1¼	quarts hot water
2	bay leaves
1¼	ounce chicken base
¼	tsp oregano
1	tsp garlic powder
¼	cup peanuts, finely chopped
¼	cup brown sugar
1	tsp onion powder
1	lb chicken strips or tenders, washed, drained and patted dry

Dissolve mole paste in hot water. Add the next seven ingredients and simmer for approximately 15 minutes. Lightly dust chicken strips in seasoned flour (see recipe) and sauté for 5 minutes. Add chicken to the sauce and simmer until chicken is tender. May be made ahead and reheated just before serving. Wrap in warm flour tortillas and serve with a bed of rice. Yield: 4 servings.

Seasoning for coating chicken:

½	cup flour
1	tsp garlic powder
1	tsp black pepper
1	tsp salt

RESIDENCE FOR EDWIN H. OLIVER. MANCHESTER ROAD.

There were once stops along Manchester Road for travelers and horses to rest. They were located roughly a mile apart, with distances marked from the Mississippi River or, by some accounts, the Old Courthouse. The Nine Mile House is today the Trainwreck Saloon and while the original Eleven Mile House building has been lost to progress, a more recent incarnation remains at roughly the same area. The Charcoal House was originally the Ten Mile House.

Charcoal House Batter-Fried Lobster
Shared by owners George and Steve Angelos

For tempura style batter:

- ⅓ cup all-purpose flour or more if necessary
- 2 Tbsp cornstarch
- ½ tsp salt
- 1 egg, separated
- ½ cup cold water

Stir together flour, cornstarch and salt; set aside. In a medium bowl, beat egg yolk and water until very light and frothy. Gradually beat flour mixture into egg yolk mixture. Beat egg white until medium peaks form, fold into batter. If batter is not thick enough to cling to lobster, beat in more flour 1 tablespoon at a time. Refrigerate until ready to use.

For lobster tails:

- 2 lobster tails (preferably from cold water lobsters)
- • Old Bay Seasoning
- • salt
- • ground black pepper
- ⅓ cup all-purpose flour
- 1 egg, beaten
- • vegetable oil for deep frying

Remove and discard shells from lobster tails. Rinse tails and pat dry. Butterfly tails by cutting into but not through the back (as you would to devein a shrimp). Season lightly with Old Bay, and (small amount of) salt and pepper. Dredge tails in flour, dip in beaten egg, then in tempura batter. Deep fry at 350 degrees for 8 to 10 minutes until golden brown. Yield: 2 servings.

The Big Chief was originally an entire Route 66 complex that included cabins, a gas station, and a restaurant with dancing. After being bypassed, it lacked traffic due to its remote location and gradually fell into disrepair. The beautiful Mission-style restaurant remains today, currently leased by Steve and Jill Smith.

Big Chief Dakota Grill's - Wild Mushroom-Merlot Sauce for Wild Game*

Recipe by Mike Hirons and Steve Lautenbach, owners in 2000, from a feature story in the March 11, 2000 St. Louis Post-Dispatch

1½ Tbsp beef base and 2 cups water
   (or 2 cups beef broth)
1 tsp fresh chopped rosemary
1 tsp minced garlic
½ cup tomato juice
¾ cup Merlot
2 cups diced fresh Portobello mushrooms
5½ Tbsp clarified butter**
¼ cup all-purpose flour

Put beef base, water, rosemary, garlic, tomato juice and Merlot into a 2-quart pot. Bring to a boil. Reduce to a simmer, cook for 10 minutes. Strain liquid through a fine strainer; return liquid to pot. In a sauté pan, sauté mushrooms in butter over high heat until tender. Sprinkle with flour, reduce heat. Cook 10 minutes, stirring constantly. Stir into sauce. Simmer 5 minutes. Skim off impurities that rise to the top. Serve hot. Yield 3 cups/ 6 to 8 servings.

*Use for bison, or ostrich but also works for tenderloin, rib-eye or sirloin.
**To clarify butter, melt slowly over medium-low heat. Skim off the foam and discard. Pour off the golden liquid and discard the milky solids that form in the bottom of the pan. Need 1 stick of butter for 5 ½ Tbsp clarified butter.

Dining Room of Big Chief Cabin Hotel

The Purina Research or Experimental Farm ("Farm") was near Route 66's Original alignment and continued to be close by when the new (Historic) Highway 66 alignment through Pacific was completed to the south. For decades, the Farm's focus was on nutritional research for farm animals. Visitors to the Farm came to see the latest on animal feed and while there were treated to wonderful meals, made from scratch at the Farm using beef, chicken, and pork raised on site and fresh eggs and fresh milk from the Farm. Because of the need for around-the-clock care for the animals, some employees lived on the Farm and ate meals at the boardinghouse on the premises. John Wear began working at the Farm in 1927 and he served as Farm Manager until he retired in 1967. In 1929, his daughter Laura Wear was the first baby born at a home at Purina Farm. Laura grew up there, worked at the boardinghouse, and married Alvin Frisch, also a Ralston Purina employee. During World War II when men were away at war, the Farm hired older workers to look after the animals and this included John's father. Today, Laura's son, Jim Frisch, works at the Farm and represents the fourth generation of the Wear/Frisch family to be employed there. About 20 years ago, the dog and cat divisions were split off and today are part of Nestlé Purina PetCare Company. The livestock and other farm animal areas are owned today by Land O' Lakes.

Purina Farm Gingerbread

This 1930 recipe was used at the original boardinghouse at Purina Farm.
Shared by Laura (Wear) Hischier and Purina Farms

½ cup sugar
½ cup lard (or use vegetable shortening or half shortening and half butter)
1½ tsp (baking) soda
1 tsp ginger
1 tsp cinnamon
1 hen egg
1 cup molasses
½ tsp salt
1 cup hot water

Put sugar and lard in bowl; add beaten hen egg and molasses. Then add dry ingredients and stir. Add hot water last and beat until smooth. Bake until straw comes out clean when put into gingerbread, maybe thirty minutes. Note: This recipe was made using wood, and later, coal stoves. Other gingerbread recipes today roll the dough out to ¼ inch thickness, cut with cutters then bake the cookies at 375 degrees for 10 to 12 minutes.

Purina Farm Mashed Potato Cakes

This is a very old recipe that was brought to the Farm. Nothing was wasted and these pancakes made good use of leftover mashed potatoes. *Shared by Laura Hischier and Purina Farms*

2 cups leftover mashed potatoes
1 small onion, chopped
2 hen eggs, well beaten
4 Tbsp flour
1 tsp salt
• small amount lard (or vegetable oil)

Mix everything except lard in a bowl. Heat lard in skillet. Drop mashed potato mixture by spoonful into hot lard and flatten each. Fry until light brown then turn over and fry other side.

Shredded Ralston

This 1939 recipe was given out to guests with the sweet treat placed inside a checkerboard box. The note said, "Our farm women have prepared Purina's newest cereal in this unusual manner, especially for their guests at the farm. We believe that you will like it so well you will want to take the recipe home."
Shared by Laura Hischier and Purina Farms

1	cup brown sugar
¼	cup water
4	tsp butter
¼	tsp salt
¼	tsp vanilla
2	cups Shredded Ralston
	(use Wheat Chex squares as a substitute)

Put sugar, water, butter and salt in a pan. Boil until a few drops form a firm ball when dropped into cold water. Add vanilla. Spread the Shredded Ralston (Wheat Chex squares) in a shallow pan (with an edge) and pour the syrup over it. Break apart when cool. Note: Break like you would peanut brittle. Yield: about 3 servings.

Historic Route 66 Alignment (to 270)

Eleven Eleven Mississippi

Soulard's Restaurant

Anheuser-Busch Brewery

Hodak's

Bevo Mill

Lemmons

Steak 'n Shake

Southtown Famous-Barr

White Castle

66 Café, Stan Musial & Biggie's, and the Flaming Pit

Pietro's

Pagliacci's Pizzeria

Garavelli's

Ted Drewes Frozen Custard

Johnny Gitto's

Shop 'n Save

Velvet Freeze Ice Cream

Dierbergs Markets

Tippin's Restaurant and Pie Pantry

Lubeley's Bakery

Grone Cafeteria

Malone's Neighborhood Grill and Pub (and Romine's)

Grant's Farm and White Haven

Katz Drug and Howard Johnson's

Dillard's Garden Room

Sappington Barn Restaurant and Tea Room

Schnucks

McDonald's and Chuck-A-Burger

Rich & Charlie's

The Pasta House Co.

Sesame Chinese Restaurant

Nelson's Café and Viking Restaurant

Helen Fitzgerald's Irish Pub

House of Maret

Marty's Watermelon Stand in Marlborough

BAUER'S RANCH HOUSE
5805 CHIPPEWA   FLanders 6769   ST. LOUIS 9, MO.
"A Bit of the West — Just East of Hampton"

The Ranch House was at 5805 Chippewa, near Hampton Village.

"EDMOND'S"
Home of Unusual Sea Foods

Edmonds, an upscale seafood restaurant, was at Gravois (66) & Compton.

The Cloverleaf Bridge in Sunset Hills

Compliments of STAN MUSIAL & BIGGIE'S RESTAURANT

Stan the Man

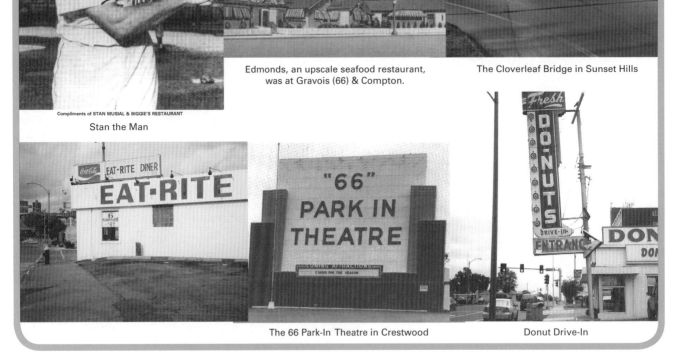

The 66 Park-In Theatre in Crestwood

Donut Drive-In

Eleven Eleven Mississippi

IIII Mississippi Ave (♦ Lafayette Square)
314-241-9999 www.IIII-m.com;
Vin de Set 2017 Chouteau Ave, 314-241-8989

Paul Hamilton, a 1990 hotel and restaurant management graduate of Penn State with lots of experience in food service management decided to open up his own place and, more interestingly, share his adventure with St. Louis, which followed his progress in the *St. Louis Post-Dispatch*. This was risky in itself, considering the high failure rate for new restaurants, with roughly 50% going under within the first year. Paul and his wife Wendy chose a Lafayette Square 1922 building that once housed the Star Shoe Co.'s factory. They shopped carefully at auctions for kitchen equipment, incorporated a gently used bar and Paul did much of the tuck pointing and painting himself, even converting some old teak deck chairs bought from Clipper Cruise Line (where he had once been in charge of food and beverage operations) into table tops for the wine room. Despite this, the restaurant cost $750,000 before he ever even opened the doors. Paul made another wise decision early on, hiring Chef Ivy Magruder, who Paul saw as a creative type with a business sense. It all paid off and the restaurant has been a huge success. The Hamiltons, with Magruder still on board, went on to open a sister operation, Vin de Set, which is noted for its great food and stunning rooftop views. It is on the Chouteau stretch of the Original route.

Eleven Eleven Mississippi Gooey Butter Cake
Shared by Chef Ivy Magruder and owners Paul and Wendy Hamilton

- nonstick cooking spray or butter to prepare pan
- ½ cup (1 stick) unsalted butter at room temperature
- 1 (18.25 ounce package) yellow cake mix
- 4 eggs, divided
- 5 cups powdered sugar, divided
- 8 ounces cream cheese, at room temperature
- 1½ tsp vanilla

Preheat oven to 350 degrees. Coat a 9- by 13- inch baking pan with cooking spray or grease lightly with butter. Combine softened butter and cake mix in a large bowl. Beat on low speed with an electric mixer until combined, then on medium speed until well blended, about 2 minutes total. Reduce mixer speed to low; add 1 egg; mix thoroughly. Add 1 more egg; mix thoroughly. Spread then press the mixture into prepared pan. Set aside 4 teaspoons powdered sugar to use as a garnish. In a clean bowl with clean beaters, beat remaining powdered sugar and cream cheese on low speed until combined, then on medium speed until well blended, about 2 minutes total. Reduce mixer speed to low; beat in remaining 2 eggs, 1 at a time, mixing thoroughly after each addition. Beat in vanilla. Pour into pan. Bake until set and lightly browned, about 30 minutes in a metal pan or 35 minutes for glass pan, rotating the pan after 15 minutes. Serve warm or let cool and refrigerate. Sprinkle with reserved 4 teaspoons powdered sugar before serving. Yield: 12 to 16 servings.

Soulard's Restaurant
1731 S. Seventh (1 block south of historic ⚡ Soulard Market)
314-241-7956
www.soulards.com

The Badock family has been serving the public for decades. Great-great grandparents operated a confectionary by the Hi-Pointe Theatre where they sold soda and sundaes for 5 cents. More recently, Raymond Badock Sr. (who had owned a Fina station in Kirwood from 1960 to 1976) stopped pumping gas and began pumping out great food when he and his wife, Margaret Phelan Badock, opened Soulard's Restaurant in 1977. (It is located in the Soulard neighborhood, just south of the downtown St. Louis area.) Daughter Kay Noble was in the restaurant business in San Francisco where she was the first to introduce alfalfa sprouts to the dining public. Kay joined up with her parents at Soulard's where Kay was known for her innovative offerings while Margaret was known for her comfort food recipes, winning numerous awards. Sons Tim and Dan took over for the family in 1985 and they continue the Badock commitment to quality food, still offering both comfort food and innovative recipes. They also put out a cookbook featuring their mother's recipes. Many restaurants have come on the scene since 1977 but Soulard's is a favorite with who matters most -- the customer. Soulard's peppered pork tenderloin and pork tenderloin with raspberry sauce are very popular items but it also known for some outstanding desserts including its bread pudding and this pumpkin cheesecake.

Soulard's Restaurant Pumpkin Cheesecake
Shared by owners Tim and Dan Badock

For crust:

⅓ cup packed brown sugar
¾ cup ground walnuts
1¼ cups all-purpose flour
½ cup (1 stick) melted butter
½ tsp almond extract

Mix sugar, walnuts and flour in a large bowl. Combine melted butter and almond extract; pour over dry ingredients, mixing well. Pat mixture over the bottom and ⅔ of the way up the sides of a 9-inch springform pan. Set aside.

For cheesecake:

16 ounces cream cheese
8 ounces ricotta cheese
1½ cups canned pumpkin
1 cup packed brown sugar
1 tsp pumpkin pie spice
1½ tsp vanilla
3 eggs

Preheat oven to 350 degrees. Beat cream cheese and ricotta cheese with an electric mixer until light and fluffy. Add pumpkin; beat well. Add brown sugar, pumpkin pie spice and vanilla. Add eggs 1 at a time, beating well after each addition. Pour batter into prepared crust. Bake for 1 ¼ to 1 ½ hours or until a knife inserted in the center comes out clean. Let cool completely. Refrigerate at least 4 hours or overnight. Yield: 12 to 16 servings.

The Anheuser-Busch Brewery is located near the Historic route, just south of Soulard. Anheuser-Busch has been a St. Louis institution for more than 150 years and has contributed heavily to the betterment of the community, giving St. Louisans everything from professional baseball to Grant's Farm to conservation areas. For all of its contributions to the community, its greatest was the sense of pride that the King of Beers and other A-B products were St. Louis based and American owned. A-B, however, was the latest St. Louis corporation to be purchased by an outside interest, Belgian based InBev, proving that even the King was not invincible.

A-B's Creamy Lager and Jalapeño Soup
Adapted from Great Food, Great Beer: The Anheuser-Busch Cookbook

- 2 Tbsp butter
- 3 jalapeño chiles, finely chopped
- ½ medium to large onion, chopped
- 1 carrot, peeled and grated
- 2 Tbsp all-purpose flour
- 4 cups American-style lager beer (make it Budweiser)
- 2 cups chicken stock
- ¾ cup Half-and-Half
- 2 Tbsp finely chopped fresh cilantro
- 1 tsp salt
- 1½ cups shredded Monterey Jack cheese, divided, optional

In a large, heavy-bottomed saucepan, melt butter over medium-high heat. When foam subsides, stir in jalapeños, onion and carrot. Cook, stirring often, until vegetables are softened, about 5 minutes. Sprinkle in flour; cook, stirring constantly, for 2 minutes. Pour beer and stock into pan in slow, steady streams, whisking constantly. Bring just to a boil, then immediately reduce heat to medium-low. Simmer for 30 minutes, stirring occasionally. Strain through a fine-meshed sieve placed over a bowl. Transfer solids and about 1/2 cup of the liquid to a blender or food processor; process to a smooth purée. Return purée to saucepan. Stir in remaining strained liquid; cook until hot over medium-low heat. Pour in Half-and-Half, stirring well until mixed and heated through. Remove from heat; stir in cilantro and salt. Ladle the soup into six bowls and sprinkle each serving with ¼ cup cheese. Yield: 6 first-course servings.

TO MAKE A GRAND EVENING COMPLETE, ENJOY THE WORLD'S MOST FAMOUS BEER

Budweiser. Leads All Beers in Sales Today ... and Through the Years!

ANHEUSER-BUSCH, INC.
ST. LOUIS   NEWARK   LOS ANGELES

Helen Hodak started this restaurant with her husband in 1961 and relocated to the current location on 66 shortly after. The Hegels bought the restaurant from the Hodak family in 1989 and continue it today. There is a reason people are willing to wait in line: good food and affordable prices. The chicken plate with 4 pieces of chicken, fries and coleslaw is the biggest seller but there is a large menu and daily specials and soups, such as this popular one.

Hodak's Southwestern Black Bean and Chicken Soup
Shared by Hodak's

½ cup dry black beans
2 Tbsp chicken base
5 cups water
½ cup diced yellow onion
⅔ cup chopped celery
1 cup chopped carrots
1 (14 ounce) can diced tomatoes, undrained
1 (4 ½ ounce) can diced green chiles
2 to 3 skin on, bone-in, chicken breast halves
5 ounces (about 1 ¼ cups) frozen corn kernels
1 Tbsp sliced pickled jalapeños, with juice
1 cup Kansas City style (sweet) barbecue sauce
¼ tsp ground black pepper or to taste

Cook beans according to package directions until tender; drain and set aside. In a large soup pot, stir chicken base into water until dissolved. Add onion, celery, carrots, tomatoes and their juice, chiles and chicken. Place over medium-high heat and simmer 30 to 40 minutes or until chicken is cooked through. Lift chicken from the pot; let stand until cool enough to handle. Discard skin and remove meat from bones. Dice or shred meat and return it to the pot. Add cooked black beans, corn and jalapeños. Stir in barbecue sauce and black pepper; cook 10 minutes more. Serve immediately. Yield: about 14 (1-cup) servings.

The Bevo Mill, a St. Louis landmark opened in 1917, is just a few short blocks south of the Gravois and Chippewa turn on Route 66 and is definitely worth the short road detour. For over 90 years, the restaurant has been known for its four-story windmill and Old World setting as well as its wonderful food. Before being acquired by InBev, A-B decided to transfer ownership of the historic building to the city of St. Louis. The deal formally closed on January 9, 2009. These are some of the popular recipes through the years.

THE WORLD RENOWNED

SCHNEITHORST'S
BEVO MILL
ST. LOUIS, MO.

Bevo Mill Sauerbraten

From the 1954 <u>Symphony of Cooking</u> cookbook, courtesy Saint Louis Symphony Volunteer Association

4   lbs sirloin butt
2   cups vinegar
1   cup water
1   tsp whole cloves
1   bay leaf
1   tsp whole black peppercorns
1   Tbsp salt
½   tsp ground black pepper
1   clove garlic
2   medium onions, sliced
1   medium-sized orange, sliced
1   cup red wine
¼   cup tomato purée

Cut meat into slices about 1-inch thick or leave in 1 piece. Combine all ingredients, except tomato purée, to make a marinade and pour over meat. Let stand for 36 hours in refrigerator, turning meat over in marinade two or three times. Remove meat and drain. Brown slices of meat. Add strained marinade and tomato purée (enough to cover meat) and simmer until tender (from 1 to 3 hours, depending upon whether the meat is in one piece and how tender the cut is.) Strain sauce and thicken. Yield: 6 servings.

Bevo Mill Seafood Salad

Shared by Bevo Mill

Seafood Salad:

2   lettuce leaves
4   ounces (about 1 cup) mixed greens
4   ounces (about ½ cup) seafood
      salad mix (see recipe)
2   tomato wedges
1   Tbsp diced red bell pepper
1   Tbsp green peas
1½ tsp sliced black olives

Arrange lettuce leaves in salad bowl. Fill bowl with mixed greens. Top with seafood salad mix. Arrange tomato wedges on each side of bowl. Sprinkle salad with diced bell pepper, peas and olives.

Seafood Salad Mix:

1   lb imitation crabmeat (or use crabmeat
      or mix of crabmeat and imitation)
½   cup diced celery
½   cup diced onion
2   pinches cracked black pepper
⅓   cup green peas
¼   cup diced red bell pepper
¼   cup Thousand Island dressing
½   lb bay shrimp

In a large bowl, combine all ingredients and stir until mixture is well blended. Yield: 8 to 10 seafood salads.

Bevo Mill's Cheddar Cheese & Chives Biscuits
Shared by Bevo Mill

2 lbs flour
2 tsp salt
4½ Tbsp baking powder
⅔ cup sugar
¼ cup dried chives
¾ cup Cheddar cheese, grated
½ cup oil
⅔ cup melted margarine or butter
2¾ cups milk

Mix all dry ingredients together thoroughly. Add butter and oil, stirring until oils are mixed in. Add milk and knead just until mix pulls away from side of bowl. (Do not overmix.) Drop onto baking pan from a large spoon. Each biscuit should weigh about 2 oz. Bake at 400 degrees about 20 minutes or until done. Yield: 30 2-oz biscuits.

Lemmons--in operation as The Black Thorn at Lemmons
5800 Gravois
314-481-4812

Lemmons (also just off the Route 66 path) was a St. Louis favorite since the 1940s. It was known for its fried chicken, house (French) salad dressing and its lemon meringue pie. Joe and Alleen Tucci bought the place in the 1980s and inherited the help and the signature items but added a few Italian dishes. More recently, the restaurant was remodeled and became entertainment venue The Black Thorn at Lemmons, known for its pizza. The old Lemmons food is gone but the vintage neon sign remains.

Lemmons Lemon Meringue Pie
Shared by former owners Joe and Alleen Tucci (who inherited the original Lemmons recipes) for an
April 12, 1992 feature story by the <u>St. Louis Post-Dispatch</u>

¾ cup granulated sugar
4½ Tbsp cornstarch
• pinch of salt
3 beaten egg yolks
3 Tbsp butter
• juice of 4 small lemons (approx ¼ cup and 1 Tbsp with some of the pulp added)
1 Tbsp grated lemon rind
1 9-inch baked pie shell
• Meringue (see recipe)

In the top of a double boiler over simmering water, combine sugar, cornstarch, and salt. Gradually add 2 cups water. Stir; cook over simmering water until mixture thickens. Cover and cook for about 5 minutes, stirring mixture occasionally. Using a whisk, blend in egg yolks. Turn off burner and continue stirring over hot water for about 5 minutes more. Add butter, lemon juice and lemon rind. Blend thoroughly. Pour into a cooled 9-inch pie shell. Top with meringue.

Lemmons Lemon Meringue Pie continued

Meringue:

4 egg whites
½ tsp cream of tartar
6 Tbsp granulated sugar, divided
½ tsp vanilla

Whip egg whites until frothy. Add cream of tartar, whipping until egg whites are stiff and stand in limp peaks. Beat in 1 Tbsp of sugar at a time. Add vanilla. Beat until stiff but not dry. Spread on top of cooled lemon pie. Bake in a preheated 325 degree oven for about 5 minutes. Watch closely and remove as soon as the meringue turns golden brown.

◆ Steak 'n Shake

There are currently 56 Steak 'n Shake restaurants in Missouri including the one at 4640 Chippewa. Get information at www.steaknshake.com

Steak 'n Shake has long ties to St. Louis. Founders Gus and Edith Belt opened the first two St. Louis Steak 'n Shakes in South St. Louis on Highway 66, just one month apart from each other. The first at 6622 Chippewa opened December 4, 1948 and the location at 4298 Chippewa at Morganford followed in January 1949. There were several others on Route 66 in St. Louis including Webster Groves (66 and Elm), Crestwood (Steak 'n Shake Jr. at 66 and Sappington and now an Imo's Pizza) and the one on the Bypass 66 route on Lindbergh Blvd. in Sunset Hills. Gus and Edith Belt resided in St. Louis (Ladue) for many years.

Steak 'n Shake-Style Chili (unofficial St. Louis customer version)
This is a longtime favorite with unknown origins.
Contributed by various readers for the <u>St. Louis Post-Dispatch</u> *Recipe Exchange column*

2 Tbsp vegetable oil
1½ lbs ground beef
½ tsp salt
1 (10 ½-ounce) can condensed onion soup
1 Tbsp chili powder
2 tsp ground cumin
½ tsp ground black pepper
2 tsp unsweetened cocoa powder
1 (15-ounce) can kidney beans, undrained or
   additional drained beans if desired
1 (6-ounce) can tomato paste
1 (8-ounce) can tomato sauce
1 cup regular cola soda (not diet)

Heat oil in Dutch oven; add crumbled beef and salt. Pack firmly in skillet and cover. Cook over low heat 20 minutes. Drain fat. Put soup in blender; blend 1 minute. Add soup to beef. Mash beef until it looks like rice. Cover; let simmer 5 minutes. Add chili powder, cumin, pepper, cocoa powder, beans, tomato paste, tomato sauce, and cola. Heat through. Yield: 6 servings.

The Southtown Famous store operated at the corner of Chippewa (66) and South Kingshighway from August 1951 to January 1992. The store held a lot of memories for many St. Louisans, particularly those in South St. Louis and areas near the Historic 66 route. The building was demolished on February 26, 1995.

Southtown Famous Bakery Blueberry Muffins

These blueberry muffins were sold at the Famous-Barr bakeries.

Contributed by readers for the October 24, 1994 St. Louis Post-Dispatch Recipe Exchange column

1½ cups all-purpose flour
¼ tsp salt
2 tsp baking powder
½ tsp ground cinnamon
¼ cup solid vegetable shortening, butter or margarine
½ cup granulated sugar
2 eggs
½ cup milk
1 cup blueberries (drained, if canned)

Sift flour, salt, baking powder and cinnamon into a large mixing bowl. Beat together shortening and sugar until fluffy; beat in eggs. Add shortening mixture and milk to flour mixture. Stir just until moistened. Fold in blueberries. Spoon batter into greased regular-size muffin cups. Bake in a preheated 350 degree oven about 20 minutes or until done. Yield: 12 muffins.

Southtown Famous at Chippewa (66) and South Kingshighway

St. Louis has the distinction of being White Castle's longest-running market, starting in 1925. The first location was on Walnut and 18th Street near Union Station. It was lost to the "new" post office development in 1932. In order to expand their clientele in 1932, local St. Louis newspapers were the first to run a White Castle coupon ad featuring 5 hamburgers for 10 cents, carryout only. It proved a huge success. The White Castle at the corner of Hampton and Highway 66 was in a porcelain-steel building and was loved by locals. Sadly, it was razed in 1983. White Castle continues to have a very loyal customer base that some call a cult following.

White Castle Turkey Stuffing

In 1992, White Castle began a cook off competition that requires the use of 10 White Castle burgers without the pickles. The contest has generated quite the variety of entries. This recipe, developed by the company in 1991, is a favorite. *Recipe courtesy White Castle*

10	White Castles (no pickles)
1½	cups celery (diced)
1¼	tsp ground thyme
1½	tsp ground sage
¾	Tbsp coarsely ground black pepper
¼	cup chicken broth

In a large mixing bowl, tear the hamburgers into pieces and add diced celery and seasonings. Toss and add chicken broth. Mix well. Stuff cavity of turkey just before roasting. Makes about 9 cups (enough for a 10- to 12-pound turkey). Note: allow one hamburger for each pound of turkey, which is equivalent to ¾ cup of stuffing per pound.

1932 ad

This location at 6435 Chippewa is of importance because it was the first restaurant in St. Louis to use 66 in its name, opening soon after the Highway came through and listed in the City Directory by 1936. Biggie Garagnani and a partner bought the 66 Café and after they split up, it became Biggie's 66 Café. Stan Musial was one of many celebrities who frequented the popular establishment. He and Biggie became friends and in 1949 they became business partners in Stan Musial &

Biggie's. In 1961, they relocated to Oakland Avenue. The 66 site became a Flaming Pit, one of two on this stretch of Highway 66. The other was located in Crestwood at 9735 Highway 66 (Watson and Sappington roads), near the Highway 66 Schnucks, the Crestwood Bank and the Bel-Air Motel. Although I was unable to find a recipe, here are the 1976 menus for the Flaming Pit and Stan Musial & Biggie's.

The Flaming Pit's six locations throughout St. Louis offer fine family dining at affordable prices. American food is served in a comfortable steak house setting. All locations offer a large salad bar which is included with your dinner. Charcoal broiled steaks are the house specialty. Flaming Pits are open on all holidays and Sundays and all have cocktail lounges.

A
Chill
Tomato Juice .50
Shrimp
Cocktail 2.45

Salad Bar
Alone 2.60

Sandwich Board
Salad Bar not included
Steak
Sandwich 3.95
Steerburger .. 2.10
Frontier
Frank 1.85
Sole
Sandwich 2.25
Above includes French Fries
Baked Potato
(a la carte)... .65
French Fries
(a la carte) .... .60

Desserts
Sherbet .... .60
Dish of
Ice Cream .... .60
Pecan Pie .... .85
Apple Pie .... .60
Cherry Pie ... .60
Cheese Cake .85
w/strawberries .95

Beverages
Coffee or
Ice Tea .... .30
(all you can drink)
Hot Tea or
Sanka .... .30
Soda/Milk .... .35

For Little Wranglers
Frank 1.65
Steerburger.. 1.65
Filet of Sole 1.65
Chicken....... 1.65
Fried Shrimp 1.95
w/French Fries, small milk or soda

Cocktails

HOUSE SPECIALTY, FRESH STRAWBERRY DAIQUIRI ... 1.50

MARTINI	1.10	OLD FASHIONED	1.10
MANHATTAN	1.10	BLOODY MARY	1.10
WHISKEY SOUR	1.10	APRICOT SOUR	1.10
DAIQUIRI	1.10	BRANDY ALEXANDER	1.50
BACARDI	1.10	GRASSHOPPER	1.50

MICHELOB ON TAP .... .60
WE PROUDLY PRESENT FROM THE VINEYARDS OF CALIFORNIA
Red Burgundy   White Chablis   Vin Rose'
1/4 Carafe – 1.25
1/2 Carafe – 2.00   Full Carafe – 3.75

Flaming Pit

Dinners include:

A Trip through
OUR EXTRAORDINARY SALAD BAR

Choice of:
Baked or French Fried Potato

Sour Cream with Chives — Rolls and Butter

A word about our steaks
Charcoal Broiled All our Steaks are aged to insure tenderness. We season all Steaks with our very own "Special Recipe Garlic Seasoning."

Steak Delight
A small steak of FINE QUALITY
4.75

Steak Kabob
Beef skewered with green peppers, onions and mushrooms
4.65

Ranchers Steak
Boneless top sirloin broiled to your liking
5.75

Steerburger Dinner
Lean ground sirloin thick, juicy & delicious
3.50

T-Bone Steak
The great all-American steak
6.95

Sirloin Strip
A large preferred cut
7.45

Filet Mignon
A tender treat—truly a gourmet's favorite
7.25

Petite Filet
Bacon wrapped Tender and Juicy
4.95

Fried Chicken
3.45

CHILDREN
10 years and under
2 pieces w/French Fries
1.85

Pork Chops
2 Center Cuts Juicy - Delicious Charcoal Broiled
5.25

Catfish
Fried to a golden brown, with garnish and sauce.
4.25

Seafoods
Filet of Lemon Sole Fried to a golden brown 3.95

Fried Jumbo Shrimp Served with shrimp sauce
4.75

Ferguson975aaa

Baseball fans from every corner of the country have enjoyed this monument to two men—one who had great ability with the baseball bat and the other who had outstanding culinary skills. Stan Musial and Biggie Garagnani are these two men. The lobby contains an interesting display of Stan's trophies. Biggie's son, Jack, has now teamed up with Stan to carry on the fine reputation enjoyed for many years. Complimentary bus rides to football and hockey games are available to dinner patrons. Piano and organ music nightly.

SEAFOODS

GENUINE ENGLISH DOVER SOLE 6.95

COLORADO RAINBOW TROUT 6.25   POMPANO 6.95
Broiled or Saute   *Broiled or Saute, Almadine*

GENUINE AFRICAN LOBSTER TAILS - *Priced Daily*

FRENCH FRIED SHRIMP 6.25   BABY FROG LEGS 6.25

MIXED SEAFOOD PLATTER 7.95

SOFT SHELL CRABS 6.50   MIXED SEAFOOD 5.95
Fried or Saute   *Au Gratin*

LOBSTER THERMIDOR 7.95

FILET OF LEMON SOLE 5.95
Fried or Saute

IMPORTED ENGLISH TURBOT 6.95
Mushrooms

FRESH CHANNEL CATFISH 5.50

ALASKAN KING CRAB LEGS - *Priced Daily*

All above entrees include Salad Bowl and Potato or Spaghetti

ENTREES

BABY BACK RIBS (Whole Slab) 6.25

TIDBITS OF BEEF TENDERLOIN 5.75
Served with Tomatoes and Mushrooms in Wine Sauce

STROGANOFF OF BEEF TENDERLOIN 6.25
with Wild Rice

GENUINE CALF LIVER STEAK 6.75
Broiled or Saute and topped with Bacon and Onion Rings

MIGNONETTE OF BEEF TENDERLOIN 8.50
*Complemented with Burgundy Sauce,
Button Mushrooms and a Broiled Tomato*

COUNTRY HAM STEAK 5.50   VEAL CUTLET 6.50
Sauteed with Pineapple Ring   *Holstein*

ROCK CORNISH GAME HEN 7.50
Served with Wild Rice, Jelly

FRIED OR BROILED CHICKEN 5.25

SAUTE CHICKEN LIVERS 5.25
Mushrooms

All above entrees include Salad Bowl and Potato or Spaghetti

DESSERTS and CHEESE

*Cherries Jubilee 2.25   Strawberry Cheese Cake 1.25
Homemade Pies .95   Gelati (Italian Ice Cream) .95
Ice Cream .85   Snow Balls .95   Spumoni .95
Parfait 1.25   Sherbet .85   Cheese Cake 1.10
Melons when in season 1.25
Roquefort, Camembert, Liederkranz, Gorgonzola Cheese 1.50*

"PRIVATE ROOMS AVAILABLE FOR BUSINESS, ORGANIZATIONAL OR SOCIAL FUNCTIONS"

FROM OUR BROILER

PRIME RIB OF BEEF au jus
Salad Bowl, Potatoes 7.75   Extra Thick 8.95

For the Gourmets   *The Ivanhoe Special*
CHATEAUBRIAND for two   PEPPERLOIN STEAK
Plank Bouquetiere, Salad Bowl, Potatoes 18.50   *For Two 17.00*

                          Two Extra Thick
T-BONE STEAK   LAMB CHOPS
Salad Bowl, Potatoes 8.50   *with Crisp Bacon, Salad Bowl, Potatoes 7.25*

For the Connoisseurs of Fine Steaks
SIRLOIN STRIP
Salad Bowl, Potatoes 8.50

Our Famous   *All-American Steak*
LADIES SIRLOIN STRIP   FILET MIGNON
Salad Bowl, Potatoes 7.50   *Salad Bowl, Potatoes 8.50*

CHOPPED BEEF TENDERLOIN
Salad Bowl, Potatoes with Fresh Mushroom Sauce 5.25

BROILED PORK CHOPS   FILET MIGNON & LOBSTER TAIL
Two Thick Chops served with Apple Sauce 7.25   *Priced Daily*

All salads served with Chef or French Dressing   All others a la carte

All above entrees include Salad Bowl and Potato or Spaghetti

FRENCH FRIED ONIONS .95   TOASTED ITALIAN GARLIC BREAD .95

ITALIAN DISHES

FETTUCCINE A LA ROMANA 4.50   PASTA VERDE A LA MARINARA 4.50
Egg Noodles with Butter and Melted Imported Cheese   *Green Noodles with Fresh Tomato, Garlic Sauce*

SPECIAL MOSTACCIOLI WITH MEAT SAUCE AND MUSHROOMS 4.25

SPAGHETTI 4.35   HOMEMADE RAVIOLI 4.50
with Meat Sauce or Meatballs   *with Meat Sauce*

BREAST OF CHICKEN CACCIATORE 6.25
Salad and Potatoes

VEAL SCALLOPINI 6.95   VEAL PARMIGIANA 7.25
Marsala, Salad and Potatoes   *Salad and Potatoes*

POTATOES and VEGETABLES

*Lyonnaise Potatoes 1.25   Cottage Fried Potatoes 1.25   French Fried Potatoes .75
Au Gratin Potatoes .95   Hashed Brown Potatoes .75   Baked Potato .85
Italian Stringbeans .85   Asparagus 1.10   Broccoli 1.10
Artichoke 1.25   New Stringbeans .95   New Peas .95   Braised Celery 1.50*

This South Side institution was started by partners John Iovaldi and Marco Griffero in 1960. John's son, John Jr. continued as a partner with Marco after John died in 1974. In more recent years, John Jr. bought Marco's share of the business. John Jr.'s wife Marianne and oldest son, John Murray, have joined John Jr. so the restaurant continues to be nurtured by the third generation. For almost 50 years, Pietro's has been serving up Northern Italian dishes as well as traditional fare. The kitchen is overseen by Chef Joseph Neri. Through the purchase of other nearby buildings, the restaurant facility has expanded four times and today has seating for 250. The menu has also evolved over the years but there are some signature items to look for. These include Breast of Chicken Maria (asparagus, crabmeat and Provel cheese), Sole Sebastian (crab, shrimp and mushroom wine sauce), Chicken Pietro (white wine mushroom sauce), made from scratch soups, and a sweet and sour dressing that became so popular, they had to bottle it and ship it nationwide. The spinach balls appetizer is also very popular.

Pietro's Meatball Soup
Shared by John and Marianne Iovaldi

For meatballs:

- 1½ lbs lean ground beef
- 6 Tbsp minced onion
- 1½ tsp minced roasted garlic
- ¾ cup canned crushed tomatoes
- 6 Tbsp grated Parmesan cheese
- about ¾ cup dry bread crumbs

Preheat oven to 375 degrees. In a medium bowl, combine beef, onion, garlic, tomatoes and Parmesan; mix thoroughly. Add just enough bread crumbs to bind the mixture. Shape into 72 meatballs; place on a parchment-lined baking sheet. Bake 15 minutes or until cooked through.

For soup:

- 3 Tbsp olive oil
- 1 cup chopped onion
- 1 cup chopped celery
- 1 cup diced carrots
- 1 cup diced zucchini
- 1 (14-ounce) can diced tomatoes
- 1¼ cups tomato sauce
- 1 tsp granulated sugar
- 1 tsp dried basil
- 1 tsp dried thyme
- ½ tsp crushed dried rosemary
- salt
- ground black pepper
- 8 cups beef stock or broth
- 1 cup uncooked orzo pasta
- grated Parmesan cheese, for garnish

Heat olive oil in a large soup pot or Dutch oven over medium-high heat. Add onion, celery, carrots and zucchini; sauté until beginning to soften, 4 to 5 minutes. Add tomatoes and tomato sauce, sugar, basil, thyme, rosemary, salt and pepper to taste and broth. Increase heat to high; bring to a boil. Add cooked meatballs; simmer for 40 minutes. Add orzo; cook 7 minutes or until pasta is al dente. Ladle into bowls; sprinkle with Parmesan and serve immediately.
Yield: 10 servings (about 14 cups).

Pietro's Spinach Balls
Shared by John and Marianne Iovaldi

1½ lbs chopped frozen spinach, thawed
2 oz chopped onions
1 tsp basil
1 tsp granulated onion
½ tsp pepper
1 Tbsp granulated garlic
1 Tbsp salt
1 lb margarine
2 eggs
6 oz Parmesan cheese
12 oz unseasoned bread crumbs

For breading:

• all-purpose flour (about 1 cup)
2 eggs beaten, well mixed with 1 cup
   milk for egg wash
1 cup dry Italian-seasoned bread crumbs

In a large sauté pan, melt margarine. Add onions and cook until clear. Add thawed spinach and spices. Cook 5 minutes more. Stir in eggs, Parmesan cheese, and bread crumbs. Refrigerate to cool. Roll into 1-ounce balls. Bread by dipping balls into flour then egg wash and then seasoned breadcrumbs. Deep fry until brown. Yield: 50 spinach balls.

Chicken Pietro
Shared by John and Marianne Iovaldi

4 skinless, boneless chicken breast halves
• salt
• ground pepper
½ cup (1 stick) butter, melted
• about 1/2 cup dry Italian-seasoned bread crumbs
• Pietro's Sauce (see recipe)

Preheat oven to 450 degrees. Sprinkle chicken with salt and pepper to taste. Dip in melted butter, then coat with crumbs. Place chicken in a baking dish or on a cookie sheet; bake until chicken is done, about 16 minutes. While chicken bakes, prepare sauce. Ladle sauce over chicken and serve.

Pietro's Sauce:

2 cups chicken stock
1 cup dry white wine
2 tsp lemon juice
½ cup (1 stick) butter
½ cup all-purpose flour
½ tsp cracked black pepper
1½ cups sliced mushrooms

In a large saucepan, bring chicken stock, wine and lemon juice to a boil. In another pan, melt butter; whisk in flour to make a roux. Add the roux to the boiling stock, stirring constantly until thickened. Reduce heat to low; stir in pepper and mushrooms. Cook about 5 minutes or until mushrooms are tender. Yield: 4 servings.

The Parente brothers, Lou and Joe, were local restaurateurs who were in business for decades. Their pizza pie recipe was very popular. Their first restaurant was Parente's Pizzeria opened in 1947 at Sarah and West Pine. Their second restaurant was Pagliacci's at Kingshighway and Manchester Road. They sold both and opened Parente's Italian Village on Chippewa (Highway 66), which closed due to a fire in 1963. They relocated to Manchester Road (now Hacienda) and had other restaurants into the 1980s. Besides their great Italian food, the brothers had personality galore and attracted all of the big names that came to town.

Brasciole a la Joe Parente

Recipe contributed by Pagliacci's Pizzeria for the 1954 Symphony of Cooking cookbook, courtesy Saint Louis Symphony Volunteer Association

For spaghetti sauce:

- 1 clove garlic, finely chopped
- ½ onion
- 3 cans tomato paste
- • olive oil

- 1 slice round steak (approx. 1 ½ lbs)
- 1 clove garlic
- 3 eggs (hard-boiled)
- 2 Tbsp grated cheese (Romano)
- 4 slices cheese (Provolone)
- ¼ bunch parsley
- 3 slices salami (thin)
- 1 tsp salt
- • a little pepper

Sauté 1 clove finely chopped garlic and ½ onion in olive oil. Season with salt and pepper. Add 3 cans tomato paste and 3 cans of water (1 for each can of paste). Boil slowly, 1 ½ hours.

Place round steak on platter; season with salt and pepper. Chop parsley and garlic fine; sprinkle evenly over steak. Cut eggs in thin slices, place on steak. Place slices of Provolone cheese over egg; do likewise with salami. Sprinkle lightly with Romano grated cheese. Roll steak evenly with ingredients to the center. Be sure ingredients do not fall out. Tie steak roll with kitchen string or skewers. Fry in olive oil until brown. Then cover with spaghetti sauce and cook 1 ½ hours. Place on platter, cover with spaghetti sauce and garnish. May be cut in half or thin slices. Yield: 2 servings.

Joe Garavelli had several restaurants in the area from 1914 to 1941 when he retired and sold his business. His most famous location was the original at De Baliviere and De Giverville in the Central West End. The Garavelli's on Chippewa is the only remaining restaurant with ties to Joe. The building started out in 1940 as Mittino's Club Shangri-La, became Parente's, Saro's Sunny Italy, and Hagiparis' before becoming Garavelli's.

Garavelli's Boston Scrod
Recipe shared by owner Sam Hawatmeh

For sauce:

- 4 lemons
- 4 sticks margarine (or 2 sticks optional)
- 1 10-ounce jar pimento stuffed queen Spanish olives, drained and sliced
- ½ lb mushrooms, sliced
- 4 Tbsp capers (one 3 ¼ ounce jar, drained)
- 1 cup chopped parsley
- 2 Tbsp diced red bell peppers (or ¼ cup optional for more color)
- 2 tsp Worcestershire sauce
- 1 cup water

Wash lemons, cut in half lengthwise then slice thickly. In a saucepan, combine lemons, margarine, olives, mushrooms, capers, parsley, red pepper, Worcestershire sauce and water. Bring to boil; remove from heat and set aside.

For fish:

- ½ cup milk
- 1 egg
- ⅔ cup all-purpose flour
- 1 Tbsp plus 2 tsp paprika
- 6 (8-ounce) pieces baby Icelandic cod, about 1-inch thick
- 2 Tbsp vegetable oil for frying

Preheat oven to 350 degrees. Beat milk and egg together to make egg wash. Stir flour and paprika together in a shallow dish. Dip fish into egg wash, roll in flour mixture and panfry in oil over medium heat until browned on both sides, about 2 minutes per side. Place fried fish in baking pan. Pour sauce over fish; bake 20 minutes. Serve with tartar sauce or cocktail sauce. Yield: 6 servings.

Garavelli

CORNER DE BALIVIERE AT DE GIVERVILLE

Garavelli's Sirloin Steak Tips and Noodles
Shared by owner Sam Hawatmeh

- nonstick cooking spray
- 2 lbs sirloin steak tips
- all-purpose flour
- a dash salt
- a dash ground black pepper
- 2 medium onions, cut into matchstick-size pieces
- 2 Tbsp minced fresh garlic
- 3 bay leaves
- 4 cups beef stock
- 2 cups diced tomatoes
- 3 cups sliced mushrooms
- 3 medium green bell peppers, diced
- egg noodles, cooked

Preheat oven to 350 degrees. Coat a 12 by 17 by 2-inch roasting pan with cooking spray. Cut tips into pieces ½ inch wide and 1¾ inches long. Lightly flour tips, then season with salt and pepper. Bake tips for 30 minutes, uncovered, stirring occasionally. Add onions, garlic, and bay leaves to pan. Cook uncovered for 15 minutes, stirring occasionally. Add beef stock. Cover; bake for 30 minutes, stirring occasionally. Reduce temperature to 300 degrees. Add tomatoes, mushrooms, and green peppers. Cook covered, for 20 minutes or until meat and vegetables are tender. Discard bay leaves. Serve over cooked egg noodles. Yield: 8 to 10 servings.

Early Garavelli's menu, original location

Ted Drewes sold custard with the carnival circuit in 1929 then opened his first custard stand in 1930 at Natural Bridge and Goodfellow. The Grand Avenue store followed in 1931 then ten years later he opened the Highway 66 store. Ted Jr. continued his father's commitment to personal service and quality. In 1959, Ted Jr. came up with the concrete, starting a St. Louis tradition that is also enjoyed by many Route 66 travelers. Request your custom mix or try these two favorites at home.

The Highway 66 Ted Drewes with original sign on roof

Johnny Rabbitt Concrete
Recipe shared by Ted Drewes

- Start with Ted Drewes Frozen Custard (no substitutions);
- Add hard shelled chocolate cone coating (for dipping cones);
- Add crushed maraschino cherries with small amount of cherry liquid.
- Blend very slightly on low speed, just until mixed.
- Note: Amounts of toppings will vary depending on the amount of custard you are using. Adjust to suit your own taste.

Hawaiian Delight Concrete
Recipe shared by Ted Drewes

- Start with Ted Drewes Frozen Custard (no substitutions);
- Add sliced bananas;
- Add crushed canned pineapple in its syrup;
- Add dry, roasted unsalted macadamia nuts;
- Lastly, add flaked, unsweetened coconut.
- Blend very slightly on low speed just until mixed.
- Note: Amounts of toppings will vary depending on the amount of custard you are using. Adjust to suit your own taste.

This unassuming building near Ted Drewes, the old Parkmoor, and Garavelli's and just inches from the River Des Peres, has housed many Highway 66 businesses. Some of them include the Red Sleigh, El Chars, Mascara's from 1966 to 1981, J.R. Federhofer's, and Michael G.'s.

Since 1996, it has been owned by Johnny Gitto, son of Charlie Gitto, owner of the Charlie Gitto's Pasta House downtown, and brother of Charlie Gitto Jr. who owns Gitto's on the Hill and other restaurants.

Johnny Gitto's Primavera Pasta
Shared by Johnny Gitto's

 1 zucchini, cut into nickel-size pieces
 1 tomato, cut into bite-size pieces
 3 stalks fresh broccoli, cut into bite-size pieces
 1 carrot, cut into 2-inch sticks
 1 oz fresh mushrooms, cut
12 pieces baby corn
 1 lb of your favorite pasta, cooked
 3 Tbsp olive oil
 1 tsp cornstarch
 4 cloves of garlic, minced
 6 oz chicken bouillon
 • red pepper flakes, fresh basil, salt and pepper
 • Parmesan cheese

Put oil and garlic into a hot skillet or wok. Get it very hot, then add vegetables, leaving the tomatoes for last. Stirring briskly so as not to burn, but brown, add the following spices to taste: salt & pepper, red pepper flakes, and fresh chopped sweet basil. Let cool; stirring for about 5 minutes; then add chicken bouillon and the tomatoes. Dissolve cornstarch in cold water and add to ingredients. (The cornstarch is to give the dish a shiny appearance while marrying all the ingredients.) Fold the pasta into the mixture. Place on a large platter; sprinkle with Parmesan cheese and serve immediately. (Can also cook adding chicken breasts and shrimp.)

Restaurants that have been at 6997 Chippewa (66)

The Shop 'n Save store located at the St. Louis city limits is at the site of ◆Hi-Land Miniature Golf and the old Liberty Market. There is also another store on old Highway 66 in Crestwood, near the site of the former Bel-Air Motel and the Colonial Hotel.

Shop 'n Save Deli Greek Salad
Shared by Shop 'n Save

```
  ¼  cup plus 2 Tbsp vegetable oil
  ¼  cup plus 2 Tbsp olive oil
  ¼  cup plus 2 Tbsp vinegar
  1  Tbsp plus 1/2 tsp garlic powder
4 ¾  tsp coarsely ground black pepper
  1  Tbsp plus ½ tsp Greek seasoning (such as
       Cavender's Greek seasoning)
  3  lbs shredded cabbage ( ½-inch shreds) *
  ¾  cup stuffed green olives
  ⅓  cup pitted black olives
  1  cup hot banana pepper rings
  3  Tbsp plus 1 tsp juice from jar of pepper rings
  ⅓  cup pepperoncini (about 7)
  5  tsp juice from jar of pepperoncini
```

In a large bowl, whisk together oils, vinegar, garlic powder, pepper and Greek seasoning. Add cabbage, green olives, black olives, pepper rings and juice, and pepperoncini and juice. Toss well. Cover; refrigerate until ready to serve. Salad is best made 24 hours before serving. It will keep in the refrigerator for 5 to 7 days. Yield: 20 cups. *Do not use preshredded cabbage, which is too thin for this recipe.

Founded in 1932, Velvet Freeze is one of the oldest retail ice cream companies in St. Louis. At one time, the company had 58 retail stores including Highway 66 locations on Chippewa and in Yorkshire Village. There was also one near 66 on Gravois that closed in 1984. The oversized fiberglass cone from that Affton location is now at Mesnier Primary School, located at 6930 Weber Road. You can still get your Velvet Freeze favorites at the only remaining location, 7355 West Florissant in Jennings. The ice cream is made fresh daily from the original recipes.

Velvet Freeze Strawberry Shortcake Sundae
Shared by owners John and Barbara McGuinness

- Start with a slice of Sara Lee pound cake;
- Add a generous scoop of genuine Velvet Freeze strawberry cheesecake ice cream;
- Smother with strawberry sundae topping;
- Finish with real whipped cream and a cherry on top. Yield: 1 serving.

There is a Dierbergs store at what was once Resurrection Cemetery property on Highway 66. Dierbergs is a family-owned St. Louis chain with roots in an 1854 country store on Olive Boulevard in Creve Coeur, Missouri. Dierbergs continued with only one location until 1967. Today, the company is run by the fourth generation of the Dierberg family and has 23 stores in the St. Louis metro area. In 1978, Dierbergs was the first supermarket in the United States to offer a cooking school. The classes are varied and include children's and couple's classes. The popularity of the cooking schools (now in 5 locations) led to the *Everybody Cooks* magazine, which includes recipes and is given away for free in the stores, as well as a very popular television cooking show and Dierbergs cookbooks.

Dierbergs Grilled Bratwurst with Onion Sauerkraut Relish

This recipe was adapted from the September 2001 Everybody Cooks magazine. Reprinted courtesy Dierbergs Markets

For relish:

¼ cup vegetable oil
½ cup granulated sugar
2 cups coarsely chopped onion
1 (16-ounce) can sauerkraut, well drained
¼ teaspoon salt
½ cup cider vinegar
½ teaspoon caraway seeds

Heat oil in large skillet over medium heat. Add sugar; cook, stirring constantly, until mixture turns a light caramel color, about 10 minutes. Add onion, sauerkraut, and salt (some sugar may harden, but it will melt as cooking continues). Cook over medium heat for 15 minutes, stirring frequently. Add vinegar and caraway seeds; simmer for 30 minutes. Use immediately or cover and refrigerate up to 3 weeks.

For bratwurst:

8 fresh bratwurst
1 (12-ounce) can beer or 1 ½ cups water
8 hot dog buns

Heat grill. In large saucepan, combine bratwurst and beer. Heat until almost boiling. Cover; simmer 10 minutes. When ready to grill, place bratwurst on grill over medium-hot coals. Grill 6 to 10 minutes or until browned, turning frequently. Serve bratwurst on buns with relish. Refrigerate any remaining relish. Yield: 8 servings.

Dierbergs French Almond Cake

This recipe is adapted from the December 2005 Everybody Cooks magazine. Reprinted courtesy Dierbergs Markets

1 box (18.25 ounces) French vanilla cake mix
1½ tsp almond extract (divided)
1 jar (12 ounces) seedless strawberry jam
2 cups heavy whipping cream
1 box (4-serving size) instant white chocolate pudding mix
2 cups slivered almonds, toasted and coarsely chopped
• fresh strawberries

Lightly coat two 9-inch round cake pans with no-stick cooking spray. Line bottoms of pans with parchment paper. Lightly coat parchment with no-stick spray; set aside. Prepare cake mix according to package directions, adding 1 teaspoon of the almond extract to batter. Divide batter evenly into prepared pans; bake as directed. Cool in pans for 5 minutes; invert onto wire racks, remove parchment, and cool completely.

In medium bowl, stir together jam and the remaining ½ teaspoon almond extract; set aside. In mixing bowl, beat cream and pudding mix until light and fluffy. Split each cake round in half horizontally. Place one layer cut-side up on cake plate. Spread about ¼ cup strawberry filling over cake. Stack remaining half of cake cut-side down. Spread about 1 cup of the whipped pudding over top. Repeat layers, spreading cut side of cake with ¼ cup strawberry filling, and spreading remaining whipped pudding over top layer. Brush remaining strawberry filling around sides of cake. Gently press almonds into filling until sides of cake are covered with nuts. Refrigerate cake until ready to serve. Just before serving, garnish with fresh strawberries. Yield: 16 servings. Tip: To split cake layers, wrap a long piece of unflavored dental floss around the center of the outside edges of the cake. Cross the ends, then slowly but firmly pull on each end. The floss will cut cleanly through the cake.

Many restaurants come and go. This Kansas City-based chain was started by James Kerwin around 1981. He originally named the restaurant Pippin's but was forced to change it when he discovered the Pippin's name was already taken. Tippin's arrived in St. Louis in 1985 and had two locations on Watson Road, one at Watson Plaza in Crestwood and one across from Resurrection Cemetery. Although it came in just as the last Missouri stretch of 66 was being bypassed, it served up comfort food and great pies for almost 20 years. The restaurant attracted customers of all types including the elderly, families, and young couples, all of whom enjoyed the great food and 36 varieties of freshly-made pies, including a monthly "feature" pie. Customers pre-ordered holiday pies (particularly a deadly pumpkin pie with fresh whipped cream) and these would be boxed and stacked high for customers who lined up out the door to pick up their pies. The cornbread, Shepherd's pie, and steak soup were also favorites. In January 2003, all four St. Louis Tippin's restaurants were suddenly closed. The CEO blamed the low-carb craze as its final blow. These delicious pies can be found locally at Dierbergs Markets-www.dierbergs.com.

Tippin's Banana Cream Pie

Shared by Tippin's for a St. Louis Post-Dispatch April 23, 1989 feature story

1¼ cups whole milk
 • pinch salt
½ cup Half and Half or light cream
¾ cup granulated sugar
2 Tbsp cornstarch
1 Tbsp all-purpose flour
2 Tbsp butter (no substitutes)
3 bananas, peeled
1 (9-inch) deep-dish pie shell, baked and cooled

For topping:

2 cups heavy (40 percent) cream
1 cup granulated sugar
 • chopped pecans (optional)

Combine milk, salt, Half and Half, sugar, cornstarch and flour in a deep, heavy-bottomed saucepan. Set over medium-high heat and bring to a boil, stirring constantly with wire whisk. Remove from heat and whisk in butter. Cut peeled bananas into ¾ inch slices. Place slices around bottom of baked deep-dish pie shell. Pour filling over bananas. Allow to cool to room temperature, then chill in refrigerator.

Combine cream with sugar. Using rotary mixer or whip attachment of electric mixer, beat cream until stiff. Decorate top of chilled pie with dollops of whipped cream or pipe whipped cream through pastry bag into pyramids. Sprinkle pie with pecans.
Yield: 6 to 8 servings.

♦ Lubeley's Bakery
7815 Watson Road
314-961-7160
www.lubeleysbakery.com

Ed Lubeley and Helen Maret met at a bakery in downtown Kirkwood (on Route 66) in the early 1930s. After the bakery folded due to the Depression, Ed and Helen opened their own bakery in 1937, the same year they married. They returned to Highway 66 as an original tenant in the new Yorkshire Village Shopping Center and moved a few blocks east to their current location in 1982. Ed passed away in 1992 and the bakery is now run by their children, Helen Murray, Bob Lubeley and Susan Suardi, along with Bob's wife, Carol. Known by everyone in these parts as Mrs. Lubeley, Helen, 96 in 2009, still comes in 5 days a week to help out. Lubeley's is known for its cakes and wonderful pastries. They also sell "a ton" of these lace cookies.

Lubeley's Florentine Lace Cookies
Shared by Lubeley's Bakery

- ½ cup butter
- 1 Tbsp flour
- ½ cup sugar
- 1 Tbsp heavy whipping cream
- 1 Tbsp milk
- ¾ cup ground almonds or ½ cup blanched, shelled almonds ground in a blender

For chocolate coating:

- 4 ounces semi-sweet chocolate chips
- 8 ounces cocoa butter, solid

Preheat oven to 350 degrees. Grease and flour cookie sheets. Place butter, flour, sugar, heavy cream, and milk in a saucepan. Heat slowly until butter is melted. Stir in almonds. Spoon out by heaping teaspoons, 5 well-spaced cookies per sheet, as cookies will spread. Bake 8 to 9 minutes. Remove from oven and cool for 1 minute then set cookies on paper towels, top side down. Repeat until all batter has been used. Cool cookies for 1 hour. Melt chocolate chips and cocoa butter in a double boiler and drizzle chocolate over cooled lace cookies. Yield: 25 cookies. Notes: Cocoa butter is butter made from coconut milk and is available at most grocery stores. If your chocolate chips already contain cocoa butter, you do not need to add this ingredient. The lace cookies can also be made into a sandwich cookie, with the chocolate piped into the center of two cookies.

L to R: Susan Suardi, Helen Murray, Pillsbury Doughboy, Helen Lubeley & Bob Lubeley

Grone Cafeteria (called Grone's by most locals) was started in 1931 at South Grand and Lafayette Avenue (near the Compton reservoir and standpipe tower) by Louis Henry Grone who immigrated to St. Louis from Germany. Through the years, there were many Grone relatives involved in the business. In 1969, I-44 was being built just outside the cafeteria so the Grones relocated to Woodson Terrace that year. Cousins George G. Grone and Louis H.

Grone III operated the restaurant for 54 years. The Grones opened a second location in 1986 in Webster Groves, taking over the site of what started as a Perkins Cafeteria in Yorkshire Village on Highway 66. By 2001, three Grones continued in the business -- Lou III and his sons Greg and Lou IV. After 73 years in business, both Grone Cafeteria locations closed in 2004.

Grone Cafeteria Stir-Fry Chicken

Recipe shared by Grone Cafeteria for the April 23, 2001 <u>St. Louis Post-Dispatch</u> *Special Request column*

For chicken, marinade and vegetables:

1½	lbs skinless, boneless chicken breasts (about 3 breast halves)
¼	cup soy sauce
⅓	cup vegetable oil
½	tsp minced garlic
½	tsp ground ginger
2	lbs frozen stir-fry vegetables

Cut chicken into ½ inch cubes. Combine soy, oil, garlic, and ginger in a resealable plastic bag; add chicken. Marinate overnight in refrigerator. Drain chicken, discard marinade. Sauté chicken rapidly in a large nonstick skillet. When chicken is cooked through, drain and set aside in a warm place. Add frozen vegetables to nonstick pan; cover and cook over medium heat until crisp tender, 8 to 10 minutes.

For sauce:

2	(14.5 ounce) cans chicken broth
¼	cup soy sauce
½	tsp minced garlic
¼	tsp ground ginger
2	Tbsp plus 2 tsp cornstarch
1	cup pineapple juice

In a medium saucepan, combine broth, soy sauce, garlic and ginger; bring to a boil. Whisk cornstarch into pineapple juice; whisk cornstarch mixture into sauce and cook over medium heat until thickened. Add cooked chicken to sauce. Drain vegetables, add to sauce. Stir to combine well. Yield: 6 to 8 servings.

Grone Cafeteria Orange Fluff Cake

This recipe was shared by Lou Grone IV in the July 5, 1999 <u>St. Louis Post-Dispatch</u>. *The reader had requested the cornbread recipe and Lou sent this as a substitute he was willing to share. He said it was his grandmother's favorite spring/summer dessert because of its light texture and orange flavor.*

•	zest and juice from 3 to 4 medium oranges, divided (with some for icing-recipe below)
8	eggs, separated
1½	cups granulated sugar
1	tsp salt
1½	cups sifted cake flour (sift before measuring)
1¼	tsp cream of tartar

Preheat oven to 350 degrees. Grate the zest (colored portion of the peel) from the oranges; set aside 2 tablespoons. Juice oranges; set aside 3/4 cup. Separate eggs into two large bowls. Beat yolks, granulated sugar and salt until light and fluffy. Add 1/2 cup orange juice; continue to beat. Add flour; mix briefly, just until flour is incorporated. Stir in 4 teaspoons zest. Using clean beaters, beat egg whites until foamy. Add cream of

Grone Cafeteria Orange Fluff Cake continued

tartar; beat until soft peaks form. Do not overbeat. Using a rubber spatula, gently fold yolk mixture into whites. Pour mixture evenly into an ungreased 10-inch tube pan. Bake 35 to 45 minutes or until cake is lightly browned and the center springs back when touched lightly. Remove cake from oven. Invert cake in pan on a rack, the neck of a bottle or the neck of a funnel; let cool completely.

Icing:

3 Tbsp butter or margarine, softened
3 cups powdered sugar

While cake is cooling, prepare icing. In large bowl, combine butter, powdered sugar, remaining 1/4 cup orange juice and remaining 2 teaspoons orange zest. Stir until smooth. Using a knife, gently separate cooled cake from sides of pan. Invert cake onto plate. Frost top and sides of cake. Yield: 12 servings.

Malone's Neighborhood Grill and Pub (and Romine's)
8742 Watson Road 843-9904
www.malonesgrillandpub.com

Malone's on Watson Road (along with the rest of Watson Auto Plaza) is at the site of the 66 Auto Court, an early motel that stood on Highway 66 for almost 50 years. The Evergreen Motel was right across the highway. Malone's owner, Steve Schafermeyer, also owned Romine's, the Route 66 landmark on Riverview Blvd. and continues to offer its famous fried chicken at some Malone's locations.

Malone's Potato Soup

This potato soup is a customer favorite and has been on the Malone's menu since day one. *Shared by owner Steve Schafermeyer*

For roux:

6 Tbsp (¾ stick) butter
½ cup all-purpose flour

In a small pot, melt butter over low heat; whisk in flour until evenly blended. Cook, stirring, about 5 minutes; do not let brown. Set aside.

For soup:

2 Tbsp (¼ stick) butter
½ cup chopped onion
4 cups water
1½ lbs potatoes, peeled and diced into ½-inch cubes
2 Tbsp chicken base
1½ tsp beef base
¼ tsp ground white pepper
¼ tsp ground black pepper
¼ tsp celery salt
1 cup Half-and-Half
• crumbled cooked bacon, for garnish
• shredded Cheddar cheese, for garnish

In a large saucepan, melt butter; add onion and cook until translucent, about 5 minutes. Add water, potatoes, chicken base, beef base, white and black pepper and celery salt. Bring to a boil, reduce heat and simmer until potatoes are almost tender, 25 to 30 minutes. Add Half-and-Half; whisk in roux. Return to a boil, then reduce heat and simmer, stirring constantly, until soup thickens to desired consistency. Ladle into soup bowls; top with bacon and Cheddar. Yield: 7 (1-cup) servings.

Grant's Farm
10501 Gravois Rd.
314-843-7100
www.grantsfarm.com

White Haven
7400 Grant Road
314-842-3298
www.nps.gov/ulsg

When Highway 66 came in along what had once been an old wagon road, sometimes called the Watson Trail, it bordered what had once been the northern edge of President Ulysses S. Grant's farmland. White Haven (the family home) and Hardscrabble (the log cabin he built) both stand today very near former Highway 66. Years later, the Breihans developed part of his land into the General Grant Shopping Center, which at one point included the General Grant restaurant and later, Grant's Cabin restaurant, housed in a replica of Hardscrabble.

Grant's Farm and Tower Grove Chowder

This chowder was cooked outdoors and served 30 people. The "receipt" originated at Grant's Farm then was used by Henry Shaw at the Tower Grove country house. It would be a great choice for a historic reenactment event.

Recipe from the 1963 Shaw House Cook Book

 3 lbs bacon, diced fine
10 lbs lean beef, diced
 4 fat hens, jointed
 1 peck* tomatoes, quartered
 1 peck potatoes, quartered
½ peck onions, peeled and quartered
 2 dozen ears of corn
 1 dozen sweet peppers
 2 lbs butter
 2 cups salt
 2 or 3 Tbsp black pepper

Do not use ground beef. Place bacon, beef, and hens in a big kettle over an outdoor fire; add water to cover and when it comes to a boil, cook for 1½ hours. While it is cooking, peel and quarter the tomatoes, potatoes and onions. Add these when the water boils. Bring back to a boil; cook 1 hour stirring frequently, then add the corn and peppers. Bring back to a boil, cook 30 minutes, then add butter and seasonings. Check the seasoning. Cook 20 minutes, replenishing the liquid as it boils away. Yield: 30 sevings. * Note: A peck is about 8 quarts.

Grant's Cabin at its original location

At the corner of Highway 66 and Elm in Webster Groves, there were two very popular places to eat. Katz Drug, which started downtown at 700 Locust then grew and expanded to the suburbs, opened its 8th store in 1960 at the northeast corner. The site had been Gus Keehn's grocery store. Katz sold to Walgreens who continued in the Katz building until recent years when the Katz building was razed and replaced. The northwest corner, now Steak 'n Shake, was a Howard Johnson's restaurant, pictured here in this 1960 ad.

HOWARD JOHNSON'S RESTAURANT

and the only Howard Johnson's Drive-In in the Midwest

US City 66 & Elm Ave.   •   Webster Groves, Mo.

Come for dinner before the show...
Stop for a snack after the show
Choice Clams and Steak Dinners

There were tea rooms at several of the Dillard's department stores in the St. Louis area, including the one on Highway 66 at Crestwood Plaza. It was a popular stop for shoppers. There are no Dillard's tea rooms operating in St. Louis today.

Dillard's Garden Room Frozen Fruit Salad
Shared by Dillard's Garden Room for the December 22, 2004 St. Louis Post-Dispatch Special Request column

1 (16-ounce) tub frozen whipped topping, thawed
1 Tbsp mayonnaise
10 maraschino cherries, halved
3 Tbsp juice from cherries
2 Tbsp powdered sugar
1 (15-ounce) can fruit cocktail,
   not chunky style, drained
1 tsp vanilla

Place whipped topping in the large bowl of an electric mixer; beat until stiff. Add mayonnaise, cherries, cherry juice, sugar, fruit and vanilla; mix to blend thoroughly. Freeze in individual molds or a small (8-inch by 4-inch) loaf pan that has been lined with plastic wrap. (Can mold in a clean Pringles potato chip can.) For easier slicing, thaw in the refrigerator for 30 minutes before serving. Yield: 6 to 8 servings.

Dillard's Garden Room Chicken Salad
Shared by Dillard's Garden Room in the October 2, 2000 St. Louis Post-Dispatch

2 lbs cooked white chicken meat, diced
½ cup chopped celery
1 tsp celery salt
½ tsp ground white pepper
2 tsp Worcestershire sauce
2 cups mayonnaise

In a large bowl, combine chicken, celery, celery salt, pepper, Worcestershire sauce and mayonnaise. Stir until well-blended. Serve for a sandwich. Yield: 8 servings.

Dillard's Garden Room Navy Bean Soup
Shared by the Dillard's Garden Room for the February 7, 2000 St. Louis Post-Dispatch

1 lb dried navy beans
1 large onion, peeled and diced
2 carrots, peeled and diced
2 ribs celery, diced
½ lb diced ham
1 Tbsp ham base
1 tsp chicken base
¼ cup brown sugar, loosely packed,
   or less to taste
1 Tbsp A-1 steak sauce
1 pinch dried thyme
1 cup canned diced tomatoes (½ of a 16-ounce can)
2 Tbsp ketchup

Pick over and rinse beans, discarding any stones or other debris. Place in stockpot. Add water to cover by at least 2 inches. Cover pot; let beans soak overnight. Drain beans. Add 8 cups water. Bring to a boil; reduce heat and simmer until beans are almost tender, about 1¼ hours. Add onion, carrots, celery, ham, ham base, chicken base, brown sugar, steak sauce, thyme, tomatoes and ketchup. Add more water if desired. Cook an additional 30 minutes or longer, stirring occasionally, until beans and vegetables reach desired texture. Yield: 6 to 8 servings.

Sappington Barn Restaurant and Tea Room

1015 Sappington Road
314-966-8387

John Sappington came to Missouri about 1801 and he bought a large amount of land in the area. In 1808, his son Thomas married and John gave him 200 acres of land. The home Thomas Sappington built that same year (in a Federal style, which is rare for the Midwest) has been restored and is believed to be the oldest brick home in St. Louis County. It is open for tours. Part of the complex includes a tea room that is housed in the Sappington Barn. The historic Sappington Cemetery (which was along the old Watson Road and later Highway 66) and Father Dickson Cemetery are both nearby and worth a visit.

Sappington Barn Restaurant and Tea Room Vegetable Salad
Recipe from the 1968 A Book of Favorite Recipes by the Sappington House Foundation

1 (20-oz) pkg frozen mixed vegetables
½ cup chopped celery
½ cup chopped green pepper
½ cup chopped onion
1 small jar pimento
¾ cup sugar
½ cup vinegar
1 Tbsp dry mustard
1 Tbsp flour

Cook vegetables per package instructions. Combine all vegetables in large bowl. In small saucepan combine sugar, vinegar, mustard and flour. Stir and bring to a boil. Continue boiling until thickened, stirring constantly. Pour over vegetables. Refrigerate overnight. Makes about 12-15 servings.

Schnucks

www.schnucks.com
314-994-4400

Schnucks had several locations on Highway 66. One was located on Highway 66 and Sappington Road, near the Crestwood Bank Building and the Flaming Pit. Today there is a Schnucks at the site of the 66 Park-In Theatre, at historic Hampton Village and at Lindbergh Blvd. and Clayton Road, on the Bypass route. The company started in north St. Louis in 1939 and has grown to include over 100 stores in seven states.

Schnucks St. Louis Salad
This St. Louis favorite is served at the Schnucks Deli Counters. *Shared by Schnucks*

2½ cups broccoli florets
2½ cups cauliflower pieces
1 small red onion, sliced thinly
5 strips bacon, cooked and chopped
1 cup mayonnaise
⅓ cup grated Parmesan cheese
¼ cup granulated sugar
• salt, to taste
• ground white pepper, to taste

Combine broccoli, cauliflower, onion, and bacon in a bowl. Toss to combine. To make dressing, combine mayonnaise, cheese, sugar, salt and pepper. Pour over salad. Cover and refrigerate several hours or overnight. Yield: 8 to 10 servings.

Schnucks Springtime Quiche
This recipe was part of the March 2008 *Schnucks Cooks* newsletter. *Shared by Schnucks*

1   refrigerated pie crust
6   slices precooked bacon, chopped
1   package (8 ounces) Schnucks shredded
    sharp Cheddar cheese
2   Tbsp chopped fresh chives
8   asparagus spears (about ½ pound)
4   large eggs
1½ cups Schnucks Half and Half
¼   tsp salt
¼   tsp ground white or black pepper

Preheat oven to 350 degrees. Unroll dough onto work surface. With rolling pin, for 11-inch tart pan, roll dough into 13-inch round. If using 9½ inch tart pan, roll dough into 12-inch round. Transfer dough to ungreased tart pan, gently pressing dough into bottom and up side of pan. Run rolling pin over top of pan to trim excess dough. Sprinkle bacon, cheese and chives over bottom of crust. Cut tough ends from asparagus, trimming to fit into tart pan. Place asparagus spears in spoke pattern over cheese, with asparagus alternating tip to stem. In medium bowl, with whisk, lightly beat eggs. Add Half and Half, salt and pepper and whisk until well blended. Pour egg mixture over asparagus. Bake 40 to 45 minutes or until golden and set in center. Cool quiche in pan on wire rack 10 minutes. Serve warm. Yield: 6 to 8 servings.

The new Highway 66 Schnucks, June 1964 (now the Kohl's site)

McDonald's
9915 Watson Road
www.mcdonalds.com

In addition to Danny Donuts, which served up doughnuts that are still remembered fondly, the north side of Route 66 on this western end of Crestwood had two places that were very popular stops. The McDonald's at 9915 Highway 66 was the first McDonald's in Missouri. It was a walk up location with neon arches on either side of the building. There is still a McDonald's at the site today.

Highway 66 McDonald's

Chuck-A-Burger
9025 St. Charles Rock Road
www.chuckaburger.com

Chuck-A-Burger was located at 9955 Highway 66 and was a popular place for eating in your car and cruising. It was the third location for the local chain, which grew to 8 stores. (There is a Kentucky Fried Chicken at the site today.) Chuck-A-Burger continues today under the Stille family with its classic St. Charles Rock Road store located in St. John and a new store in St. Charles.

Highway 66 Chuck-A-Burger

◆ Rich & Charlie's

9942 Watson Road and various locations
314-822-4909
www.richandcharlies.com

Rich & Charlie's, a local Italian restaurant chain, was started in 1967 by Rich Ronzio and Charlie Mugavero. The Pasta House became part of the organization then split off. Both chains continue to be very popular. The Rich & Charlie's site on Highway 66 started off as

Krabbe's Grill, was Gus Vogelgesang's tavern in the late 1940s and early 1950's, and is remembered fondly as il Vesuvio, which was there for about 22 years. After a brief stint as a Pasta House, it became Rich & Charlie's in 1981.

Rich & Charlie's Chicken Vesuvio
Shared by owners Emil Pozzo and Marty Ronzio

- 2 (6-ounce) boneless, skinless chicken breast halves
- 2-3 Tbsp blackened meat seasoning
- 1 lb cavatelli or other shell pasta
- ⅔ cup plus 1 Tbsp extra virgin olive oil
- ½ cup (1 stick) butter
- 2 cloves garlic, minced
- 6 Tbsp teriyaki sauce
- 1 (6-ounce) can roasted red and yellow peppers, drained (about 1 cup)
- 2 cups frozen peas, thawed
- 2 cups frozen broccoli florets, thawed
- 6 ounces fresh mushrooms, sliced

Preheat a cast iron skillet over high heat on a well-ventilated burner. Rub a liberal amount of blackened meat seasoning on both sides of chicken; sear in the hot skillet for about 3 to 4 minutes per side. Remove from skillet, cut into strips and set aside. Cook cavatelli according to package directions until al dente. While pasta is cooking, place oil, butter, garlic and teriyaki sauce in an 8-quart pot on medium-low heat. Cook until butter melts but do not allow to boil. Add cooked chicken. (This releases some of the seasoning and adds flavor to the sauce.) Stir in peppers, peas, broccoli, and mushrooms. Drain pasta; add to chicken mixture. Toss and serve immediately. Yield: 4 large servings.

The Pasta House Co.

300 Crestwood Plaza and various locations
314-961-6260
www.pastahouse.com

While Rich & Charlie's has stayed small and family-owned, The Pasta House Co., owned by Kim Tucci and Joe Fresta, has expanded tremendously and has over 25 locations, some franchised. One location is inside Crestwood Plaza on Highway 66, now Crestwood Court.

The Pasta House Co. Special Salad
Recipe courtesy The Pasta House Co. Italian Restaurant

1	head Iceberg lettuce
½	head Romaine lettuce
1	ounce thinly sliced red onions
6	pieces artichoke hearts
½	ounce pimentos, diced and drained well
4 to 6	ounces salad dressing (use 4 parts of olive oil blended with 1 part of red wine vinegar)
1	tsp salt
¼	tsp ground black pepper
½	cup grated Parmagiano cheese

Clean and wash lettuces and drain. Break lettuce into desired pieces (do not use knife). Place Iceberg and Romaine pieces in large bowl. Add artichoke hearts, onions and pimentos. In separate bowl, combine oil, vinegar, salt, pepper and cheese; add to lettuce in bowl. Toss until mixed completely and serve chilled. Yield: 4 servings. Note: This recipe is different from one published in 1996 in the *St. Louis Post-Dispatch*, which called for ⅓ head Romaine lettuce, 1 cup canned artichoke hearts (in brine and drained well), 1 cup diced pimentos, ⅔ cup olive oil and ⅓ cup Regina red wine vinegar, and ⅔ cup grated Parmesan cheese, instead of the measures given here.

Sesame Chinese Restaurant

10500 Watson Road
314-821-5038

Sesame Restaurant had its roots at the House of Hunan, located south of the cloverleaf bridge on S. Lindbergh Blvd in the space that is now Smugala's Pizza. The Watson Road site was once home to a trailer sales business and a Godfather's Pizza.

Sesame Szechwan Eggplant
Recipe shared by owners Robert and Lindy Ly

2	Tbsp granulated sugar
1½	Tbsp Kikkoman soy sauce
2	Tbsp white vinegar
1	Tbsp oyster sauce
1½	Tbsp water
1	tsp chopped garlic
½	tsp chopped fresh hot pepper (such as serrano)
1	(1-lb) eggplant
1	egg
¼	cup plus 1 tsp cornstarch, divided
5	cups vegetable oil
1	green onion, chopped

In a large saucepan, whisk together sugar, soy sauce, vinegar, oyster sauce, water, garlic and chopped pepper; set aside. Peel eggplant; cut into 1-by-1-by-2 inch rectangles. Beat egg in a large bowl; add eggplant and toss to coat thoroughly. Sprinkle on ¼ cup cornstarch; toss to coat eggplant evenly. In a wok or large skillet, heat oil to medium-high (375 degrees). Add eggplant in a single layer; fry until golden brown on all sides. Remove with a slotted spoon and set aside. Bring the soy sauce mixture to a boil. In a small dish, mix the remaining 1 teaspoon cornstarch into 1 teaspoon water; stir into the sauce and cook until the mixture thickens, about 1 minute. Add eggplant and green onion; toss to mix well. Serve immediately. Yield: 1 to 2 servings.

◆ Nelson's Café and Viking Restaurant

The northwest corner of Watson Road and Lindbergh Boulevard (where the Historic and Bypass 66 paths converged) once housed an early AAA Tourist Camp (similar to a campground site) then became the Park Plaza Courts with the Nelson's Café. In the mid 1960s, it became the Ozark Plaza Motel and the Flame Restaurant. In the 1970s, it became a Quality Inn with the Norsemen Lounge and Viking Restaurant. It then became the Viking Lodge, originally a Best Western and then a Holiday Inn. Throughout its years at this busy corner, it has been a popular place to stay, eat and drink.

Helen Fitzgerald's Irish Pub
3650 S. Lindbergh Blvd.
314-984-0026
www.helenfitzgeralds.us

Helen Fitzgerald's is at the site of the old Holiday Inn South (currently Days Inn) whose food service was run by the Schneithorst family. The Syberg family, which brought shark to St. Louis, owns the Syberg's restaurants in town and named this one after their grandmother.

Helen Fitzgerald's Cajun Grilled Shark Chunks
Recipe shared by Helen Fitzgerald's

- 1 lb shark steaks, skinned and cut into 1-inch chunks
- 3 Tbsp Syberg's Cajun Seasoning (see recipe), divided
- ⅓ cup butter
- • lemon wedges, for garnish

Combine shark chunks and 1 tablespoon Cajun Seasoning; toss to coat well. Charbroil or grill 3 minutes, turning twice. Meanwhile, melt butter in a skillet. When shark is done, transfer to skillet; sprinkle with remaining 2 tablespoons seasoning. Sauté over medium heat for 30 seconds, tossing occasionally. Pour shark with butter and seasoning into a serving dish; garnish with lemon. Yield: 2 servings.

Syberg's Cajun Seasoning:
- 1 Tbsp paprika
- 1 Tbsp seasoned salt
- 2 tsp onion powder
- 2 tsp granulated garlic
- 2 tsp cayenne
- 1½ tsp ground white pepper
- 1 tsp dried thyme
- 1 tsp dried oregano

Mix all ingredients thoroughly. Store in a cool, dry place. Yield: about 5 tablespoons.

House of Maret—in operation as Growler's Pub
3811 S. Lindbergh Blvd.
314-984-9009
www.saucemagazine.com/growlerspub

The House of Maret had humble beginnings as a gas station serving sandwiches and beer from an iced tub. Originally started in 1930 by Bill Maret Sr. and his wife Bertha, it continued in the family for decades and developed into an upscale French and German restaurant whose popular beer garden was the setting for many wedding parties. The building and beer garden remain, today housing Growler's Pub.

House of Maret Austrian Cabbage
Recipe shared by Rita Maret

- 1 large green cabbage, chopped
- ⅓ lb diced bacon
- 1 medium onion, chopped
- ¼ green pepper, chopped
- 1 rib celery, chopped
- ½ cup sugar
- 1 tsp salt
- • dash of black pepper
- • several dashes Tabasco
- ½ cup cider vinegar
- 1 scant cup caraway seeds
- 1 can tomatoes, chopped

Sauté bacon and onion in skillet. Add green pepper and celery and sauté until crisp tender. Add sugar, salt, pepper, Tabasco, cider vinegar, caraway seeds and chopped tomatoes. Add cabbage to mixture. Cover and cook gently until cabbage is tender.

The House of Maret

Unique German BIER GARTEN
Before or after the Show   3811 S. Lindbergh Blvd.   TA. 1-2626

Appetizers

Fresh Oyster Cocktail on Half Shell (in season) 1.95	Sauteed Fresh Oysters on Melba Toast with Lemon 2.95
Hickory Smoked Rib Bites 2.25	
Deviled Biloxi Crab with Mornay Sauce 1.95	Bismark Herring with Sour Cream and Onion 1.95
Swiss Fondue 1.95	Oysters Rockefeller Supreme 2.95

Dinner Entrees
ALL DINNERS INCLUDE SOUP, SALAD AND A BREAD PLATE.

SAUERBRATEN This remarkable entree is marinated weeks before it is deemed ready to be pot roasted. It is served with dark brown ginger sauce and is excellent with pan fried dumplings with mushroom, onion and celery, burgundy cabbage and spiced apples 5.95

BEEF ROULADEN A choice beef roll filled with ham, swiss cheese, onion, mustard and dill. Baked until tender in wine mushroom sauce. Red cabbage in wine sauce, crisp German potato pancakes or spaetzle and spiced apples are suggested. 5.95

CREPE MARET Tender young veal cutlet sauteed with mushrooms, accented with sherry wine in a crepe with mornay sauce. Served with asparagus tips . . 7.95

THE DEUTSCHLANDER For the adventurer—a sampling of the German cuisine—delectable morsels of tender sauerbraten, Austrian Pork Loin, Bratwurst, Knackwurst and a host of other German treats 7.25

WIENER SCHNITZEL Tender young veal sauteed in butter. We recommend an egg on top, special baked potato, spiced apples and creamed spinach 6.25

GERMAN POT ROAST A marinated Beef Pot Roast with our tempting beer mushroom sauce. Great with either spaetzle dumplings or crisp potato pancakes, burgundy cabbage and spiced apples 5.95

HUNGARIAN GOULASH A piping hot Beef Casserole over egg dumplings with spiced apples 4.95

KOHL ROULADEN A cabbage leaf filled with delicious meat dressing and baked slowly in beer sauce. Perfectly served with crisp German pancakes and spiced apples 3.95

BRATWURST Famous white sausage, browned over a charcoal fire, topped with a pinch of horseradish. Spiced apples, sauerkraut, creamed spinach and potato pancakes recommended 4.95

AUSTRIAN PORK LOIN Smoked Pork Loin on a bed of cabbage, tomato, green pepper, celery and onions, finished with beer sauce. Wunderschoen! We recommend our potato pancakes, spinach and spiced apples with this entree 5.95

TWIN PORK CHOPS Two thick center cut chops, charcoal broiled to perfection with barbeque sauce on the side. Delightful with twice baked potato 5.95

SINGLE PORK CHOP Served as above 4.75

PORK ROULADEN Lean pork loin butterflied and filled with tempting bread dressing 5.95

Chain of Rocks Alignments
City 66 "Connector" Path

Lombardo's

Bissell Mansion Restaurant
and Dinner Theatre

Crown Candy Kitchen

Vess Soda

Brooks Tangy Catsup

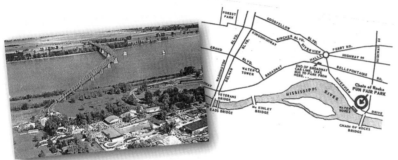

Chain of Rocks Fun Fair Park

The Swooper at Chain of Rocks Fun Fair Park

"The Chain of Rocks Bridge," Highway 66 over Mississippi River near St. Louis, Mo.

New/ Red Water Tower

Old/ White Water Tower

Lombardo's
10488 Natural Bridge Rd.
314-429-5151
www.lombardosrestaurants.com

The original Lombardo's location was just north of the City 66 routing, across from Calvary Cemetery at Riverview Blvd. and West Florissant. Patriarch Angelo Lombardo Sr. started the business as a produce stand in the early 1900s, after arriving here from Italy. The restaurant was added next door in 1934 and prospered for decades. In 1965 the produce stand was razed for a new, larger restaurant building, which remained in service until 1993 when the restaurant moved to its current location near Lambert Airport. The family also has two other restaurants, Carmine's Steak House and Lombardo's Trattoria. The Lombardos are celebrating 75 years in the restaurant business in 2009.

Lombardo's Black Russian Pie
Recipe shared by Lombardo's Restaurant

- 2 cups Oreo cookie crumbs, plus 2 Tbsp for garnish
- 3 Tbsp butter, melted
- 1 lb marshmallows
- ¾ cup milk
- ⅓ cup Kamora coffee-flavored liquer
- 3 cups heavy (40 percent) whipping cream, divided
- whole Oreo cookies, for garnish

Combine 2 cups crumbs with melted butter; press into pie pan and chill. In a large pot over low heat, melt marshmallows with milk, stirring until completely melted. Pour into a large mixing bowl; set the bowl on ice and stir until the marshmallow mixture is cool. Stir in Kamora. Whip 2 ½ cups of cream to soft peaks. Slowly fold the whipped cream into the cooled marshmallow mixture. Spoon into the crust. Freeze until firm, then cover. Store in the freezer. Transfer the pie from the freezer to the refrigerator 1 hour before serving. Whip the remaining ½ cup cream; spread or pipe over pie. Sprinkle on the reserved 2 tablespoons Oreo crumbs; garnish with the whole cookies. Yield: 8 servings.

Lombardo's Famous Green Noodles
Lombardo's is known for its house-made offerings including these creamy spinach noodles.
Recipe shared by Lombardo's Restaurant

- 1½ cups uncooked green (spinach) noodles
- salt
- ¼ cup (½ stick) butter, melted
- ¼ cup heavy (40 percent) cream
- 3 Tbsp grated Romano cheese

Boil green noodles in salted water until tender; drain. Add to pan with melted butter, cream and cheese. Stir to coat noodles; serve. Yield: 1 serving.

Bissell Mansion Restaurant and Dinner Theatre
4426 Randall Place
314-533-9830
www.bissellmansiontheatre.com

The Bissell Mansion is the oldest brick home in the city of St. Louis. It was built in the mid 1820s for Captain Lewis Bissell on property that steamboat captains used as a landmark they called Bissell Point. The home was rescued from demolition and today houses a restaurant and murder mystery dinner theater. It is located north of the McKinley Bridge in the Hyde Park area.

Bissell Mansion's Zucchini Bread
Recipe shared by the Bissell Mansion

- 3 eggs
- 1 cup vegetable oil
- 2 cups granulated sugar
- 2 tsp vanilla
- 2 cups grated zucchini (about 2 small zucchini)
- 3 cups all-purpose flour
- ½ tsp baking soda
- ½ tsp baking powder
- 2 Tbsp ground cinnamon
- ½ cup chopped pecans

Grease and flour two 9-by-5-inch or 8-by-4-inch loaf pans. Preheat the oven to 350 degrees. In a large bowl, combine eggs, oil, sugar and vanilla; beat with a fork or a whisk until smooth. Stir in zucchini until well blended; set aside. In a medium bowl, stir together flour, baking soda, baking powder and cinnamon until thoroughly combined. Add to egg mixture, 1 cup at a time. Beat until blended. Stir in pecans. Pour batter into prepared pans. Bake about 50 minutes or until a wooden pick inserted in the center comes out clean. Let cool 10 minutes, then remove from pans. Cooled loaves may be frozen. Yield: 16 servings (2 loaves).

Crown Candy Kitchen
1401 St. Louis Ave.
314-621-9650
www.crowncandykitchen.net

Crown Candy is a St. Louis institution, dating from 1913. It was near both the Original path and the City 66 Connector path and is south of the McKinley Bridge.

Crown Candy Kitchen Chocolate Banana Malt
Shared by Andy Karandzieff

- 3 scoops vanilla ice cream
- ½ of a banana
- 3 ounces chocolate syrup
- 1 Tbsp Carnation malted milk powder

Blend ingredients, adding milk to desired thickness of malt.

The Vess lemon-lime soda rotating bottles once shone in neon glory around St. Louis. This landmark was rescued and restored thanks to former Vess owner Don Schneeberger and many workers but sadly the restoration did not last long. The bottle can be found today where I-70 and Broadway come into downtown.

Vess Watermelon Popsicles
Recipe shared by Don Schneeberger

½ Missouri watermelon
2 tsp fresh lemon juice
½ cup sugar
½ cup Vess Distilled Water*

Cut watermelon into cubes and rub through a strainer to removes seeds, making 3 cups watermelon juice. In a small saucepan, mix together sugar and water; simmer 3 minutes. Remove from heat; stir in watermelon juice and lemon juice. Pour into two ice trays. Freeze until very mushy and insert a popsicle stick in each cube. Freeze. Makes about 36 small popsicles.
* If no longer available, use a substitute distilled water.

Restored Vess Soda rotating bottle

Treesh Neon, the company that made the Vess rotating bottles, first made the rotating Brooks Catsup bottles. Nearby Collinsville, Illinois embraced its landmark Brooks Catsup Water Tower and, with the help of many volunteers, restored it and preserved it for future generations. See www.catsupbottle.com for more information.

Brooks (Tangy Catsup) Super Chili

This recipe uses four Brooks products, including Brooks Tangy Catsup (now ketchup).
Adapted from a recipe on the Birds Eye Foods website and reprinted with permission of Birds Eye Foods, Inc.

- 2 cans (15.5 oz each) Brooks Chili Hot Beans
- 1 can (14.5 oz) Brooks Just For Chili Diced Tomatoes
- 4 Tbsp Brooks Rich and Tangy Ketchup
- 1 lb ground beef
- 1 lb ground pork
- 1 beaten egg
- ½ cup milk
- 1 packet (1.25 oz) Brooks Secret Chili Seasoning
- 1½ cup water
- 3 Tbsp chopped onion
- 1 small can tomato paste
- 2 tsp sugar

Mix beef, pork, egg, milk, and 3 teaspoons Brooks Secret Chili seasoning. Form into 1-inch balls and brown in 1 tablespoon vegetable oil. Combine remaining ingredients (including remaining Brooks Chili Seasoning) in Dutch oven and bring to boil. Add meatballs. Cover and reduce heat. Cook slowly for 1½ hours, stirring occasionally. Notes: Beef and pork meatballs make this recipe unique. Slow cooking results in a rich blending of flavors.

Brooks Catsup Water Tower in nearby Collinsville, Illinois

Chain of Rocks Alignments
Path Around St. Louis/
Bypass Route

Yacovelli's

Henry VIII Inn and Lodge

Kreis' Restaurant

Don Breckenridge, Highway 66,
and St. Louis-Breckenridge Inn

Schneithorst's

Sunset 44 Bistro

Spencer's Grill

Citizen Kane's Steakhouse

Manor Grove (formerly the Old Folks Home)

Green Parrot Inn

Howard Johnson's/Layton's

Airway Drive-In

Chuck-A-Burger, St. Charles Rock Road

Lambert Field postcard postmarked 1942

Early postcard King Bros. Motel

Downtown Kirkwood

Yacovelli's is one of the longest-running restaurants in St. Louis, started in 1919 and housed at various locations around St. Louis. The Yacovellis invented the salad bar and even had a rotating one that could be filled from the kitchen.

Yacovelli's Shrimp Ponchartrain
Shared by owners Jack and Jan Yacovelli

    36   (21 to 25 count) shrimp
     1   lb cream cheese, at room temperature
     1   ounce crumbled blue cheese (about ¼ cup)
    ½   cup cream
     1   dash Worcestershire sauce
     4   drops Tabasco
     2   cups milk
     2   eggs
     1   cup all-purpose flour or more as needed
    1½   cups dry bread crumbs or more as needed
     •   vegetable oil, for deep frying

Peel and devein shrimp. (For ease of handling, leave tails intact.) Steam shrimp just until cooked through. Let cool. Cut a "pocket" in the back of each shrimp, ¼ through from head to top of tail section. Combine cheese, blue cheese, cream, Worcestershire and Tabasco; mix thoroughly. Spoon filling into pocket of each shrimp, pressing to fill cavity. Place stuffed shrimp on a tray; refrigerate for 1 hour. Combine milk and eggs in measuring cup or narrow bowl, whisking until well blended. Place flour and crumbs in two separate shallow dishes. Dip each stuffed shrimp in egg mixture, roll in flour, dip back into egg mixture, then roll in crumbs. Arrange in a single layer on a cookie sheet; place in freezer for at least 1 hour or until ready to cook. Add oil to a deep skillet to a depth of 1 inch; heat to 325 degrees. Fry shrimp until lightly browned, 2 to 3 minutes. (Do not overcook or filling will melt away.) Drain on paper towels; serve hot. Yield: 36 stuffed shrimp, 9 appetizer or 6 main-course servings.

The Henry VIII Inn and Lodge began as the 1964 Red Carpet Inn then merged with the Henry VIII restaurant and lounge next door. The luxurious 384-room hotel had oak paneling and chandeliers, expensive paintings and mirrors, indoor pools, 18 rooms with whirlpool tubs (usually rented by honeymoon couples), and it was host to many wedding receptions, family reunions, company meetings and conventions. The landmark hotel was lost in 2000 to Lambert Airport's westward expansion. Bargain hunters flocked to the hotel where silverware sold for a quarter and 19-inch televisions were only $79. The bar inside Duffy's, the hotel's lounge, sold for $32,000 while a life-size painting of King Henry VIII sold for $1500.

Henry VIII Shrimp Scampi Sauce

Recipe from Pierre's Secrets, a 1980 cookbook by the Mother's Club at De Smet Jesuit High School

3 shallots
1 clove garlic
1 ounce Worcestershire sauce
• salt to taste
½ pint fresh lemon juice
½ pint sherry
1 lb butter, softened
1½ cups prepared mustard

Grind the shallots and clove of garlic; add the Worcestershire sauce, the lemon juice and the sherry. Mix the mustard with the butter until smooth and add this to the first mixture. Boil for 5 minutes, with constant stirring. This note accompanied the recipe: This sauce can be made in 15 minutes and the lemon juice helps preserve the sauce indefinitely in the refrigerator.

OF GRAPE AND GRAIN

KING HENRY VIII COOLER
A blend of orange, lemon and lime juice with rum from the British West Indies, served in a special glass 1.75

RED PRINCE
A combination of champagne and cranberry juice 1.75

HURRICANE
Passion fruit juice and rum, served in an iced special glass 1.75

BOTTLED UP

Michelob on Draft 1.25

Heinekens Beer 1.50

SAVOURIES

JUMBO SHRIMP COCKTAIL SUPREME 2.50

TOASTED RAVIOLI, Italian Sauce 1.75

OYSTER ROCKEFELLER, In season 3.00

OYSTERS on the HALF SHELL, In season 2.50

SHRIMP SCAMPI 3.25

ESCARGOTS, Garlic butter, served on mushroom cap 2.95

ASSORTED HORS D'OEUVRES PLATTER, per person 2.25

SOUPS

LONDONSHIRE SOUP .50

SOUP of the DAY 50

HENRY VIII SALADS

MIXED GREENS, With choice of Londondary, Thousand Island, Bleu Cheese, Italian or French Dressing, topped with chopped bacon and croutons 1.00

FRESH TOMATOES, Red Onions and Anchovy Salad, topped with whipped vinegar and oil dressing 1.25

HEARTS OF PALM, Tossed with Bib Lettuce, hearts of palm, green pepper, tomatoes and red onions 1.50

CAESAR SALAD, Tossed at table, Romaine Lettuce blended with our own Caesar dressing prepared at the table
With Dinner 1.50
Ala Carte 3.00

HENRY VIII SPECIALTIES

BROILED ENGLISH SHISHKEBAB
Marinated tenderloin tips skewered with tiny whole onions, green peppers, mushrooms and tomatoes on savory rice, flamed at the table 6.95

ROAST BONELESS BREAST OF CHICKEN
Stuffed with rice, with a white wine sauce 5.75

TOURNEDO'S OF BEEF
Slices of filet mignon braised with fresh mushrooms in a delicate wine sauce, served with broccoli and parmesan tomato 7.95

BONELESS ROAST DUCK
L'Orange Sauce with Cointreau and Honey 6.95

VEAL WINDSOR
Fresh milk fed veal dipped in egg batter, sauteed with parmesan cheese, served with fresh broccoli and parmesan tomato 6.95

PRIME RIB OF BEEF

Roasted in rock salt to preserve all of the delicate natural juices An extra cut for hearty appetites
7.95   8.95
Served with Yorkshire Pudding, Horseradish Mousse

TO COMPLEMENT ANY ENTREE

FRENCH FRIED ONION RINGS, Basket 1.25

SAUTEED FRESH MUSHROOMS, In steak butter 1.25

FRENCH FRIED MUSHROOMS, Basket 1.25

FRESH ASPARAGUS, Prepared to order 85

FRESH BROCCOLI, Prepared to order 85

FROM OUR BROILER

All steaks are aged for tenderness and are carefully selected from only choice or prime beef.

RIB EYE STEAK, 8 ounces 6.95

TUDOR STRIP SIRLOIN
10 ounces of aged choice sirloin 6.95

HENRY VIII STRIP SIRLOIN
14 ounces of well marbled steak 8.95

CHOPPED SIRLOIN STEAK
With mushroom sauce 4.50

FILET MIGNON
8 ounces of Beef Tenderloin 8.95

STEAK DIANE
Medallions of filet mignon prepared at your table with a special wine sauce 8.95

FILET MIGNON (6 ounces) and LOBSTER 9.95

LAMB CHOPS, with mint sauce 5.95

Henry VIII Dinners include Baked Potato, Rolls and Butter

CHATEAUBRIAND

For two, carved at your table
Served with fresh vegetable, potatoes, parmesan tomatoes, mushrooms, bordelaise sauce

19.50

Kreis' Restaurant
535 S. Lindbergh Blvd.
314-993-0735

It is believed that Kreis' (pronounced Chrises) started off as a roadhouse owned by Fred Kreis. Subsequent owners kept the Kreis' name and the clam chowder and the oyster sauce recipes were passed down as well. The Tompras family assumed ownership in 1983.

Kreis' Lamb Shanks with Rice Pilaf
Shared by owners George Tompras and Renée Bogdanos

6 lamb foreshanks (about 1 ½ lbs each)
• salt, to taste
• freshly cracked black pepper, to taste
1 Tbsp granulated garlic
2 medium onions, diced
1 (28-ounce) can whole tomatoes, diced, juice reserved
1 Tbsp granulated sugar
1 to 2 cups beef broth
1½ Tbsp dried oregano

Preheat oven to 400 degrees. Season lamb shanks with salt, pepper and garlic. Put in a heavy pan and roast about 25 minutes. Turn lamb shanks over; add onions and continue roasting until lamb is brown, about 20 minutes longer. Add tomatoes and their juice, sugar, 1 cup broth and oregano. Reduce the heat to 350 degrees. Cover the pan and cook until tender, about 1 ½ hours. Add more broth during cooking if necessary. Serve over rice pilaf.

Rice Pilaf:

1 small onion, diced fine
½ Tbsp butter
3 cups chicken broth
1½ cups uncooked rice
1 bay leaf
• salt and ground white pepper, to taste

Preheat the oven to 350 degrees. Sauté the onion in butter in an ovenproof pan until onion is transparent. Add broth, rice, bay leaf, salt and pepper; stir to mix well. Bring to a boil. Remove from heat; cover and transfer to oven. Bake for 20 minutes or until rice is tender. Remove bay leaf and serve. Yield: 6 servings.

JACK KANE'S
Kreis' Restaurant and Bar
Our Daily Specials

MONDAY: Old Fashioned Pot Roast,
   Home-Made Noodles 4.50
   Boiled Spare Ribs with Sauer Kraut 4.50
TUESDAY: Hungarian Goulash, Home-Made Noodles 4.50
   Bratwurst with Red Cabbage and Potato Dumplings 4.50
WEDNESDAY: Chicken and Home-Made Noodles 4.50
   Boiled Spare Ribs with Sauer Kraut 4.50
THURSDAY: Pot Roast of Beef with Home-Made Noodles 4.50
   Corned Beef and Cabbage 4.50
FRIDAY: Chicken Livers with Mushrooms & Rice 4.50
   Shrimp Creole with Rice 4.75
SATURDAY: Tenderloin Tips with Mushroom Sauce 4.75
   Old Fashioned Pot Roast, Home Made Noodles 4.50

Served with Chef Salad Bowl, our own Dressing

Taken from the Jack Kane's Kreis' 1976 menu

WE ARE CELEBRATING OUR 25TH ANNIVERSARY OF SERVICE TO ST. LOUIS

Hotelier and developer Donald Breckenridge had ties to several places on Route 66 in the St. Louis area including the former King Bros. Motel on the Bypass route, the Fenton Ramada Inn on 66/I-44, and the upscale Legends residential community, just blocks from old 66 in Eureka, Missouri. He also purchased pristine farmland on Highway 66 in Allenton/Eureka from the Wallach family, pioneer farmers in St. Louis County. Breckenridge, the son of a concrete maker, started out as a candy salesman for Brach Candy Co. His first development was Thornhill Estates for which he used only $3500 of his own money. His enthusiasm convinced an investor to put up the rest. He put that same vision and enthusiasm to use in 1964 when he saw a need for a hotel in Jefferson City, putting the Ramada Inn deal together while investing little of the cash and associated risk.

From that start in the hotel business, by 1980 his business had grown to ownership of 13 hotels and management of six or so more. Along the way, he saved part of the King Bros. Motel when he redeveloped it into the Breckenridge Inn (later Breckenridge Frontenac) and he found a use for the old Spanish Pavilion (which Mayor A. J. Cervantes brought to St. Louis from the 1964 New York World's Fair), making it into the Breckenridge Pavilion hotel. After he read in 1997 that the Edison Bros. warehouse, (originally a J.C. Penney warehouse from 1928, complete with its interesting trompe l'oeil murals by Richard Haas) might be torn down, he acquired it and redeveloped it into a successful complex of Sheraton Hotel rooms, condos, restaurants, health club and parking garage.

Despite a few projects that fell short of his expectations, Breckenridge never stopped believing. He had his keen eye on the Municipal Courts Building on Market and wanted to renovate the Kiel Opera House when his life was cut short in 2005 by lung cancer. He was a non-smoker. The Breckenridge Frontenac is now the Hilton Saint Louis Frontenac, the Breckenridge Pavilion is now the St. Louis Marriott Downtown and the Fenton Ramada Inn is now the Stratford Inn.

Breckenridge Inn Shrimp De Jonghe

This recipe from the Breckenridge Inn was during Don's heyday as a hotelier. *Recipe shared by Chef John Glisan, for Pierre's Secrets, a 1980 cookbook by the De Smet Jesuit High School Mother's Club*

- 16 ounces shrimp pieces
- 5 ounces butter, cut into small pieces
- 2 cloves fresh garlic, chopped
- 1½ Tbsp salt
- 4 ounces Chablis wine
- 1 ounce lemon juice
- ⅛ cup parsley, chopped
- ¼ cup bread crumbs
- ¼ cup Parmesan cheese

Preheat oven to 375 degrees. In a small casserole lay out shrimp pieces. Add white wine and lemon juice. Sprinkle with butter, chopped garlic and chopped parsley. Top with a mixture of bread crumbs and Parmesan cheese. Bake in oven for 15 minutes. Serve over rice or as an appetizer.

The Schneithorst family has been active in the St. Louis restaurant scene since 1917. They were part of the foodservice at the airport, the Bevo Mill, and the early St. Louis Holiday Inns. In 1956, they opened a place bearing their name on Highway 66. It was a popular place serving up German food in an Old World atmosphere for decades. The family remodeled the complex in 2002 and much of the original restaurant was lost to progress. Today, Schneithorst's is known for its casual dining and rooftop bar.

Schneithorst's Rouladen
Shared by Schneithorst's

12	ounces top sirloin steak
2	Tbsp prepared mustard
4	thick slices bacon
¼	cup dill pickle slices
•	salt
•	toothpicks

Preheat oven to 350 degrees. Trim any fat off the meat and cut it against the grain into ¼ inch thick slices. Place the meat between two pieces of plastic wrap and flatten with a mallet. Fill any holes with scrap meat. Spread with mustard. Distribute the bacon and pickles over the meat. Season with salt to taste; roll the meat up. Tuck in edges so that there are no flaps and secure with toothpicks. Place in a pan just big enough to hold the meat in one layer. Cover meat with special sauce (see recipe). Cover with foil; bake for 45 minutes.

Special Sauce:

2	cups brown gravy, chilled
⅓	cup pickle juice, chilled
½	tsp mustard

Put all ingredients into a bowl and mix well.

Schneithorst's Potato Pancakes
Shared by Schneithorst's

2	lbs potatoes, peeled
1	lb onions, peeled
•	juice of 1 lemon
2	eggs
¼	tsp salt
⅛	tsp pepper
¼	cup all-purpose flour
¼	cup matzo meal
¾	cup salad oil

Preheat oven to 375 degrees. Grind or grate the potatoes and onions together and add the lemon juice to prevent discoloration. Let stand 5 minutes and then drain off excess liquid. Add eggs, salt, pepper, flour, and matzo meal. Heat oil and then drop batter onto hot oil. When bottoms are brown, flip.

Your enjoyment of this historic restaurant begins about a block away as you approach the authentically decorated replica of a Bavarian inn. The interior is generously appointed with beer steins and other artifacts to help you enjoy an old-world atmosphere in this west county setting. The Schneithorst's family restaurant traditions are maintained in the quality German, continental, and seafood specialties.

 ## Schneithorst's Hofamberg Inn

Vorspeisen

kalt
Oysters on the half shell (in season). 2.75
Fresh fruit supreme. .95
Chilled shrimp a la Rhine. 2.75
Chilled tomato juice. .50

heib
Mushrooms en Skillet. 1.75
Soup of the day, made kettle-fresh every day from our own recipes. .75
Toasted ravioli. 1.75
French-fried onion rings. 1.25

Broodies

Club House Sandwich
with soup of the day and potato chips. 3.95

Ham and Eggs
with hash browned potatoes, buttered toast and pineapple ring. 3.75

The Claytonia
Chopped beef steak on toasted bun with broiled onion, French-Fried potatoes, and relishes. 3.75

Salat

Shrimp Salad Bowl
French Louisiana shrimp and anchovies with tomato wedges, slices of hard boiled egg, diced Pascal celery and green pepper ring with crisp lettuce and celery stick. Chef's special dressing or Thousand Island. 3.75

Haupt Salat Bowl
Julienne of chicken, baked sugar-cured ham, Swiss cheese, tomato wedges, hard boiled egg, and fresh June garden peas tossed with shredded lettuce and Thousand Island dressing. 3.75

Imported Roquefort Dressing
Imported from Europe, this Roquefort cheese is the only one in St. Louis awarded The **French Red Sheep** Seal for genuine excellence. Marinated and tossed at your table. Extra on all salads. .85

Hofamberg Beef

THE BARON'S T-BONE STEAK 8.50

CHOICE CHOPPED HOFAMBERG BEEF STEAK 4.50

SIRLOIN STRIP STEAK 8.75

FILET MIGNON 8.75

Der Sizzler
Special Sirloin Steak. 6.50

Chateaubriand For Two
served with vegetables. 24.00

MUSHROOMS EN SKILLET 1.75

For the Little Baron
Choice of chopped beef steak, fried sole or fried chicken leg and thigh, served with potato, jello dessert and a beverage. 2.95

We Modestly Boast of a Fine Wine Cellar
please ask the maitre d' for the wine list

Fisch

A Gourmet's Delight
Fillets de sole Saute Amandine 4.95

Tiny Cape Cod Bay Scallops
sauteed, tartar sauce. 6.95

Fresh Channel Catfish
pan fried. 5.25

Broiled Lobster Tail
served with hot drawn butter sauce.

Broiled Halibut Steak
served with hot drawn butter 6.50

French Fried Jumbo Shrimp
with tartar or cocktail sauce. 5.25

Fillets of Lemon Sole
broiled or fried. 4.75

Schneithorst's Special Seafood Platter
French fried shrimp, tiny bay scallops, broiled fillet of sole and Baked Haddock Ala Creole 8.25

Hauptspeisen

Baron's Special
Broiled chopped Hofamberg beef on crusty Vienna bread topped with molten cheese rarebit sauce and crisp bacon and brightened with onion rings. 4.95

Roast Prime Rib of Beef
A generous cut of aged beef roasted slowly to preserve all the natural juices. 8.25

Our Roast Beef Special
Roast sirloin of Hofamberg beef served on Vienna bread with fluffy whipped potatoes, au jus sauce. 4.95

Sauteed Fresh Calf's Liver
with a rasher of bacon. 5.25

Sauerbraten
Two special cuts of Hofamberg beef marinated in vinegar and spice brine and then braised to a juicy goodness in rich wine sauce. Served in a flaming casserole with German potato pancakes and applesauce. 5.50

Wienerschnitzel A La Holstein
A tender cut of choice veal steak, breaded and pan-fried to a golden brown, garnished with country fried egg, lemon wedge, anchovy and topped with a zesty tomato sauce. 6.95

Skewered Brochette of Beef
with fried brown rice. 6.75

Country Fried Chicken
Country Fried Chicken or if you prefer, broiled. Peach melba. 4.25

Sauteed Chicken Livers
4.95

ALL ENTREES SERVED WITH . . . Tossed Green Salad or Salad of the Day . . . Vegetable DuJour or Baked Idaho Potatoe with Choice of sour cream or butter or Potato of the Day

Nachtisch

Hot Apple Strudel with Brandy Sauce

Philadelphia Cream Cheese Pie topped with Smetna cheese

Homemade Apple Pie with a wedge of cheese

Sunset 44 was originally located on Highway 66 in Sunset Hills, just west of the cloverleaf bridge. It has relocated to the heart of Kirkwood, on the former Bypass route. Owner Bob Menendez followed his father, who owned the Pilot House restaurants, into the restaurant business.

Bob, who sold pretzels on St. Louis street corners as a boy, started out in the restaurant business by frying up chicken in his father's restaurant then became a Culinary Institute of America-trained chef and wine expert.

Sunset 44 Bistro Pork Tenderloin with Cranberry Ginger Chutney
Shared by owner Bob Menendez

For chutney:

       2   (12-ounce) bags fresh cranberries
       1   lb (3 cups lightly packed) brown sugar
    1½   cups currants
       1   cup dried apricots, quartered
       1   tsp ground cinnamon
     ⅛   tsp ground red (cayenne) pepper
       1   cup cranberry juice
       1   Tbsp plus 1 tsp minced peeled fresh ginger

Combine cranberries, sugar, currants, apricots, cinnamon, cayenne pepper, cranberry juice and ginger in a heavy saucepan. Cook over medium heat, stirring until sugar is dissolved. Increase heat to high; boil 10 minutes. Pour into a bowl. Refrigerate leftovers in an airtight container. Yield: 5 cups.

For pork:

    •   nonstick cooking spray
    ¼   cup soy sauce
    ¾   cup Burgundy wine
    1   Tbsp dried oregano, crushed
    1   tsp garlic powder plus more to taste
    ¼   cup corn oil
    2   lbs pork tenderloin, excess fat and
          silver skin removed
    •   salt
    •   ground black pepper

Preheat the oven to 350 degrees; place a cake rack over a shallow baking pan (e.g., jellyroll pan) and coat the rack with cooking spray. Set aside. Combine soy sauce, wine, oregano and 1 tsp garlic powder in a bowl; slowly whisk in oil to emulsify. Add pork; marinate 10 minutes at room temperature (or refrigerate overnight). Drain pork, discarding marinade. Season pork with salt, pepper and garlic powder to taste. Arrange pork on prepared rack; bake about 35 minutes or to an internal temperature of 165 degrees. Let pork stand about 5 minutes, then slice ½ inch thick. Spoon some warm chutney onto each serving plate; arrange pork slices on top. Yield: 6 servings.

Spencer's Grill has been in the current building since March 1947. Bill Spencer operated it until October 1973. Since then there have been six other owners. When Chris Powers took over (late 2003/early 2004), he restored the neon sign and clock. The place continues as a hub for locals.

Spencer's Grill St. Louis Slinger

The slinger is a St. Louis institution at all diners, popular with the late-night crowd. Some diners use shredded Cheddar cheese and use the toast as the bottom layer. Some variations are even topped with tamales and burritos. *Shared by owner Chris Powers and manager/daughter Katherine Powers*

Cook ham, bacon, sausage or hamburger patty and set aside. Cook hash browns separately and set aside. Cook two eggs to order (scrambled, over easy/hard, etc.) Place eggs, hash browns and meat side by side on a serving plate. Top with a slice of American cheese. Smother entire thing with chili. Top with chopped yellow onions. Serve with toast.

Spencers Grill

WE SPECIALIZE IN CARRY OUT ORDERS

223 S. Kirkwood, Rd.   Phone, Ki-0561

BREAKFAST		PLATE LUNCHES	
2 eggs, toast, butter & jelly	.30	T-Bone Plate	1.25
		Sirloin Steak Plate	1.00
2 eggs with bacon, ham or		Cube Steak Plate	.50
sausage; toast butter &		Pork Chop Plate, 2 chops	.65
jelly	.50	Pork Chop Plate, 1 chop	.50
(American Fries .05 Extra)		Hamburger Plate	.45
(Poached or soft boiled		Ham Plate	.50
.05 extra per egg)			
Hot cakes with bacon, ham or			
sausage	.40	DRINKS	
Cereal with cream	.20		
Cereal with milk	.15		
Order toast, butter & jelly	.10	Coffee	.05
Donuts	.05	Milk	.10
Rolls	.05	Hot Chocolate	.10
Juices	.10	Hot Tea	.05
		Bottle Soda	.10
SANDWICHES		Fountain Soda	.05
Burger Special with slaw &		Malted Milk	.25
French Fries	.25	Ice Cream Soda	.25
Hamburger	.10		
Cheeseburger	.20		
Cube Steak	.25		
Pork Chop	.25	SPECIALS	
Bacon, Lettuce & Tomato	.30		
Hot Dog	.15		
Cheese, Plain	.15	Sliced Tomatoes	
Cheese, Grilled	.20	(With Salad Dressing)	.15
Ham	.25	Soup, Heinz	.10
Ham & Cheese	.35	Chef Salad	.50
Ham & Egg	.30	Chili	.20
Bacon & Egg	.30	Chili Mac	.35
Bacon	.20	French Fries	.10
DeLuxe Burger	.20	Lettuce Tomato Salad	.15
Sausage	.25	Slaw	.10

DESSERTS

Pie	.15
Poe Ala Mode	.20
Sundae	.20

Take Home a Quart of Ice Cream .60

Curb Service
Starting Friday June 17
(CURB SERVICE AFTER 5 P.M. LARGE PARKING AREA AT REAR OF GRILL)
WHERE FRIENDS MEET AND EAT

June 1949 Menu

Citizen Kane's Steakhouse

133 West Clinton Place (Kirkwood)
314-965-9005
www.citizenkanes.com

Starting at age 14, Frank Kane, a Kirkwood native, worked for ten years doing a variety of jobs on the Admiral. From there, he worked for Ruth's Chris Steak House and Sam's St. Louis Steakhouse. When he decided to strike out on his own, he returned to Kirkwood and bought an 1884 Victorian home, which had been used as a boardinghouse, a tea room and an Irish pub. He took the name for his restaurant from the nickname "Citizen Kane," which his high school football coach had given him, taken from the Orson Welles classic movie. Located just a few blocks south of the historic Kirkwood Train Station and near Spencer's Grill, the restaurant opened in December 1993 and has been going strong ever since. Known for its great steaks in a warm atmosphere, Citizen Kane's is a consistent favorite. The restaurant is open Tuesdays through Saturdays, only for dinner. Besides its steaks, which are hand cut on the premises, Citizen Kane's makes its own sauces, soups, salad dressings and desserts.

Citizen Kane's New Orleans Style Barbecue Shrimp

This is a special appetizer at the restaurant. *Shared by Frank Kane*

2 cups (4 sticks) butter, at room temperature
2 Tbsp chopped garlic
2 Tbsp crushed dried rosemary
1 Tbsp paprika
1 Tbsp ground black pepper
1 tsp ground white pepper
1 tsp ground red (cayenne) pepper
   or more to taste
¼ tsp salt
1 Tbsp Worcestershire sauce
• juice of 1 large lemon (about 2 Tbsp plus 2 tsp)
2 to 3 lbs (10- to 15-count) shrimp

Combine butter, garlic, rosemary, paprika, black, white and red peppers, salt, Worcestershire and lemon juice in the bowl of an electric mixer; beat until light and fluffy. Refrigerate until ready to use. Peel and devein shrimp, leaving the last shell section and tail intact. Heat skillet over medium-high heat, then add butter and shrimp. Cook, stirring frequently, just until shrimp are done. Serve with crusty bread for dipping in the extra butter sauce. Yield: 8 appetizer servings.

Citizen Kane's Boardinghouse Potatoes

These potatoes take their name from previous tenants at the building. They are a tasty and colorful side dish. *Shared by Frank Kane*

¼ cup extra-virgin olive oil
½ medium onion, diced
1 clove garlic, chopped
¼ each red, yellow and green bell peppers, chopped
3 large potatoes, cooked, peeled and diced
• seasoning salt
• ground black pepper

Pour olive oil into a heavy skillet. Add onion, garlic and red, yellow and green bell peppers. Sauté until vegetables are soft. Stir in potatoes until heated through. Season to taste with seasoning salt and black pepper. Yield: 6 side-dish servings.

Manor Grove (formerly the Old Folks Home)
711 S. Kirkwood Road (Kirkwood)

The Old Folks Home was on Highway 66 for the duration. It was begun in 1907 by a small group of women who wanted to help poor, elderly senior citizens who needed a place to live. The 1927 building has been expanded several times and the name has been changed to the more politically correct Manor Grove but they continue to provide great care for seniors. Residents throughout the years have also enjoyed their meals there.

Baked Eggplant and Mushrooms
From the 1964 The New Saint Louis Symphony of Cooking cookbook, courtesy Saint Louis Symphony Volunteer Association

1 eggplant
½ lb chopped fresh mushrooms
¾ cup milk or 1 can condensed cream
   of mushroom soup
2 beaten eggs
1 small onion, chopped
1 cup soft bread crumbs
¼ cup melted butter
¼ tsp salt
⅛ tsp pepper

Cut ends off eggplant and peel. Cut into large pieces. Boil in a small amount of salted water about 15 minutes. Drain and mash. Stir in rest of ingredients. Pour into greased 1½ quart casserole. Sprinkle with topping. Bake at 350 for 25 to 30 minutes. Makes 6 servings.

For topping:
½ cup dry bread crumbs mixed with
2 Tbsp melted butter

The Green Parrot Inn, owned by the Toothman family, was a destination restaurant at 12180 Old Big Bend Road, near the Bypass route in Kirkwood. It served its famous family-style fried chicken dinners from 1938 to 1983. Today the building is a private residence.

Waldorf-Astoria Fabulous $100 Chocolate Cake, courtesy Green Parrot Inn

The Green Parrot Inn recipes were closely guarded secrets and remain so today. When a customer asked for a recipe, this one is what they handed out. *Shared by the Toothman family*

½ cup butter
2 cups sugar
4 ounces bitter chocolate
2 eggs
2 cups flour
2 tsp baking powder
⅛ tsp salt
1 cup black walnuts (ground)
2 tsp vanilla
1½ cups milk

Cream butter and sugar. Melt chocolate. Beat eggs; add to sugar mixture. Add melted chocolate. Mix dry ingredients and add alternately with liquid (milk). Add vanilla and nuts. Bake in loaf or flat pan at 350 degrees for about 45 minutes. (Batter will be very thin.)

Frosting:
¼ cup butter
2 ounces bitter chocolate
1 Tbsp vanilla
1 Tbsp lemon juice
⅔ package powdered sugar
1 egg, beaten (whole)
1 pinch salt
1 cup black walnuts, chopped

Melt butter and chocolate. Add egg, salt, sugar, vanilla and lemon juice. Beat until creamy. Add nuts.

◆ Howard Johnson's/Layton's Restaurant
Best Western Kirkwood Inn: 1200 S. Kirkwood Road (Kirkwood)
314-821-3950
www.bestwesternmissouri.com

The Giessow family owned the Howard Johnson's on the Lindbergh/Bypass 66 route. It opened around 1953 and a Howard Johnson's Hotel was added in 1973. The Giessows also owned the Howard Johnson's at 7950 Clayton Road in Richmond Heights, by Tropicana Bowl and the Galleria. That location was a Howard Johnson's from 1955 to 1984 then became Layton's. The Howard Johnson's on the Bypass route closed in 2002 as the last Howard Johnson's west of the Mississippi and it made way for Chili's. The hotel is still going strong and has been the Best Western Kirkwood Inn since 1993. Layton's closed two years later in July 2004.

Karen's Meatloaf

This recipe is named for Karen Stemmermann, manager and 30-year employee at Howard Johnson's and Layton's at 7950 Clayton Road in Richmond Heights. *Recipe shared by Layton's for a November 8, 1997 feature story by the* St. Louis Post-Dispatch

For special red sauce:

- 1 (8-ounce) can tomato sauce
- 1 cup plus 1 Tbsp water
- 1 (12-ounce) can tomato juice
- 1 (10 3/4-ounce) can condensed tomato soup
- 1 Tbsp prepared yellow mustard
- ¼ cup granulated sugar

Combine tomato sauce, water, tomato juice, tomato soup, mustard and sugar in a saucepan. Mix well. Bring to a boil, then reduce heat and let simmer for three minutes. Remove from heat; set aside.

For meatloaf:

- 3 lbs ground beef
- 1 Tbsp garlic salt
- 1 tsp ground black pepper
- 2 Tbsp chopped onion
- ½ cup dry Italian-seasoned bread crumbs
- 2 eggs

Preheat oven to 350 degrees. Using your hands, gently mix ground beef, garlic salt, pepper and onion. Add bread crumbs and eggs; mix well. Add ½ cup special sauce; mix well. Shape meat into a loaf and place on a broiler pan. Bake for 40 minutes. Pour one cup special sauce over loaf; bake 10 minutes longer. Heat remaining special sauce; pass at the table to top meatloaf or potatoes, or freeze for a future meatloaf. Yield: 8 large servings.

Howard Johnson's Motor Lodge and Restaurant

Continuation of Historic Route, west of I-270

Cracker Barrel

Fenton, Times Beach, Rock City and Eureka

White Squirrel Tavern

Sites Station Café

Haymarket Restaurant

Red Cedar Inn

Henry Shaw Gardenway, Jensen Point, and
Shaw Nature Reserve

Parrett's

Cottrell's Restaurant

George's Apple Orchard and Market

The Diamonds

Key's Twin Bridge Café

Ben Kraus at Valley
Mount Ranch

Lone Elk Park

1982 Times Beach Flood

Highway 66 near Devine's
Tavern in Allenton, MO

Cave Café in Pacific, MO

Crest Restaurant, west of
Pacific, MO

Farmer's Wayside Market
west of Pacific, MO

The Diamonds in Villa Ridge, MO

American Inn in Villa Ridge, MO

Cracker Barrel

www.crackerbarrel.com

The Cracker Barrel story begins with Dan Evins who spent hours on the new interstate system in the 1960s where he drove from town to town as a Shell Oil jobber. He saw firsthand that many of the small family places that had once served up old-fashioned cooking were quickly being displaced by the fast food chains. He decided that he could offer the traveler the type of food and atmosphere he was looking for on the road. With friend Tommy Lowe as a business partner, they opened the first Cracker Barrel Old Country Store in Lebanon, Tennessee on September 19, 1969. From the outset, it had a retail store/restaurant combination as part of the concept and featured vintage décor and products. Like today, it had rocking chairs on the front porch and a fireplace but also featured gas pumps out front--something that went by the wayside due to the 1970s gas shortage.

The restaurant prospered. By 1977, there were 13 stores. Now a publicly traded corporation, in 2009 there are over 580 Cracker Barrel stores across the country. Many are along the former 8-state path of Route 66. (In St. Louis, the Fenton, Missouri store is located right on former Highway 66, near what was Weiss Airport and across from the Chrysler plant.) So, if you want a taste of old-fashioned country cooking in a family-friendly environment, look for a Cracker Barrel on the highway. If there is a line, you can shop in the store. While you wait for your food, you can try your luck at the Cracker Barrel peg board game to see if you're genius material or "just plain eg-no-ra-moose." In 2008, Cracker Barrel was voted #1 among family dining chains in the Restaurants and Institutions Consumer Survey.

Cracker Barrel Country Cornbread Dressing
Recipe courtesy Cracker Barrel

- ⅔ cup chopped onion
- 2 cups chopped celery
- 2 quarts of day old, grated cornbread
- 1 quart of day old, grated biscuits
- ¼ cup dried parsley flakes
- 2 tsp poultry seasoning
- 2 tsp ground sage
- 1 tsp coarse ground pepper
- 4 oz margarine
- 1 quart (32 oz) plus one-14-ounce can chicken broth

Preheat oven to 400 degrees. Mix onion, celery, grated cornbread and biscuits, parsley, poultry seasoning, sage and pepper in a large mixing bowl. Add melted margarine to mixture. Stir until well blended. Add chicken broth to dry ingredients and mix well. The dressing should have a wet but not soupy consistency like a quick bread batter such as banana bread or cornbread. Divide mixture evenly into two 8 x 8 inch pans that have been sprayed with non-stick cooking spray. Bake uncovered for 1 hour at 400 degrees or until lightly brown on the top. Remove from oven and serve warm. Yield: 16 (6-ounce) servings.

◆ Fenton, Times Beach, Rock City and Eureka

There were several restaurants in the Fenton/Valley Park area on Highway 66 starting with Sylvan Beach Restaurant (officially in Sunset Hills near the Meramec River), the Stage Coach Inn next to the Sunset Ranch Motel (currently a Super 8 motel), and the Red Coach Inn and Kessler's, both at the busy corner of 66 and 141 in Peerless Park. Continuing into Times Beach there were several well-known restaurants. These were the Bridgehead Inn/Steiny's, Times Beach Café, and the Chicken Coop.

Just beyond Times Beach, the complex known as Rock City had two restaurants, Keeton's Rock City Café and LaMar's Ozark Café. Continuing west on 66 in Eureka, there were Gerwe's Log House Café and the Brown Mug (both near Central) and just a bit west, Wetzel's Café. The Al-Pac owned by Fred and Jean Miller, located west of Allenton and east of Pacific, served weary travelers a great meal for years. Unfortunately, no recipes surfaced for any of these Route 66 restaurants.

Sylvan Beach Restaurant in Sunset Hills, MO

Kessler's at SE Corner of 66 and 141

Today's Route 66 State Park Visitor Center
in Eureka, MO

Aerial view of Times Beach Café

STEINY'S INN

TIMES BEACH   EUREKA, MISSOURI

...MENU...

(FULL COURSE)

Steak Dinner	2.50
Chicken Dinner	1.80

Butter Crusted Spring Chicken, Slaw, French Fries	1.25
Charcoal Broiled Steak (Filet Mignon), Cole Slaw, French Fried Potatoes, Mushroom Sauce	1.80
Grilled Lamb Chops, Apple Sauce, French Fried Potatoes	1.15
Hot Turkey Plate, Cranberry Sauce, French Fried Pot., Veg.	1.05
Chicken Raviola and Grated Cheese	.75
Italian Meat Balls and Spaghetti	.75
Chicken Livers With Rasher of Bacon, French Fried Pot.	.90
Ham and Eggs, French Fried Potatoes	.75
Bacon and Eggs, French Fried Potatoes	.75
Pork Chops and Apple Sauce, French Fried Potatoes	.90
Breaded Veal Cutlet, Slaw and French Fried Potatoes	.90

COLD CUTS

Cold Sliced Chicken, Slaw and Potato Salad	1.25
Cold Assorted Meat Cuts, Slaw and Potato Salad	1.00
Cold Baked Virginia Ham, Slaw and Potato Salad	1.00
Cold Roast Beef or Pork, Slaw and Potato Salad	1.00
Cold Alaska Salmon, Slaw and Potato Salad	1.00
Cold Tuna Salad	1.05
1 Dozen Shrimp on Ice (Cocktail)	1.05
Shrimp Cocktail	.60

STEINY'S SPECIAL SANDWICHES

No. 1—.65 — Double Decker — Steiny's Special, Ham, Lettuce and Tomato, Melted Cheese and Potato Salad

No. 2—.65 — Double Decker — Combination, Ham, Swiss Cheese, Lettuce, Tomato and Potato Salad

No. 3—.65 — Double Decker — Chicken Salad, Bacon, Lettuce and Tomato, Potato Salad

No. 4—.65—Double Decker—Tuna Salad, Lettuce and Tomato, Steiny's Dressing and Potato Salad

No. 5—.75—CLUB SANDWICH—Double Decker
Sliced Chicken, Bacon, Lettuce and Tomato, Potato Salad

SANDWICHES

Hamburger	.25	Lettuce, Bacon and Tomato	.40
Frankfurter	.20	Ham Salad	.25
Cheese - Burger	.30	Egg Salad	.30
Bar-B-Q Ribs	.65	Toasted Cheese	.30
Baked Ham	.30	Ham and Egg	.45
Roast Beef	.30	Bacon and Egg	.45
Roast Pork	.30	Sliced Chicken	.60
Chicken Salad	.30	Sliced Turkey	.60
Cheese	.25	Tuna Salad	.40

Sandwiches on Toast, 5c Extra

SALAD ORDERS

Chicken	.90	Fruit	.90
Tuna	.90	Ham	.90
Shrimp	.90	Egg	.90
Salmon	.90		

SET-UPS—30c Each Per Person. CORKAGE CHARGE—30c Per Person Where No Set-Ups Are Purchased. (Corkage Charge—15c Per Bottle of Beer.) All Sodas—15c Per Bottle.

These Prices Prevail After 9 P. M. . . . . Tax Included

We Close Every Tuesday

Steiny's Inn Menu

The Chicken Coop at Times Beach

Ed LaMar at his Ozark Café, part of Rock City

Deke Keeton's Rock City Café

Lou Gerwe's Log House Café

Wetzel Family at Wetzel's Café

The Al-Pac owned by Fred and Jean Miller

The White Squirrel was a popular family tavern on the south side of Highway 66, just east of Central Avenue in Eureka. Fred Hagemeister opened the tavern in 1933 and operated it into the late 1940s/early 1950s. When Fred Jr. wasn't interested in the tavern business, Fred sold his place and the new owners continued it for a few years until it was purchased by the Highway Department for what would eventually become I-44. It was gone by 1956.

White Squirrel Doughnuts

Fred's first wife, Edna, served up these delicious doughnuts at the tavern, particularly at Christmas. Notice that the recipe calls for riced potatoes. Apparently, there is a utensil that makes boiled potatoes into particles that resemble rice. If you don't have one of these, mash the potatoes finely. *Recipe shared by Fred Hagemeister Jr. and his wife Hetty*

6	cups all-purpose flour
2	tsp salt
2	Tbsp sugar
¼	cup vegetable shortening
1	package yeast
1½	cups to 1¾ cups warm water
2	medium white potatoes-1 cup fluffy riced potatoes

Mix 6 cups flour, salt and sugar. Add ¼ cup shortening and work with fingers as for pie crust. Boil two potatoes in jackets. Peel and rice the potatoes while still hot. Cool. Measure 1 cup (fluffy). Add to flour mixture and blend with fingers. Add yeast to ½ cup of warm water. Let stand 5 minutes. Stir to mix. Add the yeast and ½ cup water mixture to other ingredients with remaining water. Knead dough in bowl until it sticks together. It should be a stiff dough but not dry. Place ¼ cup flour on board and knead the dough with all your might for 5 or 10 minutes. Knead dough well. When dough gets smooth and satiny and no longer sticks to your hand, dough is kneaded enough. Make into a ball. Grease a deep bowl all around and turn ball of dough all around to grease the dough. Cover with a tea towel and let rise until dough is very light. Test: press finger deep into dough. If depression remains, the dough has risen enough. To make doughnuts, shape into balls. Set deep fryer to 370 degrees. Drop doughnuts into vegetable shortening and fry until golden brown, turning once. Drain on paper towels. Spread with sugar or powdered sugar. This recipe can also be used to make doughnuts with a cutter or rolled out to make long johns.

White Squirrel Spanish Spaghetti Bake

This recipe was prepared and served at the tavern by Fred's second wife, Wilhemenia.

Shared by Fred Hagemeister Jr. and his wife Hetty

- 1   lb ground beef
- ½   cup chopped onion
- ¼   cup chopped green pepper
- 2   Tbsp butter
- 1   can Campbell's cream of mushroom soup
- 1   can Campbell's tomato soup
- 1   cup water
- •   sprinkle of garlic salt
- 2   cups shredded Cheddar cheese, divided
- ¼   lb spaghetti, cooked and drained

In large skillet, cook first three items in the butter until meat is light brown. Stir frequently to separate the meat. Add next 4 ingredients and heat thoroughly. Add 1 cup of cheese and spaghetti. Place in 3-quart casserole dish. Top with 1 cup cheese and bake at 350 degrees for 30 minutes or until bubbling hot. Note: Italian sausage may be substituted for ground beef.

Sites Station Café

This little diner was in a converted railroad car and sat next to a Site gas station. It was located between Eureka and Allenton on Highway 66, east of Long Ford. All the locals added an "s" to the name. It was known for this chili, which simmered all day long on the stove and had a sobering-up effect.

Sites Station Café Chili

Recipe courtesy Carnahan family

- 2   lbs ground beef
- 1   large onion, diced
- 2   tsp garlic powder
- 2   Tbsp chili powder
- •   salt and pepper to taste
- 1   6-oz can tomato paste with 2 cans water
- 1   #10 (foodservice size) can red chili
      beans plus ½ can water

In a large cast iron Dutch oven, brown ground beef with 1 large onion. Sprinkle in dry ingredients. Add tomato paste and water. Mash one half of the red beans and keep the other half unmashed. Add all to pot. Fill the large can halfway with water and add to pot. Let items simmer all day.

◆ Haymarket Restaurant
4901 Six Flags Road (Eureka)
636-938-6661

This restaurant is centered around a historic barn that was part of a stagecoach stop. It was salvaged when the Eckelkamp family built the Ramada Inn, today Holiday Inn Six Flags.

Haymarket Minnesota Wild Rice Bisque
Shared by the Haymarket Restaurant

½	cup raw wild rice
¾	cups (1 ½ sticks) butter, divided
1	cup all-purpose flour
½	medium onion, diced
2	ribs celery, diced
6	ounces mushrooms, sliced
¼	tsp dried thyme leaves
•	salt
•	ground white pepper
1½	tsp chicken base (very concentrated bouillon)
½	cup white wine, divided
10	cups chicken stock
1	cup heavy (40%) whipping cream

Cook rice according to package directions; drain. Set aside. In a heavy saucepan, melt ½ cup plus 2 tablespoons butter. Whisk in flour to make a thin roux. Cook over medium heat 3 to 4 minutes, whisking constantly. Do not let brown. Remove from heat; set roux aside. Melt remaining 2 tablespoons butter in a heavy saucepan; add onion, celery, mushrooms, thyme, ¼ teaspoon salt and 1/8 teaspoon white pepper. Cook, stirring occasionally, until vegetables are translucent, about 8 minutes. Add chicken base; cook 1 minute. Let cool slightly, then add ¼ cup wine. Purée vegetables in small batches in a food processor; set aside. In a very large, heavy soup pot, bring chicken stock to a simmer. Stir in roux; cook, stirring frequently until soup thickens. Let simmer 20 minutes. Stir in puréed vegetables and additional salt and pepper to taste. Simmer 30 minutes, stirring often to prevent scorching. Add remaining ¼ cup wine, cooked rice and cream; bring to a simmer. Taste; adjust seasonings. Yield: 6 (2 cup) servings.

The historic barn that is now part of the Haymarket Restaurant

The historic Red Cedar Inn, a Route 66 institution, served up great food in a welcoming atmosphere from 1934 to 2005. The Smith family took a brief hiatus when they leased out the restaurant from 1972 to 1986. The log building, on the National Register of Historic Places, currently sits vacant with the city of Pacific, Missouri considering whether it can afford to purchase the site and convert it into a museum and visitor's center.

1934 view of the Red Cedar Inn, before the bar portion was added to the east end

Red Cedar Inn Carrots Delight
Shared by Katherine Smith and Ginger Gallagher

4	cups sliced carrots (cut like coins)
1½	teaspoons minced onions
1	tsp sugar
2	slices bacon
1½	tsp bacon drippings
½	cup ground onion
½	cup water from parboiled carrots
½	tsp chicken base
1½	tsp seasoning salt (Lowery's or Vandzant's recommended)

Clean and slice carrots. Parboil carrots with minced onion and sugar in barely enough water to cover. Meanwhile, fry bacon until crisp. Drain bacon on absorbent paper towels then crumble bacon. Sauté ground onion in bacon drippings, and then add water, chicken base, and seasoning salt. Continue cooking carrots until tender. To serve, top carrots with crumbled bacon. Yield: 6 to 8 servings.

Red Cedar Inn (Honeymoon) French Dressing
While on their honeymoon, Jimmie and Katherine Smith talked a restaurant manager in the Ozarks into sharing this recipe, which they then served at the Red Cedar Inn. *Shared by Katherine Smith and Ginger Gallagher*

1	can (51 ounces) tomato soup
5	cups white vinegar
3¾	cups sugar
¼	tsp pepper
5	tsp salt
5	tsp paprika
3¾	cups corn oil

Blend first six ingredients well, then add corn oil very slowly and mix well again. Makes 1 gallon.

Lars Peter Jensen, an immigrant from Denmark, served at the Missouri Botanical Garden, was the first manager of its country cousin in Gray Summit (now called the Shaw Nature Reserve), and was also the first president of the Henry Shaw Gardenway Association, which served to promote and protect a 35-mile stretch along Highway 66 from the Garden to the Shaw Nature Reserve. A rustic overlook in Pacific, just west of the Red Cedar Inn, bears Jensen's name. It was built by the Civilian Conservation Corps and dedicated in 1939. Get more information on the Missouri Botanical Garden at www.mobot.org and on the nature reserve at www.shawnature.org. Note that Jensen Point is privately owned by Wayne Winchester and you must make arrangements with him to tour the site. You can contact him at 636-257-5400.

This poem, a recipe for being good stewards of nature and our land, was written by Lars Peter Jensen around 1939 and shared with visitors to the Arboretum. *Courtesy Shaw Nature Reserve*

Lend A Hand

Come, my friend, reach out a helping hand,
To save the native beauties of our land.
Break not the bough which blossoms fair,
Nor strip the woodlands altogether bare,
Help us to plant, and not destroy
The beauties others should enjoy,
Let us pass by, and leave behind,
A part of each, of every kind
Of scenery fair, and birds in air,
Of fish in streams, and blossoms fair,
So that the ones who come our ways
In some distant future days,
May say that we have guarded well
The treasures among which they dwell.

The beauties of our charming land
We are wasting with a lavish hand;
Perhaps, because we cannot see
That to such abundance, an end could be,
Or, perhaps, our earthly selfish greed
Makes us forget what others need,
And blinds us so we cannot see
Our duty to posterity.
Therefore, my friend, let's not debate,
But lend a hand, it's not too late
To educate, to preach and teach,
In every hamlet we can reach,
To save, to hold, to add, and give
What others must enjoy to live.

Jensen Point Lookout, Pacific, MO

Henry Shaw Gardenway 1940 plaque for
Blackburn Park on Sand Mountain

Parrett's Restaurant in Pacific, at Fifth and Highway 66, was in the heart of town near Sand Mountain from 1932 to 1974. Highway 66 travelers made a special stop here for its made-from-scratch food, particularly its fried chicken, cinnamon rolls and other baked items. For many years, the restaurant was operated by three Parrett brothers, Jim, Bill and Tom, and their wives.

Parrett's, in the heart of Pacific for over 40 years

Parrett's Cinnamon Coffee Cake
The restaurant recipes were never shared but this recipe was in a vintage cookbook, contributed by Tom Parrett's wife, Viola. It is unknown if it was strictly a family recipe or was also made at the restaurant.
Adapted from Favorite Recipes of Meramec Valley Senior Citizens

2 cups flour	Preheat oven to 350 degrees. Mix flour, sugar, salt and cinnamon. Add soft butter. Set aside ½ cup of mixture for topping. Add nuts to this. Add egg to dry mixture. Mix baking soda with buttermilk. Add to egg mixture. Pour batter into two greased 9-inch pans. Sprinkle with (reserved) topping. Bake for 25 minutes.
1½ cups sugar	
• pinch of salt	
2 tsp cinnamon	
½ cup soft butter	
2 cups nuts	
1 egg	
1 cup buttermilk	
1 tsp baking soda	

◆ Cottrell's Restaurant

Cottrell's was located on Highway 66 in Pacific, west of Sand Mountain and the downtown Pacific area. It started off in 1951 as a tiny ice cream stand called Big Bob's Drive-In then grew to Cottrell's Dairy Freeze and eventually Cottrell's Travel Center with a more upscale restaurant. Today, there is a McDonald's, a BP station and a Taco Bell on what once was the Cottrell family property.

Cottrell's Famous Cheesecake
Cottrell's was known for this cheesecake. *Lorene Cottrell's recipe, courtesy Jani Cottrell Testerman*

For crust:

1½ cups graham crackers, crushed	Mix together. Save 3 tablespoons of crust mixture for top of cheesecake. Press the rest into a 9 x 12-inch baking dish.
¼ stick butter, melted	
½ cup sugar	

For filling:

> 4 eggs
> 1 cup sugar
> 3 8-oz packages Philadelphia Brand Cream Cheese
> 3 tsp vanilla

For topping, combine:

> 1 pint sour cream
> ¾ cup sugar
> 2 tsp vanilla

Beat eggs and sugar very well. Add cream cheese and vanilla and beat until very smooth and creamy. Place filling mixture into crust-lined baking dish. Bake for 1 hour at 300 degrees. Remove from oven and spread on the sour cream topping and the 3 tablespoons reserved crust mixture. Return to oven and bake for 5 more minutes. Allow to cool and then serve.

◆ George's Apple Orchard and Market

The George family apple orchard was near Highway 66 in Pacific, Missouri, predating the highway. Later, they opened George's Apple Market (at 3132 W. Osage) to take advantage of the tourist traffic on the busy road. The apple orchard stopped operating in 1995 but the market building still stands today.

George's Apple Market Bavarian Apple Torte

This is one of the recipes that the apple market handed out to customers. *Shared by Janet and Jim Daniel*

Crust:

> ½ cup margarine or butter
> ⅓ cup sugar
> ¼ tsp vanilla
> 1 cup flour

Cream margarine or butter, sugar and vanilla. Blend in flour. Spread dough onto bottom and 2 inches high of the sides of a 9-inch springform or angel food pan. (Note: can also use a 9-inch by 13-inch pan)

Filling:

> 8 oz cream cheese, room temperature
> ¼ cup sugar
> 1 egg
> ½ tsp vanilla

Combine cream cheese, sugar and egg. Mix until blended. Add vanilla and pour into pastry-lined pan.

Topping:

> ⅓ cup sugar
> ½ tsp cinnamon
> 4 cups thinly sliced and peeled Jonathan apples

Toss sugar, cinnamon, and apples and pour over cheese filling. Bake at 450 degrees for 10 minutes then reduce heat to 400 and bake 25 more minutes. Serve with vanilla ice cream if desired.

There were several versions of the Diamonds. Founder Spencer Groff started off with a roadside stand, built the Banana Stand, which was a step up, and then opened the first frame Diamonds complex in July 1927. Busboy turned manager then owner, Louie Eckelkamp, took the place to the next level and continued it for years, replacing the building in 1949 after a disastrous fire. After the (second) Diamonds was bypassed by I-44, he continued in Villa Ridge for a few years then relocated the Diamonds closer to an I-44 exit, at the crossroads of the Original 66 alignment and the Historic alignment in Gray Summit, across from the Shaw Nature Reserve. He operated the third Diamonds there from 1969 until November 1995. That building no longer remains. His previous 1949 building in Villa Ridge became the Tri-County Truck Stop, which also continued for decades under different owners but closed in 2006 and sits vacant.

Bread Pudding, Diamond Style
Recipe from Marian Clark's The Route 66 Cookbook

- 6 eggs, beaten
- 6 cups milk
- 2 Tbsp vanilla
- 1 Tbsp melted margarine
- 1 cup sugar
- ½ tsp salt
- ½ cup raisins
- 3 cups dry bread cubes
- 1 tsp cinnamon

Combine eggs, milk, vanilla, margarine, sugar and salt. Blend to dissolve sugar. Butter a 9-inch by 11-inch baking pan and fill with raisins and bread cubes. Pour egg mixture over bread and sprinkle with cinnamon. Place baking dish in larger pan containing water. Bake in preheated 350 degree oven for 45 minutes or until a knife inserted near the center comes out clean.
Yield: 10 to 12 generous servings.

The Original Diamonds with Louie Eckelkamp (behind little girl Janet Perkins) and Spencer Groff behind Louie

Last Diamonds version, (relocated across from the Shaw Nature Reserve) now razed

Second Diamonds 1949 version, built by Louie Eckelkamp after a fire destroyed the frame building

Noble and Edna Key started out at the Diamonds under Spencer Groff then became part owners with Louie Eckelkamp. They later left and opened Key's Twin Bridge Café, also on Highway 66, near the Twin Bridges over the Bourbeuse River. It had a gas station as well as the restaurant. Noble also owned a large vineyard in Steelville, Missouri. The restaurant stayed in the Key family until 1977 and the gas station was operated by Bill Key until 1993 when he retired.

Key's Twin Bridge Café Concord Grape Pie
The café's calling card was this Concord Grape Pie served a la mode. *Recipe shared by Bill and Ruth Key*

- 4 cups prepared grapes
- 1 cup sugar
- 2 Tbsp tapioca
- prepared 9-inch pie crust and pastry strips
- pats of butter

To prepare grapes, wash grapes. Pinch the middle (pulp) of each grape out and separate the skins. Continue this until pulp measures 4 cups. Place pulp in a saucepan then cook it over medium heat until pulp gets soft, being careful not to scorch. Run the pulp through a sieve to remove seeds. Place pulp in mixing bowl. Add reserved skins to pulp along with the sugar and tapioca. Mix all together in the bowl. Pour filling into prepared 9-inch pie crust. Place pats of butter over top of filling. Cover with pastry strips layered first horizontally then topped with a row set vertically. Bake at 350 degrees for 50 minutes or until the grape mixture bubbles. Serve with vanilla ice cream.

The Key's neon sign is at the Route 66 State Park in Eureka, MO

KEY'S TWIN BRIDGE CAFE

THE HOME
OF HOME MADE PIES
24 HOUR SERVICE

HWAY. 50 - 66 - - - - - - - - - - - Pilgrim 2-7755

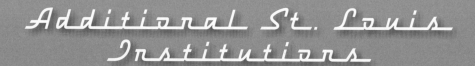

Additional St. Louis Institutions

This is by no means an exhaustive list. It is only a sample of some of St. Louis' long-standing restaurants, dining traditions, and bakeries.

Busch's Grove

Pelican's Restaurant

Lemp Mansion Restaurant and Inn

Other Historic Houses in St. Louis

Al Baker's

Café Balaban

The Edge

Ed's White Front

Goody Goody Diner

Wright City Big Boy's

Ruggeri's

Missouri Baking Company

Pratzel's Bakery

Rosciglione Bakery

Noah's Ark Restaurant

Straub's Grocery Store

Busch's Grove

The outdoor pavilions at Busch's Grove were razed for parking space.

Goody Goody Diner

Interior of Wright City Big Boy's

Ruggeri's

Noah's Ark, St Charles, MO

Busch's Grove

According to its Nomination Form for the National Register of Historic Places, Busch's Grove (originally called Woodlawn Garden) at 9160 Clayton Road in Ladue is believed to have been built in the mid 1800s (1855 to 1860 time period). It served as a stagecoach stop, grocery store, post office, pleasure resort, hotel, and saloon. It may have also been a 10-Mile House. In 1891, John Busch leased it for a restaurant (eventually purchasing the property) and it soon became the center of the area's social life. Many visitors to the World's Fair stopped there and Busch's Grove hosted parties for Theodore Roosevelt and Will Rogers. In 1909, John Busch sold Busch's Grove to his son Henry and to Henry's friend, Paul Kammerer for $6,000. They built up the reputation further and it was considered an annex to the St. Louis Country Club where many business deals were made. Henry Busch died in 1951 and it continued in the Kammerer family, owned by Bill Kammerer and Mrs. Lawrence O'Neal. Paul's granddaughter Patti Cowles and her husband Carl owned it next, until February 15, 2003. Entrepreneur Lester Miller then purchased the historic watering hole for $3 million and spent another $8 million to revamp it. The historic building was spared and improved (though removed from the National Register at that point) while the screened outdoor dining cabins (called everything from huts to pavilions to gazebos and similar to those once advertised at Grupp's 14 Mile House on Manchester Road) were lost to progress. Miller reopened Busch's Grove in 2005 but it closed in May 2008. The landmark Busch's Grove became the upscale Market at Busch's Grove, opening December 13, 2008.

Busch's Grove Bellevue Dressing
Shared by Chef Wesley Dietrich for the 1964 The New St. Louis Symphony of Cooking, *courtesy St. Louis Symphony Volunteer Association*

2 cups mayonnaise
⅔ cup cream
5 hard cooked eggs, finely chopped
2 Tbsp chopped chives
1 tsp garlic powder

Combine all ingredients until smooth. Makes 3 ¾ cups.

Busch's Grove Wild Rice Supreme
Shared by Chef Gus Marzan for the 1965 Salvation Army Women's Auxiliary of St. Louis "Clowning Around" With Cookery *and the 1964* The New St. Louis Symphony of Cooking

1 lb wild rice
2 quarts water
3 green peppers, finely chopped
2 ribs celery, finely chopped
1 large onion, finely chopped
4 ounce can mushrooms, drained and chopped
3 eggs
1 cup oil
2 Tbsp salt
¼ tsp pepper
3 cups brown gravy (recipe for "Medium Gravy" given)

Cook rice in water about 2 hours over low heat, or until tender. Watch carefully as rice swells more than four times in volume and more water may be needed. Blanch peppers, celery, onion, and mushrooms about 10 minutes. Beat each egg separately. Fry, one at a time, in oil on both sides. Remove from oil and drain on paper towels. When all eggs are fried, chop finely. Make Medium Gravy (see recipe below, which requires tripling to yield 3 cups). Mix all ingredients. Pour into 13 by 9 by 2-inch pan. Bake at 350 degrees for 15 minutes. Makes 16 servings.

Medium Gravy (from skillet or roasting pan):

2 Tbsp fat = 6 Tbsp
2 Tbsp flour = 6 Tbsp
1 cup liquid = 3 cups

Remove meat to a warm place. Pour off fat, leaving crusty brown bits in the pan. Measure amount of fat needed into the pan. Stir in flour until smooth. Stir over low heat until brown. Browning the flour develops good gravy color. Remove from heat and stir in the liquid. Return to heat and stir. Boil 1 minute. Taste, season and serve.

Pelican's Restaurant

Pelican's Restaurant was located at 2256 South Grand, on the northeast corner of Grand and Shenandoah. A saloon was present at the site since at least the 1870s, with a permit to expand the existing saloon sought in 1878. When the beer baron Griesedieck family assumed ownership, they made improvements to the building including adding the corner turret. Pelican's Restaurant served a variety of menu offerings but is long remembered for its turtle soup. Although it appears the recipe was never shared, here is the Pelican's 1976 menu from the *Gateway Gourmet*. It may have been the final menu as the building was sold by 1978.

Welcome to Pelican's
YOUR HOSTS GABE AND NICK

For a before dinner treat,
try one of our appetizers.

Toasted Ravioli . . . 1.95
Shrimp on Ice 2.25
Fried Mushrooms . . . 1.40
Citrus Compote 75
Frosty Tomato Juice . . .50
Oysters on the Half Shell .40
(In Season) Each
Onion Rings 95

Pasta

Baked Lasagna 3.75
Mostaccioli 2.50
With Hearty Meat Sauce
Meat Balls & Spaghetti . 2.60
Ravioli 2.60
With Meat Sauce

Salads

Pelican's Chef Salad
With Cheese, Salami and Anchovies
2.25
Tossed Green Salad
With Ham and Cheese
1.35
Small
Chef's Dinner Salad
.85

Dressings:
House Dressing, French, Thousand Island,
Bleu Cheese

Soup

Pelican's
Soup of the Day 55
Turtle Soup with Sherry .90

Entrees

Seafoods & Fish

Lobster Tail
South African
8.95
Seafood Platter
Lobster, Shrimp, Scallops and Sole
8.25
Fried Jumbo Shrimp
5.45

Channel Catfish
4.75
Rainbow Trout
4.75
Deep Sea Scallops
4.50
Filet of Sole
3.95
Jack Salmon
3.95

Steaks & Chops

Filet Mignon
With Mushroom Sauce
6.50
Petite Filet
5.00
Strip Steak
6.50
Top Sirloin Steak
5.45
Pork Chops
With Apple Sauce
4.75
Lamb Chops
With Mint Jelly
5.25

Best of Both

Filet Mignon and Lobster Tail
8.50

ALL DINNER ENTREES INCLUDE:
Cup of Soup or Chilled Tomato Juice
Salad with Choice of Dressing
Baked or Fried Potatoes
Vegetable of the Day

For Light Dining

Roast Beef Sandwich
On French Bread Au Jus
2.25
Hamburger on Toasted Bun
With Lettuce and Tomato
1.65
With Cheese
1.80
Reuben Sandwich
Corned Beef, Sauerkraut,
and Dressing
2.05
Fillet of Sole
1.95
Sirloin Steak Sandwich
On French Bread
2.25
Above served with potato or slaw.

Pelican's
Special Fried Chicken
3.75

Especially For the Little Ones

Mostaccioli 1.50
With Meat Sauce
Hamburger 1.25
With French Fries and Soft Drink

Fried Chicken 2.00
With Potato and Vegetable
Fillet of Sole 2.00
With Potato and Vegetable

Turkey Au Gratin
Sliced Turkey Broiled with Cheese
Sauce and Bacon
2.45

Lemp Mansion Restaurant and Inn
3322 DeMenil Place
314- 664-8024
www.lempmansion.com

The Lemps were the city's first beer barons, introducing lager beer to St. Louis in 1840. There was a cave below their mansion, which was used for beer storage among other things including a theater. The cave operated as the show cave, Cherokee Cave, from 1950 to the early 1960s but was lost to I-55 construction. (Parts of the cave are still intact and occasionally open to cave enthusiasts. The cave was filmed recently by local television show *Living St. Louis* and can be viewed online at www.ketc.org.) Besides losing their business to Prohibition, the Lemps had a long list of tragic events and are said to still hang around their mansion on DeMenil Place. The home is often described as one of the most haunted places in America.

Lemp Mansion's Cheddar-Sour Cream Potato Casserole
Recipe contributed by the Lemp Mansion Restaurant

- 1 (10 ¾-ounce) can condensed cream of chicken soup
- ½ cup (1 stick) butter, melted
- 2 cups sour cream
- 1½ cups shredded Cheddar cheese, divided
- ½ cup diced onion
- ½ tsp salt
- ½ tsp ground pepper
- 2 lbs frozen shredded hash brown potatoes (or Southern-style version)
- • paprika
- 1 tsp chopped fresh parsley

Preheat the oven to 350 degrees. Grease the bottom of a 9-by-13-inch baking pan. In a large bowl, stir together condensed soup, butter, sour cream, 1 cup cheese, onion, salt and pepper. Add potatoes; toss to combine. Press mixture into prepared pan. Bake until casserole begins to brown around the edges, about 1 hour. Sprinkle with the remaining ½ cup cheese, paprika and parsley; return to the oven until cheese melts, about 3 minutes. Yield: 12 servings.

Other Historic Houses in St. Louis

Located near the Lemp Mansion, the Chantillon-DeMenil House is one of several historic houses open to the public. The Café DeMenil is located in the carriage house. Rather than provide a recipe here, I include information on some of the houses you should try to visit.

Chantillon-DeMenil House • 3352 DeMenil Place • 314-771-5829 • www.demenil.org

Tower Grove House • Missouri Botanical Garden • 314-577-5100 • www.mobot.org

Campbell House Museum • 1508 Locust St. • 314-421-0325 • www.campbellhousemuseum.org

Eugene Field House & St. Louis Toy Museum • 634 S. Broadway • 314-421-4689 • www.eugenefieldhouse.org

Scott Joplin House • 2658 Delmar Blvd. • 314-340-5790 • www.mostateparks.org

Al Baker's

Al Baker's was located at the northwest corner of Clayton Road and Brentwood Blvd., across from what is now the Galleria. Al Baker and his partner and wife Mary opened the restaurant on March 17, 1966. It was known as a high-end establishment featuring Italian pastas, steaks, chops, fresh fish and other specialties and was also known for its extensive and expensive wine list, which at one time had 25,000 bottles. Part of the dining experience was music and dancing. The place closed on December 31, 1993 when the Bakers retired and sold off the entire contents, including the rare wine bottles, the Steinway piano for about $4800, and the Al Baker's swizzle sticks for a nickel a piece. The building was razed and made way for Linens 'n Things.

Al Baker's Veal Talleyrand
Recipe appeared in the St. Louis Dining Magazine and was shared by Diane Friedmeyer for the St. Louis Post-Dispatch Recipe Exchange Column

4 (3-ounce) veal patties, pounded thin
1 cup all-purpose flour
2 Tbsp butter
4 mushrooms, minced
1 clove garlic, minced
⅔ cup minced onion
2 Tbsp white wine
½ tsp lemon juice
⅓ cup heavy cream
1 egg yolk
• salt
• ground pepper

Dust veal with flour. Melt butter in skillet; add veal and sauté until halfway done. Add mushrooms, garlic and onion; cook, stirring constantly, until vegetables are tender and veal is cooked through. Remove veal from skillet; keep warm. Stir in wine and lemon juice. Stir in cream and egg yolk. Add salt and pepper to taste. Cook, stirring constantly, until sauce thickens. Serve over veal. Yield: 4 servings.

Al Baker's Sicilian Red Snapper
Recipe shared by Al and Mary Baker for a feature story in the St. Louis Post-Dispatch

2 medium onions, chopped
¾ cup virgin olive oil
3 large cloves garlic, minced
1 (28-ounce) or 2 (14½-ounce) cans Italian pear or plum tomatoes, undrained
¼ cup chopped fresh basil (or 1½ to 2 Tbsp dried)
1½ tsp chopped fresh oregano (or ½ tsp dried)
1½ tsp granulated sugar
• salt, to taste
• freshly ground black pepper, to taste
4 (10- to 12-ounce) red snapper fillets (or Pacific red snapper or Florida snapper)

Sauté onions in oil until transparent, about 10 minutes. Do not brown onions. Add garlic; cook 2 minutes. Chop tomatoes by hand. Add tomatoes with their juice, basil, oregano, sugar, salt and pepper to onion mixture; simmer 30 minutes. Thaw fish, if frozen. Wash fish and pat dry. Season with salt and pepper, if desired. Put snapper in greased baking dish large enough so that each fillet can lay flat. Pour tomato sauce over fish. Bake in a preheated 375-degree oven 20 minutes, or until fish flakes and is done. Yield: 4 large servings.

One of the more elegant restaurants in the area is Al Baker's. Adorned with many antiques, family portraits, and memorabilia, the scene is luxurious. The food is gourmet, and features fresh pompano, Lamb Monasteraki, and stuffed tenderloin. The wine cellar houses the largest selection in the midwest. Indicative of the pride in their establishment, the doors are never open unless Al or Mary Baker are present to greet you.

Benvenuto, we welcome you to our restaurant as we would welcome you to our home.

Al + Mary

antipasti

Poisson de Mer Aux Champignons	2.95
Shrimp de Jonghe	2.95
Fettuccini Alfredo (for two)	5.00
Toasted Ravioli	1.95
Cannelloni	1.95
Tortellini Bianco (for two)	6.50
Melone con Proscuitto	2.50
Soup du Jour	1.50
Blue Points (in season)	2.95
Baked Stuffed Oysters	2.95
Escargots de Bourgogne	3.50
Escargots Champignon	3.50
Baby Back Lamb Ribs	2.95

pasta

Linguine Marinara pear tomato, imported olive oil, anchiovy, seasoned olives, garlic	5.95
Tortellini Bianco cream, butter, early peas, proscuitto, imported parmasean	6.50
Linguine a la Carbonara butter, dry sherry, proscuitto, imported parmasean, parsley, garlic	6.95
Rigatoni a la Bolognese tomato with ground meat	5.00
Fettuccini Alfredo butter, cream, fresh parmasean	5.00
Linguine con Vongole white clams with garlic, oil	6.95
Rigatoni con Broccoli fresh flower of broccoli, mushrooms, butter, parmasean	5.95
Pasta con Pesce clam, lobster, garlic, tomato, oil	7.95
Spaghetti con Sazeetz tomato with spicy sausage	5.95

l'insalata

Classic Caesar (for two only)	5.00
Greek Style Salad (for two only)	5.00
Salada Romaine d'Asperges (for two only)	5.00
Dinner Salad	1.25

contorni

American Fried Potatoes	1.50
Italian Fried Potatoes with Scallions	1.50
Italian Fried Artichoke Hearts	2.00
Fresh Broccoli	1.50
Fresh Asparagus (in season)	2.00

dalla griglia

New York Strip Sirloin fines herbes	9.95
Filet Mignon	9.95
Chateaubriand au Bearnaise Bouquetiere (for two)	18.50

il pesce

Shrimp Marinara	6.95
Shrimp Scampi	6.95
Fresh Florida Pompano	8.95
con Provencale	9.50
Fresh Pompano Neptune	8.95
Dover Sole	8.50
Speciale	8.95
Dover Sole Princess	9.50
Maryland Soft Shelled Crabs	7.50
Lobster Supreme aux Champignons	8.95
Lobster Diablo	8.95

DESINARE

VEAL PICATTA sauté with butter, fresh lemon, Soave, chopped parsley.	7.50
VEAL PARMIGGIANO center cut veal with imported spices, tomato sauce, fresh parmasean and provelone.	7.50
VEAL SCALLOPINI nozettes of veal simmered in Marinara with mushrooms, green pepper, chopped parsley; served with imported pasta with butter.	6.95
VEAL SALTIMBOCCA baby veal tenderloin, proscuitto ham, provelone; sautéed with white wine, sliced mushrooms.	7.95
VEAL MARSALA CLASSICO tender veal sautéed with imported sweet Marsala, mushrooms, butter.	7.95
VEAL OSKAR NEW ORLEANS cutlet of young veal, whole lobster tail, garnished with fresh asparagus, topped with Sauterne creme sauce.	9.95
CHICKEN MILANESE boneless breast of chicken sautéed with butter, mushrooms; baked with proscuitto and provelone; served with imported risotta.	6.95
CHICKEN CACCIATORE boneless breast of chicken sautéed with Marsala wine, fresh tomatoes, mushrooms, green peppers, and ripe olives. Complimented by our House Salad and Vermicelli.	6.95
CHICKEN KIEV boneless breast of chicken stuffed with baby onion and butter; floured and sautéed with butter; with Chablis creme sauce with mushrooms.	6.95
RACK OF LAMB MONASTERAKI Greek style Rack of Spring Lamb, baked then sautéed with white grapes, butter, lemon, oregano.	9.95
BROCHETTES OF BEEF TENDERLOIN with broiled tomato parmasean, green pepper, onion, wild rice dressing.	6.95
TENDERLOIN SAUTÉ medallions of prime tenderloin, fresh mushrooms, green pepper, fresh tomato; sautéed in rich Sherry wine.	7.50
BEEF LILY tenderloin sautéed with scallions, fresh mushrooms, Madeira wine.	9.50
STUFFED TENDERLOIN	10.50
BEEF APRICOT with mushrooms, baby onions, rich with Apricot Brandy.	9.50
BEEF MAITRE 'D medallions of tenderloin sautéed with finely chopped scallions, mushrooms, Burgundy wine; on a bed of wild rice dressing.	9.50
BEEF MARSALA CLASSICO prime beef tenderloin sautéed with mushrooms, sweet Marsala, butter.	9.50

Café Balaban (originally Balaban's) at 405 North Euclid Avenue in the Central West End was opened in 1972 by Herb Balaban. Balaban's quickly became a favorite known for its inviting atmosphere and great food. When Herb retired in 1996, he sold to former employees Tom Flynn and Steve McIntyre. McIntyre left for a while to pursue another venture but returned full time when Tom Flynn died in a surfing accident while on vacation in Mexico. McIntyre sold to Brendan Marsden and Harlee Sorkin in December 2006. The place fell into financial problems and they closed on January 27, 2008. It sat empty for a short while then reopened in October 2008 as Herbie's Vintage 72, owned by Aaron Teitelbaum and Jeff Orbin.

Café Balaban's Sweet Potato Gratin

This recipe was shared by Chef David Timney in 1999 in response to a St. Louis Post-Dispatch *reader's request.*

- 4 lbs sweet potatoes, peeled and sliced thin, divided
- 12 ounces crumbled blue cheese, divided
- 12 ounces grated Parmesan cheese, divided
- 3 cups heavy cream, divided
- 1 Tbsp salt, divided
- 2 Tbsp ground black pepper, divided

Preheat oven to 375 degrees. In a 9-by 13-inch pan, layer in the order listed: 1/3 of the sweet potatoes, 4 ounces blue cheese, 4 ounces Parmesan, 1 cup cream, 1 teaspoon salt and 2 teaspoons pepper. Repeat twice. Cover pan with aluminum foil. Bake for 1 hour. Remove foil. Bake 15 or 20 minutes longer, until top has browned and the potatoes are tender when pierced with a fork. Let cool for 30 minutes before serving.
Yield: 10 to 12 servings.

1976 Menu

The Edge

The Edge, located at the edge of Lafayette Square in a windowless, brown brick building, was a happening place starting in the mid 1970s. It drew a varied clientele, from politicians to gangsters, cops, and lawyers including Missouri Supreme Court Justice Michael Wolff, and famed St. Louis Cardinals announcer Jack Buck. Owned throughout by Frank Bommarito (not the car dealership Bommaritos or the Tony's Bommaritos), Frank held many jobs before opening his restaurant, including construction worker, iron worker, Maitre'd and bartender at Al Baker's. Everyone felt welcome at The Edge because everyone was. The place closed sometime in late 2004 or early 2005.

The Edge Pollo Con Aragosta (Chicken with Lobster)
Shared by The Edge for a May 13, 1990 feature story by the <u>St. Louis Post-Dispatch</u>

- 1 (8-ounce) boned, skinned chicken breast
- 1 (5-ounce) lobster tail
- salt and pepper, to taste
- all-purpose flour, for dusting
- 2 Tbsp olive oil
- 2 Tbsp white wine
- 1 Tbsp brandy
- 1 tsp finely minced garlic
- 1 Tbsp Dijon-style mustard
- ¾ cup chopped fresh mushrooms (2 ounces)
- ¾ cup Half-and-Half or light cream
- 2 Tbsp cold butter

Halve chicken breast; pound pieces thin with mallet. Thaw lobster, if frozen. Remove lobster meat from shell; halve lengthwise. Place one piece lobster on each piece of chicken; roll up into long tubular shape. Fasten with toothpicks or skewers. Season to taste with salt and pepper. Dust rolls with flour. Heat olive oil in skillet over medium-high heat. Add rolls; cook 10 to 12 minutes, turning occasionally, or until evenly browned and done. Remove and keep warm while making sauce. Drain oil from pan. Add wine, brandy, garlic, mustard, mushrooms, Half-and-Half and butter. Simmer until sauce is reduced by half. Place rolls on serving plate; pour sauce over rolls. Yield: 1 generous serving or 2 average servings. Note: Rice pilaf is recommended as a side dish.

Ed's White Front

This popular barbecue restaurant was in North County at Goodfellow and Natural Bridge from 1933 to 1979. In 1933, Edwin Reinschmidt took over Rogers White Front, renaming it Ed's White Front. The restaurant had a huge charcoal-burning oven, credited as its secret weapon. The place was wildly popular and stayed in the family. During World War II it stayed open 24 hours a day to accommodate the workers at the nearby munitions plant. Throughout its 46 years in business, Ed's White Front only ran one ad, in 1958 for the 25th Anniversary, which rolled back prices. They sold out of every last piece of food that day. Many have fond memories of Ed's White Front including these famous burgers. The barbecue sauce remains a family secret but can be ordered from Ed Norman at www.edswhitefront.com or 636-477-7484.

Ed's White Front Famous Hamburgers
Shared by Edwin (Ed) Reinschmidt's grandson, F. Ed Norman for an April 26, 2006 feature story on Ed's White Front in the <u>St. Louis Post-Dispatch</u>

- vegetable oil for frying
- 3 cups barbecue sauce *
- 12 ounces ground beef
- 6 ounces ground pork
- ¾ cup plain dry bread crumbs
- ½ cup Golden Dipt fish breading
- 6 hamburger buns
- coleslaw or sweet pickle relish

Pour oil into deep fryer; heat to 360 degrees. Pour barbecue sauce into a medium pan and place over medium high heat. When bubbles appear, reduce heat to low. In a large bowl, gently but thoroughly mix ground beef, ground pork and bread crumbs. Separate into six equal portions; press into thin patties, about 3 ½ inches in diameter. Place breading in another bowl; coat patties completely, shaking off excess breading. Deep-fry patties until cooked through, 5 to 6 minutes, working in batches if necessary. Remove patties to a paper towel-lined plate for 1 to 2 minutes, patting with another paper towel if necessary to remove oil. Transfer patties to pan of barbecue sauce, coating them entirely and simmer for at least 5 minutes or until ready to serve. Serve on a hamburger bun topped with slaw or a dollop of pickle relish. Dip underside of top of bun in sauce before serving. Yield: 6 servings. * For a substitute, try Maull's barbecue sauce but thin it with water and flavor it to taste with paprika, dry mustard and a pinch of dried red (cayenne) pepper.

Goody Goody Diner
5900 Natural Bridge Avenue
314-383-3333
www.goodygoodydiner.com

The Goody Goody Diner has a long history in North St. Louis starting out in 1931 as the first walk-up A & W root beer stand. It had good company with Ed's White Front famous barbecue place, Sam the Watermelon Man, and the original Ted Drewes frozen custard stand all located by the busy corner at Natural Bridge and Goodfellow. In 1948, the root beer stand became Cecil Thompson's Goody Goody Drive-In, named after the Benny Goodman song "Goody Goody" and the words that children expressed when they first pulled up to their favorite restaurant. In 1954, Herb and Viola Connelly bought the drive-in, adding curb service to the place, with their son, Richard, helping out as the youngest carhop. Even as the neighborhood experienced a decline with many white business owners and residents leaving the area, the Connellys chose to stay, feeling that they had benefitted from the neighborhood too much to justify their abandoning it. Richard bought the place from his parents in the late 1960s and the diner celebrated its 60th anniversary in 2008. Richard and his wife Laura continue to elict the "goody goody" expression from customers, thanks to its wonderful food, and they continue the Connelly family commitment to the neighborhood. Celebrities who come to town often choose Tony's but some seek out the Goody Goody. Open only for breakfast and lunch and known for its interesting combinations and excellent versions of standard diner fare, the Connellys felt they had no real recipe to share. Instead, go for yourself and check out their recipe for embracing their neighborhood and successfully continuing the diner tradition through the decades.

Wright City Big Boy's

There were two Big Boy names in the St. Louis area. This recipe is not from the Big Boy's/Shoney's chain, which had the overall-clad boy holding up a hamburger. It is from a popular and recently-shuttered roadside restaurant along I-70, which served travelers in nearby Wright City, Missouri from 1924 to 2005. The restaurant was started by J.W. "Big Boy" Chaney after hearing a hard surface road was coming through the area. He served up all-you-can-eat fried chicken and all the fixings for years and his sons, Emory and Ray, took over after his death. When they retired in 1962 they sold to the Baseels and the King family took over in 1985.

Big Boy's Coleslaw
Shared by owner Kevin King for an August 19, 1990 St. Louis Post-Dispatch feature story

- 1 large head cabbage, shredded
- 1 medium onion, thinly sliced
- ¾ cup plus 2 Tbsp plus 2 tsp granulated sugar, divided
- 1 cup cider vinegar
- ¾ cup vegetable oil
- 1 tsp salt
- 1 tsp dry mustard
- 1 tsp celery seeds

Layer shredded cabbage and onion in large bowl, sprinkling with ¾ cup plus 2 tablespoons sugar as you layer the vegetables. Combine vinegar, oil, remaining 2 teaspoons sugar, salt, dry mustard and celery seeds in saucepan. Bring to a boil then pour over cabbage mixture. Stir. Cover and refrigerate 4 to 6 hours or overnight. Mix well before serving. Slaw can be stored in the refrigerator for 2 weeks. Yield: 10 to 12 (half-cup) servings.

Ruggeri's

Ruggeri's (pronounced roo-JE-ries) was owned by Henry "Chief" Ruggeri and his wife Erminia. It was located at 2300 Edwards on the Hill, the Italian part of St. Louis. The Hill had some famous residents, most notably Yogi Berra and brothers Joe and Mickey Garagiola who lived across the street from Yogi on Elizabeth Avenue. Yogi and Joe were both professional baseball players. Yogi went on to be a team manager for the New York Yankees and the Mets and he is famous for his Yogi-isms. Joe Garagiola went on to a television broadcasting career. His older brother Mickey was famous in his own right, as a waiter at Ruggeri's, a city hot spot for decades, which was known for its great food and as the place to be seen. Mickey was also the ring announcer for years for the television show "Wrestling at the Chase," which was taped at the Chase Park Plaza on Sundays when Ruggeri's was closed.

For years, Mickey has stood by his story that he witnessed the birth of toasted ravioli. According to Mickey, one night in the 1930s, when his shift at Ruggeri's was over, he and other waiters went over to Oldani's. Chef Fritz was supposed to be putting the wine into the scallopini but drank it instead. When he was pulling ravioli out of a pot, some fell into the deep fryer then in anger he threw the rest of them in as well. After they popped to the surface toasted, Fritz took them to the bar rather than throw them away. The guys who were drinking at the bar liked them so much they asked for another order. The next day, the owner heard what happened and said, "If they make the customers drink more, let's add them to the menu." (Subsequent versions bread the ravioli before frying and serve it up with meat sauce.) Oldani's today houses Mama Campisi's restaurant.

About Ruggeri's, Yogi said, "No one goes there anymore, it's too crowded." Ruggeri's was recommended by Duncan Hines. The restaurant's reputation was so widespread that its slogan became, "In St. Louis, it's Ruggeri's." Chief strictly enforced the closing time and is said to have turned away late arrivals Tommy Dorsey and Frank Sinatra. Ruggeri's closed its doors on June 8, 1982, after being a destination restaurant for more than 50 years. After waiting tables for forty-five years at Ruggeri's, Mickey was still not ready to retire and he went on to wait tables at nearby Pietro's on Watson Road for another 14 years until he finally retired at age 75 in 1996.

Ruggeri's

RUGGERI'S are the originators of the CHARCOAL BROILED STEAK . . . and for over four generations Ruggeri's have served only Choice Cuts — Tender, thick and juicy, with all the flavor captured through skilled broiling . . . plus a dash of Garlic (if you like) . . . to give that final touch of seasoning, and served to your order

From Our Broiler

SPECIAL BROILED FILET MIGNON
(10 oz.) *served with Bordelaise Sauce* 8.00

RUGGERI'S BROILED SIRLOIN STEAK
(16 oz.) 8.75

RUGGERI'S FAMOUS BROILED T-BONE STEAK
(20 oz.) 9.95
→ *Not Available With Birthday Or Central Hardware Certificates* ←

RUGGERI'S BROILED STEAK SANDWICH
(14 oz.) 7.70

DOUBLE RIB SPRING LAMB CHOPS
(Two) *with Mint Jelly* 6.95

BROILED PORK CHOPS
(Choice Cut), *with Apple Sauce Sec* 5.95

CHOPPED BEEF TENDERLOIN STEAK
with Mushroom Sauce and French Fried Onion Rings 4.95

**served with above
Tossed Salad with French or Italian Dressing, French Fries or
Baked Idaho Potato, Fresh Italian Bread and Butter

Steaks should be cooked Rare, Medium or Well only - we are not responsible and will not exchange any meat ordered in in-between stages - such as Medium Rare or Medium Well.

Features of The House

ROAST PRIME RIB OF BEEF, Au Jus
Served as you desire it   Rare, Medium or Well Done 7.50

SAUTEED BONELESS RAINBOW TROUT
with Fresh Mushrooms 6.00

**served with above
Tossed Salad, with French or Italian Dressing, French Fried or
Baked Idaho Potato, Fresh Italian Bread and Butter

GOURMET'S BROILED PLANKED CHATEAUBRIAND
Au Bordure, Mushroom Caps . Service for Two 18.00
→ *Not Available With Birthday Or Central Hardware Certificates* ←

Italian Bread and Butter, Salad, included with above

CHILD'S PLATE (See your waiter) 3.00

Pasta

Fettuccine Ala Ruggeri, *Ala Dente* 4.95
Cavatelli Con Broccoli 4.75
Cavatelli Con Cauliflower 4.75
Special Mostaccioli & Meat Sauce 4.25
Special Mostaccioli Rigati - Carbonara,
   with Proscuitto 5.50
Baked Lasagne with Ricotta Cheese 4.95
Our own Home Made Ravioli,
   with Savory Sauce 4.95
Chef Combination Mostaccioli, Rigatoni,
   Ravioli and Spaghetti 5.25
Canneloni, *with Meat Sauce or White Cheese Sauce* . 5.50
Linguine, *with Red Crabmeat Sauce* 5.65
Linguine, *with Clam Sauce* 5.65
Spaghetti - with Savory Meat Sauce 4.00
   With Meat Balls *and Meat Sauce* 4.75
   With Italian Sausage 4.75
   With Tomato Sauce 3.50

(if wanted - Mushrooms . .85 extra)

Italian Bread and Butter, Salad, included with above

(*May We Suggest a Bottle of Wine With Your Pasta or Gourmet Dinner*)

Gourmet's Delight

MILKFED VEAL CUTLET, PARMIGIANO, *served with Italian Spaghetti (no Potatoes)* 6.75

SAUTEED VEAL SCALLOPS, *with Proscuitto in White Wine Sauce* 6.85

BREADED VEAL VALENCIA, *with Bordelaise Sauce* 6.75

VEAL SCALOPPINI, *Marsala Wine, Mushrooms* 6.75

BONELESS BREAST of CHICKEN SAUTE, *Maria Christina* . . . 4.95

BONELESS BREAST of CHICKEN, *with White Wine and Mushroom Sauce* 5.95

BONELESS BREAST of CHICKEN, *alla Ruggeri* 5.95

CHICKEN LIVERS, *Saute, Mushrooms, Strips of Bacon, au Sherry* 4.60

MIGNONETTES OF BEEF TENDERLOIN
Saute Marsala, Mushrooms 6.75

PICANTI OF VEAL, *Madallions of Veal Sauteed with Lemon Slices and Sherry Wine, au Gratin* 6.75

EGG PLANT PARMAGIANO 4.85

COMBINATIONS

VEAL PARMAGIANO and MIGNONETTES of BEEF 7.50
BROILED ROCK LOBSTER TAIL and MIGNONETTES 8.50
BROILED SPLIT KING CRAB LEGS and MIGNONETTES 7.95
BROILED SHRIMP and MIGNONETTES 7.75

served with above Gourmet's Delights
Tossed Salad, with French or Italian Dressing, French Fried or
Baked Idaho Potato, Fresh Italian Bread and Butter

Fish and Seafood

FRENCH FRIED JUMBO FAN TAIL SHRIMP 6.95

SOFTSHELL CRABS, *Fried to a Golden Brown or Sauteed* 6.75

BROILED JUMBO SHRIMP 6.95

SEA SCALLOPS, *Sauteed or French Fried* 5.95

COMBINATION SEAFOOD ALA POULETTE, *a delicious mixture of Lobster, Shrimp and Crabmeat in White Wine Sauce* 6.50

RUGGERI'S FAMOUS SEAFOOD PLATTER 6.75
JUMBO FROG LEGS, *Saute or Deep Fried* 6.35
GENUINE WHOLE BROILED DOVER SOLE 6.75
SAUTEED FILET OF SOLE, *in Wine Sauce with Fresh Mushrooms and Crabmeat* 6.15
STUFFED RAINBOW TROUT, *Boneless and Sauteed with a stuffing of Crabmeat au Mornay* 6.50
CRAB MEAT FLORENTINE AUGRATIN 5.95

served with above
Tossed Salad, with French or Italian Dressing, French Fried or Baked Idaho Potato, Fresh Italian Bread and Butter

Vegetables and Potatoes

Fresh Spinach . . .60	with Bacon . . .90	Buttered Peas . .40	Cut Green Beans .50
	French Fried Egg Plant . .90	Buttered Sliced Carrots . .70	
Cauliflower . . .80	Broccoli . .80	Asparagus . . 1.00	with Hollandaise . 1.35
POTATOES:	French Fried . . .60	Cottage Fried . . .75	Au Gratin . . . .75 Hashed Brown .60
Baked Idaho . . .50	Lyonnaise . . .75	American Fries . . .75	Shoe String . . .75 Whipped . . .50

Desserts

Italian Spumoni 90
Creamy Cheese Cake 90
   with Strawberries 1.05
Melons in Season 80
Rainbow Parfait 90
Creamy Ice Cream and Sherberts 60
Sundaes 70
Black Forest Cake 1.00
Gelati 85
Cherries Jubilee (ea.) 1.60
Apple Pie 55
   with Cheese 70

Beverages

Coffee 40
Milk (Large Glass) 40
Iced Coffee or Tea 40
Hot Tea 40
Chocolate Milk 40

Erminia Salad with Shrimp

This salad was created by Erminia Ruggeri and appeared in the July 17, 1999 St. Louis Post-Dispatch Recipe Exchange column, submitted by Erminia's grandson Jim Ruggeri.

½ head of iceberg lettuce, quartered
1 hard-cooked egg, sliced
3 anchovy fillets, chopped
1 (about 6-ounce) can baby shrimp, drained
1 teaspoon imported Italian olive oil
1 teaspoon red wine vinegar
• Thousand Island salad dressing to taste
• Roquefort salad dressing to taste

Wash and quarter lettuce. Add sliced egg, shrimp, oil and vinegar. Cover with equal parts of Thousand Island and Roquefort dressing. Mix and serve chilled. Yield: 1 generous serving. Note: a different newspaper recipe version of the salad called for 2 sliced radishes, 1 julienned carrot and 1 Tbsp chopped onion and omitted the oil and vinegar.

Ruggeri's Ravioli Sauce

Shared by Henry "Chief" Ruggeri for the 1965 "Clowning Around" with Cookery cookbook by the Salvation Army Women's Auxiliary of St. Louis

1 lb ground beef
1 large onion, sliced
2 cloves garlic, minced
½ lb sliced mushrooms (fresh or canned)
1 Tbsp paprika
1½ cups tomato paste
3 cups beef stock
1 tsp sweet basil
1 tsp oregano
1 tsp white pepper
• salt

Combine beef, onion, garlic, mushrooms and paprika in large skillet. Sauté well for 15 minutes over low heat. Add rest of ingredients and cook for 1 hour over low heat. Yield: 6 cups sauce.

"Buono Appetito"

Missouri Baking Company
2027 Edwards Avenue
314-773-6566

This bakery, also on the Hill, is a St. Louis institution, serving the area for over 80 years. It is famous for its Italian dessert items but also carries a wide variety of baked goods. It was started in 1924 by Stefano Gambaro and at that time it only baked bread, providing the bread for Joe Garavelli's restaurant. After Stefano's death, uncles Eugene and Frank Karpiani (Stefano's brothers-in law) ran the business then trained the Gambaro children including Ben. The younger Gambaros saw opportunity in adding sweets and they expanded into desserts. Ben eventually bought the bakery from his older siblings and today Ben's son, Chris, is a baker and president of the company while daughter Mimi Lordo is in charge of the front end of the bakery. The Italian cookies are the biggest seller but this cake is also always very popular.

Missouri Baking Company continued

Missouri Baking Company Deep Butter Cake
Shared by Missouri Baking Company

- ¾ cup plus 1 Tbsp shortening
- 2 cups plus 1 Tbsp cake flour, plus more to prepare the pan
- 1⅓ cup granulated sugar
- 1¼ tsp salt
- 1 Tbsp plus 1 ½ tsp baking powder
- ¼ cup nonfat dry milk
- ⅓ cup water
- 3½ eggs (3 eggs plus 2 Tbsp egg)
- 3 Tbsp milk
- 1¼ tsp vanilla
- • powdered sugar

Measure the full amount of shortening, then use about 2 teaspoons of that amount to grease two 8-inch cake pans; dust with flour and set aside. Preheat the oven to 350 degrees. Beat together flour and shortening to blend. Add granulated sugar, salt, baking powder and dry milk; beat at low speed until blended and creamy. Gradually beat in water. Add eggs, milk and vanilla; beat 5 minutes at medium speed. Divide evenly between the prepared pans. Bake about 25 minutes, until the cakes begin to pull away from the sides of the pans and the centers test done with a wooden pick. Let cool 5 minutes on racks. Remove cakes from the pans; let cool completely. Before serving, dust with powdered sugar. Note: Beat 1 egg in a cup; measure 2 tablespoons for the ½ egg. Yield: 2 cakes; 16 servings.

Pratzel's Bakery
10405 Old Olive Road (Creve Coeur)
314-991-0708
www.pratzels.com

Max Pratzel, a baker who came to St. Louis from Poland, and his wife Sarah, who immigrated from Russia, opened a European-style corner bakery in 1914 at the corner of Carr and High Street. At the time, it was in the Jewish part of St. Louis, just north of downtown. To get started, Max went to another local Jewish bakery and asked them for a small portion of their sour culture. Today, the Pratzel's rye bread continues from that starter. Max also brought with him recipes from Germany and Russia, which have been passed on through the years. Max and Sarah's children, Nate, Al and Yetta, all were involved in the family bakery and their spouses all joined in as well. From 1931 to 1979 the business was at Eastgate Avenue near the University City Loop, where Nate and his wife Bertha lived above the bakery and worked with the rest of the Pratzel family. The bakery followed its Jewish clientele to various St. Louis neighborhoods and the wholesale operation is now in Olivette, with the only retail location inside Simon Kohn's in Creve Coeur. Nate's son, Ron Pratzel, and his wife Elaine, continue the business today but, with their son becoming a computer programmer, no fourth generation member is on the horizon to take over. Pratzel's, a Kosher bakery, is famous for its bagels, Jewish rye bread and traditional Jewish items like the hand-braided challah bread. This Kamish (Kuh-MISH) bread (a biscotti-like chocolate cookie) is also popular.

Pratzel's Kamish Bread
Shared by Ron and Elaine Pratzel

2 ounces semisweet chocolate, chopped (⅓ cup chips)
1 Tbsp corn syrup
3 whole eggs plus 1 egg white, divided
1 cup granulated sugar
¾ cup vegetable oil
1 tsp vanilla
4 cups all-purpose flour
1 pinch salt
1½ tsp baking powder
¼ cup sliced almonds
2 Tbsp cinnamon-sugar

Preheat oven to 350 degrees. Melt chocolate and corn syrup together, stir until smooth and set aside to cool. In the large bowl of an electric mixer, beat whole eggs; add sugar gradually. Beat in oil and vanilla. Sift together flour, salt and baking powder; add flour mixture a little at a time to egg mixture. (This is a stiff dough; if mixer labors, stir in remaining flour by hand.) After all flour has been incorporated, use a rubber spatula to cut down into the dough in several places to create "ditches and mounds." Add chocolate mixture in 4 or 5 dollops to dough. Fold dough carefully over chocolate just to cover, leaving distinct streaks through dough. With lightly floured hands, shape dough into 3 logs, each about 15 inches long and 1½ to 2 inches in diameter. Arrange on a greased or parchment-lined cookie sheet. Lightly beat remaining egg white. Brush logs with egg white; sprinkle with almonds and cinnamon-sugar. Bake about 25 minutes or until lightly browned. Remove from oven. Let cool, then cut logs into 1-inch slices. Turn each slice on its side and return to oven for about 10 minutes or until dry. Yield: about 45 cookies.

Rosciglione Bakery
2265 Bluestone Drive (St. Charles, Missouri)
636-947-6500

St. Charles, an area just north of St. Louis, can boast of being the starting point for the Lewis and Clark Expedition in May 1804 and of being the first (temporary) capital of Missouri from 1821 to 1826 before the Jefferson City capitol was built. It is also home to Rosciglione Bakery. Rosciglione Bakery was started by Vincenzo Rosciglione around 1900 or before on Seventh Street in downtown St. Louis in an area known as Little Italy. Vincenzo's son, Francesco, came to this country as a teenage boy to help his father with the bakery. Upon Francesco's death in 1949, his son Peter became the third generation owner followed by fourth generation and present owner Francesco Peter who continues making the family's Old World recipes such as Italian cakes, cookies, spumoni, gelati, granita, and pastries. The bakery moved to Dellwood in 1969 and followed its customers out to St. Charles in 1998. It continues as the oldest bakery in the St. Louis metropolitan area.

Rosciglione's Strufoli

Strufoli are tiny, deep-fried balls, which are honey coated then arranged in cone and cluster shapes and are often used as a centerpiece on Christmas day. *Shared by Rosciglione Bakery*

- 2 cups sifted flour
- ¼ tsp salt
- 3 eggs
- ½ tsp vanilla extract
- 1 cup honey
- 1 Tbsp sugar
- candy sprinkles
- chocolate pieces or shavings; nut pieces (optional)

Set automatic deep-fryer for deep-frying and heat to 365 degrees. Place flour and salt in a large bowl. Make a well in the center of flour. Add in eggs one at a time, mixing after each addition. Add vanilla. Mix well to make a soft dough. Turn dough onto a lightly–floured surface and knead. Divide dough into halves. Lightly roll each half ¼ inch thick to form a rectangle. Cut dough with a pastry cutter into strips ¼ inch wide. Use palm of hand to roll strips to pencil thickness. Cut into pieces about ¼ to ½ inch long. Fry only as many pieces of dough as will float uncrowded, one layer deep in the oil. Fry 3 to 5 minutes or until lightly browned, turning occasionally during frying time. Drain over fryer before removing to absorbent paper. Meanwhile cook the honey and the sugar in a skillet over low heat for about 5 minutes. Remove skillet from heat and add deep-fried pieces. Stir constantly until all pieces are coated with honey-sugar mixture. Remove strufoli with a slotted spoon. Transfer to a large serving platter and arrange in a mound. Sprinkle with tiny multicolored candies. You may also mix in chocolate or nuts with the candy sprinkles.

Noah's Ark Restaurant

The Noah's Ark restaurant was located at I-70 and Fifth Street in St. Charles, Missouri. David Flavan, an Eastern Air Lines pilot entered the restaurant business, just in case he ever failed the requisite pilot physicals that came every six months. His kids loved animals and he loved boats and this fun restaurant was the result. Initially, he planned to have a steamship called the Galway Bay Steamship Co., filled with live animals. When the health department didn't go along with his plans, he switched to the Noah's Ark theme and large fiberglass animals. The restaurant opened in 1967 and the adjoining Noah's Ark Motel, a Best Western Motor Inn, followed. The ark filled with animals was hard to miss from the freeway and the place became a destination restaurant known for its food as well as its atmosphere. The restaurant closed around 2000 and was razed in 2007. The clam chowder and the brownies were two longtime St. Louis favorites.

Noah's Ark Clam Chowder

Recipe shared for the March 20, 1995 <u>St. Louis Post-Dispatch</u> *Recipe Exchange column by Eleonora Eaves who personally received it from a Noah's Ark Chef*

- 1 (10 ¾ -ounce) can condensed cream of potato soup
- 1 (10 ¾ -ounce) can condensed New England clam chowder
- 1 soup can filled with milk
- 1 can chopped or minced clams (any size can)
- 1 Tbsp butter, optional

Combine potato soup, chowder, milk, clams and butter in saucepan; heat through. Note: Noah's Ark used only Campbell's brand soups for their recipe.

Noah's Ark Brownies

Shared by David Flavan, Noah's Ark owner, for a January 24, 1988 feature story by the <u>St. Louis Post-Dispatch</u>

- 1 lb (2 cups or 4 sticks) butter
- ¾ lb (12 squares or 1½ boxes) semisweet chocolate
- 3 cups minus 6 tablespoons all-purpose flour
- 2¼ tsp vanilla
- 7 eggs
- 4 cups granulated sugar
- 4 cups chopped walnuts

Over very low heat, melt together butter and chocolate. Watch carefully to prevent burning. Remove from heat. Stir in flour and vanilla. With electric mixer, whip eggs and sugar until mixture resembles a yellow ribbon. Blend in chocolate mixture on slow speed. Stir in walnuts. Spread batter in two pans: a greased 9-by 3-inch pan and a greased 7-or 8-inch square pan. Bake in 350 degree oven for 35 minutes for large pan and 30 minutes for small pan. Do not overbake. Yield: 24 brownies from the large pan and 16 from small pan.

Straub's Grocery Store
www.straubs.com
314-725-2121 or toll free 866-725-2121

William A. Straub opened a grocery store in 1901 at the corner of Lockwood and Gore in the heart of Webster Groves. The store delivered groceries by horse and buggy and later switched to delivery trucks. From the beginning, Straub's offered personalized service with William Straub personally greeting customers. Early on, the store became known for carrying fine products, particularly its meats. In 1941, William hired Alfred Minor, a 15-year old who attended nearby Douglass High School, the all-black high school in Webster Groves. Minor started out as a bottle jockey sorting beer and soda bottles and moved on to filling grocery orders and delivering them. He recalled that his boss made sure his customers got what they needed, even if his delivery runs included stopping for a customer's prescription first or delivering a sandwich to the school when a customer had forgotten to pack their child a lunch, or it had accidentally been left behind. He often had keys to customers' homes and routinely let himself in, put the groceries away, then went on to the next delivery. Alfred

Minor is only one example of the many long-tenured employees who enjoyed their work at Straub's. He retired as a manager after 47 years of service in 1998.

Through the years, Straub's personalized service coupled with quality goods and the Straub's in-store credit line helped the company grow. William's sons followed into the family business with son Jack joining in 1933 and staying involved well into his 80s. Jack Straub Jr. and his son, Jack "Trip" Straub continue the business today. Now in its fourth generation with five locations, Straub's has faced stiff competition as grocery stores have grown increasingly competitive. Staying true to its founder's early principles, Straub's has carved out a niche market that delivers the best available products to discerning customers. While the butcher, bakery and wine department are all very popular, the deli also is known for its signature salads. This potato salad recipe has been popular for many years and is a Straub's deli staple.

Straub's Mustard Potato Salad
Shared by Chef Fred Youngblood and Trip Straub

2½   lbs Idaho potatoes, peeled and ½ -inch diced
1½   lbs red potatoes, peeled and ½ -inch diced
1½   stalk celery, diced
¼   red bell pepper, diced
¾   cup pickle relish
½   cup yellow prepared mustard
2½   oz sugar
¼   bunch fresh parsley, chopped
¾   cup mayonnaise
1½   Tbsp Grey Poupon mustard

Season the potatoes with salt and boil until tender. Cool potatoes by placing them in a shallow pan and refrigerating until they are cool enough to handle. Add remaining ingredients to the cooled potatoes and fold in until all ingredients are incorporated. Use your hands and smash some of the potatoes between your fingers to produce a creamy potato salad. Adjust seasoning and serve. Yield: 20 4-ounce portions.

Definitely Worth Driving to in Missouri

This is by no means meant as an all-inclusive listing of places on Route 66 in Missouri.
Please contact the Route 66 Association of Missouri for more detailed listings. www.missouri66.org.

Blue Owl Restaurant and Bakery

Lewis Café

Missouri's Natural Caves

Meramec Caverns

Cuba, Missouri (Route 66 Mural City)

Route 66 Fudge Shop

Missouri Wine Country

St. James Winery

Rolla, Missouri

Zeno's Motel and Steak House

A Slice of Pie

Springfield, Missouri

Alberta's Hotel

Lambert's Café

Southwest Tip of Missouri

Ott's Famous Dressings

Bradbury-Bishop Deli

Granny Shaffer's

Meramec Caverns Entrance

Notice the Ma and Pa outhouses

Mule Trading Post in Rolla, MO

Zeno's in Rolla, MO

Alberta's Hotel in Springfield, MO

Bradbury–Bishop Deli in Webb City, MO

Blue Owl Restaurant and Bakery

Second and Mill Street (Kimmswick, Missouri)
636-464-3128 • www.theblueowl.com.

This restaurant is about 25 minutes from downtown St. Louis and is known for its many varieties of pies. It is located in historic Kimmswick, near the Mississippi River. Although not on Highway 66, it is a nice getaway.

Blue Owl's German Chocolate Pie

In addition to the Levee-High Apple Pie, which is named for the levee that volunteers built in 1993 to save the restaurant, this pie is one of its most popular. *Recipe shared by owner Mary Hostetter*

For Pie:

- 10-inch deep-dish unbaked pie crust
- 2 eggs
- 1½ cups granulated sugar
- 3 Tbsp cornstarch
- 1 tsp vanilla
- ¼ tsp salt
- 4 oz bar Baker's German sweet chocolate
- ¼ cup butter
- 12 oz can evaporated milk
- ¼ cup sweetened flaked coconut
- ¼ cup coarsely chopped pecans
- 3 oz bittersweet chocolate

Preheat oven to 350 degrees. Melt butter and Baker's German sweet chocolate together; stir to break up. In a large bowl, combine sugar, cornstarch and salt; stir to break up any lumps. Stir in eggs and vanilla, then stir in chocolate mixture. Add evaporated milk and mix well. Pour into prepared crust. Mix together coconut and pecans. Sprinkle over filling. Bake 1 hour or until the center is just set. Let cool. Melt bittersweet chocolate in microwave on medium power; spread over cooled pie. Let set.

For Frosting:

- ½ cup butter
- ½ cup granulated sugar
- ½ cup packed brown sugar
- ¾ cup evaporated milk
- 3 egg yolks, lightly beaten
- 1 tsp vanilla
- 2 cups sweetened flaked coconut
- 1½ cups coarsely chopped pecans
- 2 oz bittersweet chocolate

In a heavy saucepan, combine butter, sugars, and evaporated milk. Bring to a boil over medium heat, stirring constantly. Remove from heat. Stir a little of the hot liquid into egg yolks; continue adding until yolks are warm. Gradually stir yolk mixture into the pot. Stir in vanilla, then coconut and pecans. Gently spoon frosting onto pie. Melt chocolate and drizzle over frosting.

Blue Owl's Gooey Butter Cookies

Mary Hostetter generously shared this popular cookie recipe in the December 3, 2008 St. Louis Post-Dispatch. On visits to the Blue Owl, I try different pies but my son chooses these cookies.

- ¼ cup (½ stick) butter, softened (no substitutions)
- ¼ tsp vanilla
- 1 egg
- 4 oz cream cheese, softened
- 1 (about-18-ounce) box yellow cake mix
- 1 cup powdered sugar

In large bowl of electric mixer, beat together butter, vanilla, egg and cream cheese until light and fluffy. Add cake mix; beat until well blended. Cover dough and chill 30 minutes. Preheat oven to 350 degrees. Shape dough into 1-inch balls; roll in powdered sugar. Place about 1½ inches apart on a lightly greased cookie sheet (see note). Bake 12 minutes; do not let brown. Let cookies cool, and then sift additional powdered sugar over the tops. Yield: about 4 dozen cookies. Notes: Recipe may be doubled; it isn't necessary to shake off excess powdered sugar after rolling; and baking on a greased sheet results in just enough spreading to make the cookies a perfect two-bite size. If you bake on parchment paper, the cookies spread a bit less and are more ball-shaped. These should not brown; baking 12 minutes allows the cookies to stay soft.

Lewis Café
145 S. Main (St. Clair, Missouri) • 636-629-9975

The Lewis Café has a long history on Route 66 in St. Clair. Virgil Lewis started the place in 1938 as one of several restaurants in town catering to both the Route 66 traveler and the local International Shoe factory workers. The restaurant originally only had seven booths and seven counter stools but it prospered due to Virgil's great food. In 1966, the building next door became available and Virgil bought the place, converting it into the Café's dining room. In 1973, after 35 years of serving up his home cooking on Route 66, Virgil sold his place to his nephew, Fred Short. Fred and his wife, Marie, inherited the recipes, kept the Lewis Café name, and kept the place much the same as Virgil had it. After 22 years, Fred and Marie Short sold the Café to their son, Chris and his wife, Tracie. Other than raising their own beef, which they use at the Café, they have kept everything the same as much as possible. All of the recipes are still original to Uncle Virgil Lewis.

Lewis Café Blackberry Crumb Pie
This is a popular dessert that dates to Virgil's tenure. *Shared by Chris and Tracie Short*

For Filling:
- 1½ lbs fresh blackberries
- 1 cup sugar
- 3 Tbsp cornstarch
- 2 Tbsp melted butter or margarine
- • prepared pie crust

Mix ingredients and place in prepared pie crust. Set aside.

Crumb Topping:
- 1 cup brown sugar
- 4 Tbsp melted margarine
- ½ cup flour

Mix items together until they resemble wet sand. Place over pie filling. Bake for 1 hour and 15 minutes at 350 degrees. Yield: 6 to 8 servings.

Missouri's Natural Caves

Missouri is known for its beautiful caves, which are located throughout the state. Some are located near old Route 66 and still capitalize on the Highway's continuing tourism. These include Meramec Caverns in Stanton, Missouri (still owned by Lester Dill's descendants), Onondaga Cave and Cathedral Cave in Leasburg, Missouri, and Fantastic Caverns (a ride along tour) and Crystal Cave in Springfield, Missouri. For a complete list, visit www.missouricaves.com. A day of floating on the river, a tour of one of Missouri's caves, and a stop for ice cream on the way home make for a traveler's day in paradise. Some of the best views of the Ozarks are found while floating on a river. If you head to Springfield, Missouri you may want to overnight at a vintage Route 66 motel. The Munger Moss Motel is in Lebanon, Missouri and the Rail Haven Motel is in Springfield. Be sure to stop in Lebanon and visit Wrink's Market, a famous little grocery store where Glenn Wrinkle sold sandwiches and provisions to travelers from 1950 to 2005. The store is now owned by his son, Terry Wrinkle.

Get more information at www.mungermoss.com, and www.wrinksmarket.com, and www.route66railhaven.com.

Meramec Caverns is a natural, living wonder that has been forming for thousands of years and has amazing rooms filled with various formations, stalactites (that "hold tight to the ceiling") and stalagmites (that reach up from the floor and "just might make it there someday.") Besides the beautiful wonders and the year-round 60 degree temperature, Meramec Caverns is a Route 66 institution from 1933, which owner and legendary promoter Lester Dill transformed from a true hole in the ground into a show cave with lights and paved paths. A marketing genius and colorful character, Dill went to great lengths to see his show cave succeed. He claimed to be a caveologist, painted Meramec Caverns on barns along the country's highways, (in the early 1960s there were 300 barns), advertised on many billboards, and he tied bumper signs to customer cars then later worked until he got the stickiness just right on his new bumper stickers.

All of these brought in the tourists. Once there, Dill had plenty to capture their attention. He promoted the cave as a stop on the Underground Railroad, a hideout for Jesse James, and as the Greatest Show Under the Earth. Along the way, two episodes of *Lassie* were filmed there and Art Linkletter sent a honeymoon couple there. (They stayed in the Honeymoon Room.) Jesse James also resurfaced, old but alive and well. Kate Smith performed "God Bless America" in front of the Stage Curtain formation and she continues to be heard there today.

A wonderful storyteller, Dill was often asked if his stories were true to which he would respond, "That's the Ozark truth." Meramec Caverns continues today as a third generation, family-owned attraction and is still worth a visit. And that's more than just the Ozark truth.

Meramec Caverns Georgia Pecan Muffins
These moist and delicious muffins are a popular breakfast item. *Shared by Chef/Restaurant Manager Judith Martin*

1½	cups flour
3	cups brown sugar
3	cups chopped pecans
6	large eggs
1½	cups melted butter

In a large bowl, add flour, brown sugar and pecans. Mix well and make a well in the center. In a separate bowl, combine eggs and butter. Add to dry mixture and mix well by hand. Prepare muffin pan by placing foil liners into pan and spraying liners with nonstick cooking spray. Fill foil liners ⅔ full. Bake at 350 degrees for 20 to 25 minutes. Yield: 27 to 30 muffins. Notes: Do not use electric mixer. Muffins will not release well from paper liners or from greased muffin pans. Muffins freeze well.

Cuba, Missouri (Route 66 Mural City)

This public art project has helped revitalize this Route 66 town. It began in 2001 when People's Bank celebrated its 100th Anniversary by commissioning a mural that depicted its first cashier, A. J. Barnett, who was also the first to own a Model T in Cuba and served as the city's mayor for 10 years. A community beautification group called Viva Cuba formed with the goal of completing 12 murals by 2007, Cuba's 150th Anniversary, and with the help of many community volunteers and support, met its target. Each mural tells a story that is linked with the city's history, so pick up a brochure at the Visitor's Center to fully appreciate what you are viewing. You can also download one at www.crawfordcounty.com/murals. The Bluebonnet Train mural might bring a tear while the Bette Davis mural may bring a chuckle. While in Cuba, visit (or stay at) the Wagon Wheel Motel, a classic Route 66 motel, and stop in for a treat at the Route 66 Fudge Shop.

Route 66 Fudge Shop

705 W. Washington (Cuba, Missouri) • 573-885-1121 • www.route66fudgeshop.com

Marcia Wilson started out with an internet-based business then needed more space and moved to a building that had once housed her parents' liquor store on Route 66. She gives full credit for her recipes to her mother and grandmother. Marcia came up with a line of Route 66 candy bars and one of them is Cuba's own Mural City candy bar.

Route 66 Fudge Shop's Hard Candy
Courtesy owner Marcia Wilson

3¼ cups sugar
1½ cups light corn syrup
½ cup water
1 dram (1 tsp) oil based hard candy flavoring*
⅛ tsp food coloring

Mix sugar, corn syrup and water in a large saucepan. Stir over medium heat until sugar dissolves. Boil, without stirring, until temperature reaches 310 degrees. Remove from heat. After boiling has ceased, (265 degrees) stir in flavoring and coloring. While the candy is cooking, lightly oil the sucker molds or pans that you are going to pour your candy in. Pour candy into molds or pan and allow to completely cool. Remove suckers from molds or break candy into pieces. If you are breaking into pieces, lightly dust with fine ground sugar to keep them from sticking. Package in airtight containers or wrap suckers in cellophane.
*available at grocery stores and specialty shops

Missouri Wine Country

Missouri has many places to explore. Some of the most popular attractions are Branson and nearby Silver Dollar City, Lake of the Ozarks (which includes Tan-Tar-A, the Lodge of Four Seasons and Osage Beach outlet mall shopping), many state parks, and float trips on many scenic rivers. (Kansas City is west of St. Louis, across the state, and like Jefferson City, the state capital, is not near old Highway 66.) One lesser known "attraction" is Missouri's wine country, the oldest wine growing region in the entire United States. Wineries are located in various Missouri regions but some are right along Route 66, where their grape stands once competed with Ozark curio stands and fireworks stands for the Route 66 tourists' dollars. This includes St. James and Rosati, Missouri. Be sure to stop off the road for some Missouri grapes and take home some local wines. For a complete listing of Missouri's wineries, visit www.missouriwine.org.

St. James Winery

540 Sidney Street (St. James, Missouri) • 1-800-280-9463 • www.stjameswinery.com

St. James Winery Summertime Punch
Recipe courtesy St. James Winery

2 bottles St. James Winery Country White Wine
1 lime, sliced thin
1 orange, sliced thin
1 2-liter bottle lemon-lime soda
• Fresh mint leaves
8 large fresh strawberries

Mix the wine, orange and lime. Add the soda just before serving. Garnish with mint and strawberries.

Rolla, Missouri

There are several reasons to stop at Rolla, Missouri and some of these include exploring Route 66, eating, and shopping. Visit the remains of John's Modern Cabins (about 8 miles west of Rolla off of the Sugartree Outer Road) and the Trail of Tears Monument at the Jerome, Missouri exit. Don't miss the Big Piney River and Devil's Elbow (about 25 miles west of Rolla and said to be one of the prettiest places on all of Route 66) as well as the Elbow Inn, which was originally the Munger Moss Sandwich Shop. With the completion of the Hooker Cut, Route 66 was realigned and the area was bypassed. Get

a brochure for the area between exits 145 and 169 at the Pulaski County Tourism Bureau or download one at www.visitpulaskicounty.org and click on the historic driving tour. After all of this exploring, shop at two Route 66 classics, the Totem Pole Trading Post (573-364-3519) and the Mule Trading Post (573-364-4711). Rolla has a Maid Rite hamburger stand, the hamburger made with loose ground beef instead of a patty. At one time there were 400 restaurants in the 1926 chain but today only 60 to 80 remain. (573-364-1434). Rolla is also home to Zeno's and A Slice of Pie.

Zeno's Motel and Steak House
1621 Martin Springs Drive (Rolla, Missouri) • 573-364-1301 • www.zenos.biz

In 1957, Zeno and Loretta Scheffer opened a 20-room motel on Route 66 in Rolla. Rolla and the motel both needed a restaurant so the Scheffers added a 60-seat restaurant in 1959. As Rolla has grown so has Zeno's, which now has a 50-room motel with two pools, the

steak house restaurant, a lounge, and a banquet center. Zeno's has been a popular stop for Route 66 travelers for decades and today Michael and Tracy Scheffer continue to welcome them to their door.

Zeno's Seafood Lasagna with Asparagus and Lobster Sauce
Recipe shared by Michael and Tracy Scheffer

For Filling:
- 5 lbs ricotta cheese
- 3½ ounces finely chopped carrots
- 1½ ounces chopped spinach
- 1 tsp salt
- ½ tsp pepper
- 6 ounces grated Parmesan cheese

Mix all ingredients together in a bowl.

For Lasagna:
- 8 pasta sheets
- 8 ounces lump crabmeat
- 8 ounces cooked shrimp, chopped
- 1 lb fresh asparagus, chopped and cooked
- Ricotta filling (recipe above)
- Sauce (recipe follows)
- slices Provolone or Mozzarella cheese

Spread 11 ounces of filling on a pasta sheet. Top with 4 ounces crabmeat. Top next sheet with 11 ounces filling and 4 ounces shrimp. Top next two sheets with half of the cooked asparagus and assemble into layers. Cut into eight portions and top with one slice of Provolone cheese. Repeat for the remaining four pasta sheets.

For Sauce:
- 3 cups Marinara sauce
- 6 cups Alfredo sauce
- 1 tsp lobster base
- 2 tsp Cajun spice

Combine Marinara sauce (blended) with Alfredo sauce. Add lobster base and Cajun spice. Heat and ladle into serving bowl.

To serve: Warm individual portions in microwave for 90 seconds rotating dish every 30 seconds until hot. Top lasagna portion with sauce and fresh chopped parsley. Yield: 16 servings.

A Slice of Pie
601 Kingshighway (Rolla, Missouri) • 573-364-6203

A Slice of Pie was opened on November 8, 1986 by Ron and Mickey Hopson at 601 Kingshighway, near the Kroger store and Denny Ford. It has won the "Best of Rural Missouri" Award for Best Dessert since *Rural Missouri* magazine started the contest.

Coconut Buttermilk Custard Pie
Recipe shared by owners Ron and Mickey Hopson

- 10-inch unbaked pie shell
- 4 eggs
- 1½ cups sugar
- 1 Tbsp flour
- 1½ cups buttermilk
- ¼ cup Half and Half
- 1 stick butter, melted
- 1 tsp lemon juice
- ⅔ cup sweet flaked coconut

Combine items in a bowl and pour into an unbaked 10-inch pie shell. Bake at 350 degrees for 50 minutes to 1 hour, until top is golden brown. Yield: 8 servings.

Springfield, Missouri

Springfield, Missouri's third largest city, is known as the Queen City of the Ozarks as well as the Birthplace of Route 66. The latter name comes from the historic telegram exchange on April 30, 1926 sent from 332 St. Louis Avenue (a side entrance to the Colonial Hotel) in which Father of Route 66 Cyrus Avery and State Highway Engineer of Missouri B.H. Piepmeier advised the Bureau of Public Roads that they preferred the number 66 to 60 or 62 for the diagonal highway. The Colonial Hotel was owned by John T. Woodruff who served as the first president of the U.S. Highway 66 Association. Woodruff's Colonial Hotel has been lost to progress (now a parking lot) but the Woodruff Building, Springfield's first skyscraper at 10 stories, still stands at St. Louis and Jefferson as does Woodruff's 1926 Kentwood Arms Hotel, now a dormitory owned by Missouri State University.

Springfield was once home to Red's Giant Hamburg (claimed as the first drive through restaurant in which customers ordered through an intercom then drove up to a window to get their food), Campbell 66 Express trucking company (with its Snortin' Norton camel and Humpin' to Please slogan), and many giraffe-rocked motels, but you can rest assured that there is more to this town than just the first Bass Pro Shop and Brad Pitt's childhood hometown. Look for two vintage havens, the Route 66 Rail Haven Motel (203 S. Glenstone) and the Rest Haven Motel (2000 E. Kearney) as well as the Melinda Court (2400 W. College Street), Rockwood Court and Café (2204 W. College Street), the Rancho Court's original cottages at 1544 E. Kearney, and the vacant Wishing Well Motor Inn at 3550 W. Chestnut Expressway. The old-style Steak 'n Shake with curb service and vintage neon is at St. Louis and National Avenue while the Rex Smith Gas Station from 1932 continues in the Smith family at 2321 N. West Bypass.

Other places to explore are the Abou Ben Adhem Shrine Mosque, the Gray-Campbell Farmstead, Wilson's Creek National Battlefield, the Gillioz Theatre and Landers Theatre, the Missouri Sports Hall of Fame, the Frisco Railroad Museum located at Grant Beach Park, the Springfield-Greene County Historical Museum, the Library Station, Fantastic Caverns, and the Animal Paradise in Strafford (formerly Exotic Animal Paradise). For a favorite place to train watch, check out the Jefferson Avenue Footbridge on Commercial Street. Lastly, tour (or stay at) Mansion at Elfindale, a historic bed and breakfast.

Alberta Ellis' Hotel no longer stands in Springfield, Missouri. Located at 618 N. Benton, it was once the site of the Springfield Hospital. Alberta and her family provided food and lodging to African Americans traveling on Route 66. She also owned the Crystal Lounge on Highway 66 in Springfield. Alberta's daughter, Ora Logan, and grandson, Irv Logan Jr., live in St. Louis and recently spoke to Route 66 Association of Missouri members about the days, not so long ago, when there were things along Route 66 that money couldn't buy. For African Americans traveling on Route 66 in Missouri, these things included food and lodging, which prompted enterprising Alberta Ellis to fill that need.

Barbecued Ribs

This recipe was prepared by Alberta's husband, Robert Ellis. Alberta submitted it for the Southwestern Bell Company cookbook. *Shared by Ora Logan*

    1   large onion
    1   clove garlic
    1   green pepper
    1   (8-oz) can of tomato sauce
    1   cup water
    1   cup vinegar
    ½   cup catsup
    2   Tbsp Worcestershire sauce
    ¼   cup margarine
    1   tsp salt
    4   lbs spareribs

Finely chop onion, garlic and green pepper and combine with tomato sauce, water, vinegar, catsup, Worcestershire sauce, margarine and salt and simmer for 20 minutes. Pour into a container to use when grilling spareribs. Wipe spareribs with a damp cloth. Place with rounded side down on broiler over glowing coals, and broil on both sides, turning with a long toasting fork or tongs. Then brush with barbecue sauce, using a swab made by wrapping a clean cloth around the end of a long stick. Continue basting, then turning meat every ten minutes, until well browned and done. Allow 45 to 60 minutes. Serve remaining barbecue sauce in a bowl. Makes about 4 or 5 servings.

Alberta's Cranberry Salad

This recipe, in Alberta's own handwriting, was one she prepared at the hotel. Many family members helped out in the kitchen. *Shared by Ora Logan*

    1   pkg strawberry Jell-O
    ½   cup hot water
    1   lb cranberries
    1   large package marshmallows (1 lb)
    1   cup sugar
    1   #2 can drained crushed pineapple (2 ½ cups/20 oz)
    ½   pint whipping cream or whipped topping

Dissolve Jell-O in ½ cup hot water and set aside to cool. Grind cranberries with marshmallows. Mix together and add sugar and pineapple. Add Jell-O and mix thoroughly. Fold in whipped cream.

Lambert's Café

1800 W. State Hwy J (Ozark, Missouri between Springfield and Branson) • 417-581-7655;
original location at 2305 E. Malone (Sikeston, Missouri) • 573-471-4261 • www.throwedrolls.com

Lambert's Café was started in 1942 by Earl and Agnes Lambert who borrowed $1500 to open a small café in Sikeston, Missouri. The business, known for its excellent comfort food and southern vegetables, was a success and after Earl's death, their son Norman stopped teaching physical education and coaching football to help his mother at the restaurant. His wife Patti also joined the business. On one crowded day in 1976, Norman was passing out extra rolls in the dining room but couldn't get to a customer in the corner. The customer told him to throw the d%@# thing and Norman did, starting a fun tradition that brings plenty of smiles to this day. The restaurant continued to grow and prosper under Norman and Patti and they expanded twice. Lambert's has added two new locations, both throwing rolls, in Ozark, Missouri and in Foley, Alabama. Norman passed away in 1996 but his sons, Ben and Scott, continue to run the business today.

Lambert's Café continued

Lambert's Café Fried Potatoes and Onions

This is a popular item that is "passed around" in the dining room to all Lambert's Café customers.
Courtesy Lambert's Café

- 4 to 5 potatoes, peeled and sliced thin
- about ½ of a yellow or white onion, sliced thin
- ½ tsp black pepper
- 1 tsp seasoned salt
- ½ tsp garlic powder
- vegetable oil

Get yourself a large skillet and fill with vegetable oil enough to cover the bottom to about ⅛ of an inch deep. Get your oil nice and hot, and then layer in your onions and potatoes and then your seasonings. Let them get nice and brown and crisp before turning and then just flip everything over until done.

Southwest Tip of Missouri

Past Springfield, Missouri you will find Halltown, Paris Springs and Avilla. In Paris Springs, look for Gary Turner at the Gay Parita Sinclair Station. He can also direct you to the Red Oak II area. Next are Carthage, Webb City and Joplin, Missouri, once a lead and zinc mining area near the state border. Carthage has Civil War history, a beautiful courthouse, the Precious Moments Museum, and it is also home to a Route 66 landmark, the Boots Motel (still standing and now rented as apartments). While St. Louis lost the 66 Park-In Theatre, its namesake, the 66 Drive-In lives on in Carthage. Webb City is home to some beautiful Victorian-era architecture, the Art Deco Route 66 Music Theatre, a Webb City mural inside the Webb City Bank and a Route 66 mural outside the Bruner building. It is also home to the Kneeling Miner Monument and the Praying Hands Monument. Joplin, where many of the miners once lived, is home to historic Schifferdecker Park, which includes a golf course and the Joplin Museum Complex. Other things to see are Joplin City Hall (once Newman Mercantile Store), the House of Lords building at 407 Main Street, the Frisco Depot and the Union Depot, the George Washington Carver Monument, the Bonnie and Clyde Hideout, Grand Falls on Shoal Creek, and Sky High Castle. Be sure to look for Dale's Ole 66 Barber Shop (originally a Phillips 66/Shamrock gas station dating to the late 1920s) and the spooklights just outside of Joplin. Download a tour of Carthage, Missouri to Baxter Springs, Kansas at www.route66tvonline.homestead.com and click on tour guide.

Ott's Famous Dressings
www.ottfoods.com • 1-800-866-2585

A lesser known story pertaining to this area is about this classic, Ott's Dressings.

In the mid 1940s, Walter Ott, a petroleum engineer, and his wife Ruby, opened a restaurant on Highway 66 in Carthage, Missouri. Walter was determined to recreate his mother's ruby-red dressing and he put his chemistry know-how to good use in coming up with his secret dressing in 1947. Ott's Famous Salad Dressing (a French-style dressing) was so popular that it drew customers from across the country, including Clark Gable and Gene Autry, who bought bottles to go. Many people tried to figure out what the white specks in the dressing were, with many believing incorrectly that they were Roquefort cheese crumbles. The salad dressing business soon overtook the small Highway 66 eatery and in 1948 they closed the restaurant and went solely into the commercial salad dressing business. It proved a wise move and 60 years later, Ott's produces a wide variety of dressings and even has barbecue sauce and wing sauce. Ott's can be found at most grocery stores in the Missouri area and can be ordered through the company website. The company is still located in Carthage, Missouri. In 1990, the company revealed its secret, that the mysterious white specks are horseradish granules, long a part of the ingredient list on the label.

Ott's Catfish Fillets
Recipe courtesy Ott's

1½ lbs catfish fillets
1 small onion, diced
16 oz bottle Ott's Famous Dressing
1 tsp seasoned salt
8 oz tomato sauce
1 cup Cheddar cheese, shredded

Butter a 10-inch microwave-safe dish. In a single layer, place fish fillets. Smother with Ott's Famous Dressing and diced onion. Cover loosely and cook on High for 6 minutes. Remove from microwave and cover evenly with the mixture of tomato sauce, seasoned salt and shredded Cheddar cheese. Re-cover and cook for additional 3 to 4 minutes. Serve with the resulting sauce. Note: If you do not have a turntable in the microwave, turn every minute while cooking

Bradbury-Bishop Deli
201 N. Main Street (Webb City, Missouri) • 417-673-4047

This 1887 building served as the corner drugstore in Webb City for decades. The original soda fountain was installed in 1927 then refurbished in 1945 and again in 1988, the latter with a 1950s décor. Longtime owners were pharmacists C.S. Bradbury and his son-in-law, Harry Bishop who operated the drugstore until 1987. Subsequent owners have continued the place exclusively as a restaurant, still serving up old-fashioned phosphates, sodas, shakes and banana splits in addition to breakfast, burgers and deli sandwiches.

Bradbury-Bishop Deli's Miner's Steak Sandwich
Recipe courtesy owners Bruce and Peggy Richardson

2 lbs thinly sliced roast beef
1 green bell pepper, chopped
1 white onion, chopped
½ cup butter
½ lb Provolone cheese, sliced
6 Hoagie buns
• au jus sauce/ beef broth for dipping

Sauté green bell pepper and onion in butter. In separate skillet, cook roast beef until warm. Assemble Hoagie buns on sheet pan and place roast beef, peppers then onions on bun, topped with the Provolone cheese. Bake at 350 degrees until cheese is melted and bread is warm. Serve with warm au jus or beef broth for dipping. Yield: 6 sandwiches.

Granny Shaffer's
2728 N. Rangeline • 417-659-9393
7th and Illinois • 417-624-3700 (Joplin, Missouri) • www.grannyshaffers.com

In 1973, Karen and David Shaffer sold their family farm and purchased an old, run down drive-in restaurant on Route 66 in Webb City. After several years of operating the restaurant as a drive-in, they changed the restaurant to a full-service, 86-seat facility called Granny Shaffer's. Today there are three Granny Shaffer's with a total of 700 seats, serving up good old fashioned American cooking, all located on old Route 66 in Joplin. One restaurant is owned by Steve and Renée Shaffer and the other two are owned by Michael Wiggins. Granny Shaffer's is famous for its homemade cooking and makes all of its pies, rolls and breads from scratch. The restaurant is also known for a country fried steak (which is hand cut from fresh sirloin), catfish, and its breakfast, which is served all day. Granny Shaffer's food "tastes homemade 'cause it is."

Granny Shaffer's Breakfast Strata

This is a popular breakfast casserole dish, perfect for Christmas morning or other special event when you don't want to be stuck in the kitchen. *Recipe shared by owner Michael Wiggins*

3 cups croutons
1½ cups bulk sausage, browned and drained
4 eggs, well beaten
¾ tsp dry mustard
2 cups milk
1 can cream of mushroom soup
2 lb bag of frozen hash brown potatoes, thawed
2 cups sharp Cheddar cheese, shredded and divided
½ cup milk

Place croutons in a 9" x 13" pan. Top with a layer of 1 ½ cups of cheese and then a layer of sausage. Combine eggs, 2 cups milk and mustard; pour over strata. Cover and refrigerate overnight. Before baking, mix mushroom soup with half cup milk and pour over the strata. Cover with the potatoes and top with ½ cup cheese. Bake at 300 degrees for 1½ hours or at 325 degrees for 1 hour. Note: This recipe is very forgiving. I substituted white bread with crusts removed for the bottom layer, and one package of bacon (cooked soft, drained and blotted) for the sausage. I also accidentally forgot about the hash brown layer until the casserole was almost finished so I cooked them separately in a pan and layered them on the very top of the casserole. It all still tasted delicious.

Granny Shaffer's Black Walnut Fudge Pie

This recipe was originally shared by Karen "Granny" Shaffer who became a bit of a local celebrity in these southwest Missouri parts, appearing weekly on a morning television show's cooking segment. After she retired and sold the restaurant to Michael Wiggins, she continued to share her love of cooking and baking at Silver Dollar City for a while where she demonstrated pie baking. Granny loved Missouri-owned Hammons nuts and used them in her pies. *Courtesy Michael Wiggins*

3 eggs
1 cup sugar
1 cup dark corn syrup
½ cup cocoa
2 Tbsp melted butter
1 tsp vanilla
2 cups Hammons Black Walnuts
• 10-inch unbaked pie shell

Beat eggs slightly; add sugar, syrup, cocoa, melted butter and vanilla. Whisk until thoroughly mixed. Measure black walnuts into unbaked pie shell; cover with chocolate mixture. Bake one hour at 350 degrees. Cool to room temperature. Serve with whipped cream or ice cream. Yield: one 10-inch pie/8 servings.

Definitely Worth Driving to in Illinois

This is by no means meant as an all-inclusive listing of places on Route 66 in Illinois. Please contact the Route 66 Association of Illinois for more detailed listings. www.il66assoc.org. (Web addresses for the other six states are in the Additional Resources section.)

To explore Route 66 in Illinois, pick up these three items: Illinois Route 66 Visitors Guide by the Illinois Route 66 Association; The Classic Illinois Route 66 brochure by the Illinois Route 66 Heritage Project; and the Illinois Historic Route 66 map available at www.enjoyillinois.com. These free items are also widely available at many of the visitors' centers and Route 66 Illinois points of interest.

Pere Marquette Lodge
Ariston Café
Springfield, Illinois
Pease's Candy
Dixie Truckers Home

Funk's Grove Famous Maple Sirup
White Fence Farm Restaurant
Dell Rhea's Chicken Basket
Lou Mitchell's Restaurant & Bakery

Ariston Café in Litchfield, Illinois

Bob Waldmire, the inspiration for Fillmore in the *Cars* movie

Tall Paul in Atlanta, Ilinois

Dixie Truckers Home in McLean, Illinois

Dell Rhea's in Willowbrook, Illinois

Lou Mitchell's in Chicago, Illinois

Pere Marquette Lodge

Illinois Route 100 (Grafton, Illinois) • 618-786-2331

While not on Route 66, the lodge was built by the Civilian Conservation Corps and is definitely worth a visit. The complex includes rustic cabins in a beautiful setting. The lodge, known for its chicken and catfish, also offers a great view and a long-standing tradition, a giant chess set.

Pere Marquette Lodge Stuffed Mushrooms Supreme
Recipe shared by Pere Marquette Lodge

- 1 cup whipping cream
- ⅛ tsp seasoned salt
- 6 Tbsp butter, divided
- 2 small green onions, finely diced
- 5 ounces cooked king crabmeat, diced (or any good canned or frozen snow crabmeat)
- ½ cup cracker meal (or finely crushed saltines)
- 1½ lbs large button mushrooms (about 28 mushrooms, 1 1/2 to 1 3/4 inches wide)

Scald cream by heating it to 185 degrees, or until tiny bubbles form around edge. This is just short of boiling. (In microwave oven, heat on high power for 2 to 2½ minutes.) Add seasoned salt. Melt 3 tablespoons butter in skillet. Add green onions; sauté about 1 minute. Do not brown onions. Add sautéed green onion mixture to seasoned cream; mix. Add diced crabmeat; mix. Add cracker meal and stir to mix. You will have about 2 cups of very thick filling mixture. Wash mushrooms; remove stems (save stems for another use). Fill mushroom caps with crabmeat filling, using about 1 tablespoon per large mushroom. Place stuffed mushrooms, stuffing-side up, on rimmed baking sheet. Melt remaining 3 tablespoons butter. Spoon about 1 teaspoon melted butter over each stuffed mushroom. Bake in preheated 350-degree oven about 10 minutes, or until golden brown. Top each mushroom with 1 rounded teaspoon supreme sauce (see recipe); return to oven until sauce bubbles, about 1 minute. Serve hot. Yield: about 28 stuffed mushrooms.

Supreme Sauce:

- 1½ cups whipping cream
- • pinch of salt
- 1½ Tbsp butter
- 1½ Tbsp all-purpose flour

Scald cream by heating it to 185 degrees, or until tiny bubbles form around edge. This is just short of boiling. (In microwave oven, heat on High power for 2 to 2½ minutes.) Add salt. Melt butter in small skillet. Add flour; stir to make roux. Cook about 1 minute. Add scalded cream to roux; simmer 1½ minutes, or until mixture thickens slightly. This is like thin white sauce. Use sauce as directed for topping for stuffed mushrooms. Yield: about 1½ cups.

Ariston Café

413 N. Old Route 66 (Litchfield, Illinois) • 217-324-2023 • www.ariston-cafe.com

The Ariston Café was started by Pete Adam and Tom Cokinos in 1924 in Carlinville, Illinois. Pete Adam came to the United States from Greece in 1905 at age 15. The Adam family continues to operate the restaurant today. The building was completed in 1935 and included gas pumps out front. By several accounts, the Ariston Café is the longest-operating restaurant on all of Route 66. In 1940, a four-lane bypass was constructed just one block west of the Ariston building so they quickly added new signage to the rear of the building to draw Route 66 customers to the café. The building was added to the National Register of Historic Places on May 30, 2006 along with Lou Mitchell's 1949 building (in Chicago) and Dell Rhea's Chicken Basket's 1946 building (in Willowbrook, IL).

Ariston Café Hawaiian Wedding Cake
Recipe shared by the Adam family

Cake:

2 cups flour
2 cups sugar
2 eggs
1 tsp baking soda
1 cup coconut, shredded
½ cup nuts, chopped
1 can (20 ounces) crushed pineapple with liquid

Combine all ingredients and stir by hand. Place in a greased 9-inch by 13-inch pan. Bake at 350 degrees for 40 to 45 minutes. Cool completely.

Cream Cheese Icing:

1 8-ounce package cream cheese, room temperature
¼ lb (1 stick) butter, softened
1 cup powdered sugar
1 tsp vanilla
4 ounces whipped topping (Cool Whip)

Combine well with mixer. Spread frosting on cooled cake. Makes 10 to 12 servings.

Ariston Café Rice Pudding
Recipe shared by the Adam family

½ gallon whole milk
1 cup long grain rice (recommend Uncle Ben's)
1 tsp vanilla
¾ to 1 cup sugar
• cinnamon for topping

Place all ingredients except cinnamon into large pot. Simmer and stir <u>often</u> to prevent sticking. When rice is done, pour into bowl and top with cinnamon.

Ariston Café Cabbage Soup
Recipe shared by the Adam family

1 head cabbage, chopped
2 carrots, diced
1 small onion, chopped
2 quarts chicken broth
3 small potatoes, peeled and cut up
• chopped ham, to taste
• black pepper, to taste
• dill, to taste

Place all ingredients in a large pot. Simmer until cabbage, carrots, onion and potatoes are tender.

Springfield, Illinois

This is a great day trip from St. Louis. Don't miss the Cozy Dog Drive In, where the hot dog on a stick was invented, and its collection of Route 66 memorabilia as well as Shea's Gas Station Museum at 2075 Peoria Road. After visiting the Abraham Lincoln sites and the Abraham Lincoln Presidential Library and Museum, stop at Pease's Candy for a wonderful sweet treat. Get more information at www.cozydogdrivein.com, and www.alplm.org and call Shea's at 217-522-0475.

Pease's Candy
6th and Washington and other locations (Springfield, Illinois)
217-241-3091
www.peasescandy.com

Peases's Candy has been satisfying the sweet tooth of locals in Illinois and across the country for over a hundred years. Martin A. Pease Sr. started making candy at the turn of the twentieth century, published several candy making cookbooks, and invented the first candy thermometer. The business survived moves to Bloomington and Springfield, sugar rationing and the Depression, and was passed on to Martin's descendants. It is now in its fifth generation and is owned by Martin's great-grandson, Rob Flesher, and Doug Anderson.

Pease's Vanilla Caramels
This recipe was in Martin Pease's 1908 cookbook and is still used today. *Shared by Rob Flesher and Pease's*

- 3 lbs sugar
- 2 lbs glucose (light corn syrup)
- 2 quarts cream, divided
- 1 Tbsp vanilla

Put sugar, glucose and 1 quart of cream on fire and stir constantly and cook until pretty thick or until it will form a soft ball when dropped in cold water. Gradually add 1 pint of the remaining cream. Stir and cook up again to the same consistency as before, then add the remainder or last pint of the cream and stir and cook until it forms a good firm (but not a hard) ball when dropped in cold water. The consistency of this ball when thoroughly cooled in the water will be the same as the caramels when they are perfectly cold. This is the only practical way to test the caramel and if you do as I direct, being careful not to cook them to a hard ball, you will find that they are a very easy candy to make. As these require so much stirring in order to keep them from sticking to the kettle, it is rather difficult to use a thermometer while making them, but it may be done, and if you wish to use your thermometer, the proper degree to cook them is about 246 to 248, according to how the weather is. Two degrees in caramels make quite a difference in their consistency, so be careful not to overcook them.

In this recipe I give you the amount of cream to use, but of course you may use half cream and half milk if you wish, and still have a very fine caramel. They will stick very easily, so be careful to stir over the whole bottom of the kettle, as they commence to thicken. When cooked to the right consistency, set off the stove and add about a tablespoon of vanilla and also, if you wish to add any nuts to them, stir them in after removing from the stove. Pour batch out on a slab, which must be well greased before hand. After cooling, cut the caramels into approximately one inch squares and wrap them in 3 X 2 inch waxed paper. Yield: approximately 4 to 5 lbs.

The Dixie Truckers Home was opened on January 1, 1928 by J.P. Walters and John Geske. It is regarded as one of the oldest truck stops in the entire country. As told in a September 25, 2003 *Illinois Times* interview of C.J. (Geske) Beeler, when her grandfather (J.P.) and father (John) bought the place, it was an old mechanic's garage on Highway 66. In the early Depression years, it only had six counter stools. Still, beggars and hoboes from the trains knew they would be fed by C.J.'s mom, Viola. The Geskes had free shows for the community, usually on Saturday nights, a precursor to the drive-in theaters. In 1939, there were only two nearby gas stations, one in Shirley and one in Bloomington. When one closed and the other burned down, the Dixie had a captive audience as both travel and the trucking industry were starting to pick up, so they decided to expand. They remodeled the building many times. During the war years, the Dixie served military convoys that stopped in to eat. Although it served standard fare, John Geske developed many of the recipes and formulas that went into making the Dixie a success.

In 1949, C.J. married Chuck Beeler, a farmer who supplied all of the eggs for the Dixie and also helped out at the Dixie when he had the time. In 1965, the original building burned down and they quickly began pumping gas again, setting up shop in one of the rental cabins that they had for travelers. A new building was ready in 1967, the same year the Geskes retired and turned the Dixie over to C.J. and Chuck. C.J. and Chuck reinvented the truck stop. A vintage postcard of the new place says the Dixie featured a 24-hour air-conditioned restaurant, car and truck service, road service, automatic car wash, shopping center, barber shop, Western Union service, air-conditioned sleeping rooms, showers, and a television lounge for truckers. It also had a gift shop, which was the first in a truck stop to carry genuine Hallmark cards. (They sold a lot of "Happy Birthday to My Wife" cards to the many traveling truckers.)

C.J. and Chuck continued the Geskes' commitment to travelers. This included taking care of travelers who had no money or were stranded and needed gas, food or a place to stay, as well as being a safe haven for runaways who had gotten scared on the road. With the help of many long-tenured employees, they made the Dixie a true home for more than just truckers. The Beelers sold the Dixie on July 31, 2003 and it has had several owners since. It is now called the Dixie Travel Plaza but it is still worth a stop.

Dixie Chili

This recipe was shared by the Beelers as they said goodbye to their Dixie Truckers Home. *From the Illinois Times "End of the Road" article, September 25, 2003, with minor modifications*

10	lbs ground beef
2	#10 (commercial size) cans diced tomatoes
2	#10 cans red beans
½	cup chili powder
¼	cup sugar
2	Tbsp cumin
1	Tbsp salt
2	tsp black pepper
2	cans tomato juice
1	can V-8 juice
1	lb onion, diced
2	Tbsp granulated garlic

Brown the ground beef and the onions. Add the diced tomatoes and the red beans. Add the spices. Add the tomato juice and V-8 juice. Place in six one-gallon jars; refrigerate. Note: no size was given for the tomato juice and V-8 juice but judging from the size of the recipe, they are likely 32-ounce cans.

Funk's Grove Famous Maple Sirup

5257 Old Route 66 (Shirley, Illinois) • 309-874-3360 • www.funkspuremaplesirup.com

Funk's Grove has been making maple sirup (an old spelling) for seven generations along old Route 66. The business, started in 1891, has depended on Route 66 travelers for years and continues to do so today. Get your sirup early from March through August because when they run out, they are out until the next season.

Funk's Grove Maple Sirup Bars
These bars are simply delicious. *Recipe shared by Mike and Debby Funk*

½	cup butter
¼	cup sugar
1	cup flour
¾	cup brown sugar
⅓	cup maple sirup
1	Tbsp butter
1	egg
½	tsp vanilla
⅓	cup chopped pecans

Cream butter and sugar in food processor or with electric mixer. Add flour and process until just blended. Dough does not form a ball. Pat into bottom of a greased 9-inch square pan. Bake at 350 degrees for 15 minutes or until lightly browned. Beat brown sugar, sirup and butter to blend. Beat in egg and vanilla. Pour over shortbread. Sprinkle with nuts. Bake at same oven temperature for 25 minutes or until set. Cool and cut into bars. Yield: 24 bars.

White Fence Farm Restaurant

1376 Joliet Road (Romeoville, Illinois) • 630-739-1720 • www.whitefencefarm.com

The White Fence Farm began in the early 1920s when coal magnate Stuyvesant Peabody envisioned a restaurant serving up great food on a picturesque farm setting. The restaurant building was originally on twelve acres of a 450-acre farm. The name of the original restaurant has been lost through the years but the original rooms with the hand-hewn hardwood beams remain. (Peabody Energy continues in the coal business today, headquartered in St. Louis.)

In 1954, Robert and Doris Hastert purchased the restaurant and renamed it White Fence Farm. They remodeled it extensively and began serving up their special award-winning chicken with all the country fixings. They use soybean oil and pressure cook the fresh chickens before flash frying them but the Hastert's breading recipe is a closely-guarded secret. The coleslaw, corn fritters sprinkled with powdered sugar, and the brandy ice dessert are also popular items. In addition to the wonderful food, there are twelve named and themed dining rooms, a petting zoo, and a museum featuring classic cars and other items. The fiberglass chicken out front is a great photo opportunity as well. Doris, who had many friends, served as the hostess for years, handing customers their paper numbers and then directing them to their table. She passed away August 14, 2006 at age 93. Son Robert Hastert Jr. continues the operation today and, with the help of many long-tenured employees, upholds his parents' traditions and commitment to excellence.

White Fence Farm Creamy Coleslaw Dressing
Shared by White Fence Farm and the Hastert family

7¼	oz cider vinegar
3½	oz Wesson oil
1	Tbsp salt
1	Tbsp onion powder
⅓	lb (⅔ cup) sugar
14½	oz mayonnaise

Combine items and mix well. Add to approximately 3 heads of shredded cabbage, to taste. Yield: 1 quart dressing.

Dell Rhea's Chicken Basket

645 Joliet Road (Willowbrook, Illinois) • 630-325-0780 • www.chickenbasket.com

Dell Rhea's Chicken Basket started out as a lunch counter in a gas station owned by Irv Kolarik. Two enterprising local farm women with a great fried chicken recipe made a deal with Irv and agreed to teach him how to fry up chicken if he would buy the chickens from them. The lunch counter was joined soon after by a dining room and a new building in 1946. The Chicken Basket fell on hard times when it was bypassed but it was rescued by Dell Rhea and his wife Grace in 1963. The restaurant continues in the Rhea family today.

Dell Rhea's Chicken Basket Sautéed Chicken Livers
Recipe shared by Patrick Rhea

- ½ cup flour
- ½ tsp iodized salt
- ½ tsp granulated garlic
- ½ tsp white pepper
- ½ tsp black pepper
- 1 lb fresh chicken livers
- 3 oz largely diced onions
- 4 oz clarified butter
- 4 oz Marsala wine
- • toast points

Add seasonings to flour and sift items together. Rinse chicken livers. Toss them to coat them evenly in the seasoned flour. Clarify the butter by melting the butter and discarding both the foam on the top and the white sediment on the bottom of the pan. Heat clarified butter in skillet over medium heat. Gently place coated livers into pan. Watch carefully. Do not turn too often and be careful for splatters. Brown on one side then turn over; add onions. Lightly brown the other side; add Marsala wine; turn over one last time if necessary. Serve in casserole dish alongside toast points. Yield: 2 dinner servings or 3-4 appetizer servings.

Lou Mitchell's Restaurant & Bakery

565 W. Jackson Blvd. (Chicago, Illinois) • 312-939-3111 • www.loumitchellsrestaurant.com

Lou Mitchell's was started in 1923 by William Mitchell who named the restaurant after his son, Lou. Located at the starting point of Route 66 in downtown Chicago and predating Route 66, this place is filled with many traditions including serving donut holes to customers waiting in line and giving out Milk Duds to all the ladies. The restaurant continued under Lou himself then by Lou's cousin, Kathryn Thanas, along with her children, Nicholas and Heleen. Lou Mitchell's is a Chicago institution and is considered a "must see place."

Lou Mitchell's French Toast
Recipe shared by the Thanas family

- 1 loaf uncut day old bread (optional cinnamon raisin bread)
- 1 cup milk
- 2 eggs
- 1¼ tsp vanilla extract
- • salt to taste (just a pinch should do)

Cut 8 slices of bread approximately 1½ to 1¾ inch thick. In mixing bowl, beat together milk, eggs, vanilla extract and salt. Dip both sides of bread squeezing each slice by pressing between your hands as in prayer pose. Then place on heated lightly oiled grill or skillet; cook on both sides until golden. Do not press down. Serve hot with warm syrup accompanied with butter or cinnamon or both.

Some St. Louis Favorite Foods

Mississippi (Riverfront) Mud Pie

Mississippi (River) Mud Cake

(Mound City) Mounds Bar Cake

(Old and New) Cathedral Window Cookies

St. Louis Gooey Butter Cake

Toasted Ravioli

St. Louis Crab Rangoon

Texas Sheet Cake

Rye Bread with Dill Dip

Friday Fish Fry Beer-Battered Fish

Potato Candy

Mississippi (Riverfront) Mud Pie

A local favorite. *Recipe contributed by various readers for the March 28, 1998* <u>St. Louis Post-Dispatch</u> *Recipe Exchange column*

- 1 cup granulated sugar
- ½ cup (1 stick) butter, melted
- 1 tsp vanilla
- ¼ tsp salt
- 2 eggs
- ⅓ cup all-purpose flour
- ⅓ cup unsweetened cocoa powder
- 1 cup chopped nuts
- ¼ cup fudge sauce, plus more for drizzling on top
- 1 cup whipped topping

Preheat oven to 325 degrees. Grease an 8-inch pie plate. Mix sugar, butter, vanilla, salt, eggs, flour and cocoa powder. Stir in nuts; pour into pan. Bake until toothpick comes out clean, 25 to 30 minutes. Immediately prick holes in pie with toothpick. Spread fudge sauce over top. Let cool completely. Top with whipped topping. Drizzle with additional fudge sauce. Store in refrigerator. Yield: 8 servings.

Mississippi (River) Mud Cake

If you aren't a pie person, here is a chocolaty cake version that is very popular. *Recipe adapted from the 1981* <u>Cooking for Applause</u> *cookbook by the Backers of the Repertory Theatre of St. Louis and* <u>Food Editors' Hometown Favorites Cookbook</u>, *contributed by Barbara Gibbs Ostmann*

For Cake:

- 1 cup butter or margarine, softened
- 2 cups granulated sugar
- 4 eggs
- ¼ cup cocoa powder
- ¾ tsp salt
- 1½ cups all-purpose flour
- 1 tsp vanilla extract
- 1½ cups flaked coconut
- 1½ cups chopped nuts (preferably pecans)
- 1 jar (9 ounces) marshmallow cream or miniature marshmallows as needed

Cream butter and sugar in a large mixing bowl. Beat in eggs, one at a time with spoon. Sift flour, cocoa and salt together. Stir into creamed mixture. Stir in vanilla, coconut and chopped nuts. Pour batter into a greased and floured 9-inch by 13-inch pan. Bake in a 350 degree oven 30 to 35 minutes, or until toothpick inserted in center comes out clean. Remove from oven and, while hot, either spread with marshmallow cream or cover with miniature marshmallows and spread them after they have melted. Let cake cool, then frost with frosting.

Frosting:

- ⅓ cup cocoa powder
- ½ cup butter or margarine
- ½ tsp vanilla extract
- ⅛ tsp salt
- ⅓ cup light cream or milk
- 1 box (16 ounces) confectioners sugar

Beat cocoa, butter, vanilla, salt, cream and confectioners sugar in a medium bowl until fluffy. Spread over marshmallow cream on cake. Note: no baking powder or soda is needed in this recipe.

(Mound City) Mounds Bar Cake

A local favorite. *Recipe contributed by various readers for the March 26, 2003* <u>St. Louis Post-Dispatch</u> *Recipe Exchange column*

Cake:

1 (18¼ ounce) dark chocolate cake mix

Prepare cake as directed in a 9-inch by 13-inch pan (or in two 8 or 9-inch rounds for layers that can be split then filled). Bake cake as directed on package and let cool.

Filling:

30 large marshmallows
1 cup milk
1 cup granulated sugar
14 ounces (1 ¾ cups) shredded sweetened coconut

Combine marshmallows, milk and sugar in large saucepan; cook over low heat until marshmallows are melted. Remove from heat; stir in coconut. Gently spread mixture over the top of the cooled cake.

Frosting:

½ cup (1 stick) margarine or butter
½ cup milk
1½ cups granulated sugar
12 ounces (1½ cups) semisweet chocolate chips

Melt margarine with milk and sugar together in saucepan; bring to a boil over medium-high heat. Remove from heat and stir in chocolate chips until melted. Beat with an electric mixer until thick. Spread frosting on top of coconut layer(s). Yield 12 to 16 servings.

(Old and New) Cathedral Window Cookies

A popular no–bake cookie. *Shared by readers for the April 13, 2002* <u>St. Louis Post-Dispatch</u> *Recipe Exchange column*

1 (12-ounce) package chocolate chips
½ cup (1 stick) margarine or butter
1 cup finely chopped pecans
1 (10½-ounce) bag colored mini marshmallows
1 (7-ounce) bag sweetened flaked coconut

Melt chocolate and margarine; let cool. Stir in chopped pecans and marshmallows, mixing well. Sprinkle coconut on a large piece of waxed paper. Shape marshmallow mixture into 2 logs. Roll each log in coconut until completely covered. Wrap logs in a clean piece of wax paper. Refrigerate overnight. Before serving, slice into rounds with a sharp knife. Yield: 72 cookies.

St. Louis Gooey Butter Cake *(traditional recipe from Heimburger Bakery)*

According to local lore, a German baker got the proportions wrong on his cake batter and the result became a sweet St. Louis tradition. *From the 1994-1995* <u>St. Louis Days, St. Louis Nights</u> *Junior League of St. Louis cookbook, contributed by Fred and Audrey Heimburger*

For Crust:

1 cup all-purpose flour
3 Tbsp granulated sugar
⅓ cup butter or margarine, softened

Preheat oven to 350 degrees. In mixing bowl, combine flour and sugar. Cut in butter until mixture resembles fine crumbs and starts to cling together. Pat into the bottom and sides of a greased 9-by 9-by 2-inch pan.

For Filling:

1¼ cups granulated sugar
¾ cup (1½ sticks) butter or margarine, softened
1 egg
1 cup all-purpose flour
⅔ cup evaporated milk
¼ cup light corn syrup
1 tsp vanilla
• powdered sugar for sprinkling

In mixing bowl, beat sugar and butter until light and fluffy. Mix in egg until combined. Add alternately flour and evaporated milk, mixing after each addition. Add corn syrup and vanilla. Mix at medium speed until well blended. Pour batter into crust-lined baking pan. Sprinkle with powdered sugar. Bake for 25 to 35 minutes until cake is nearly set. Do not overcook. Let cool in pan. Yield: 9 servings.

Toasted Ravioli *(Lower fat version)*

Adapted from 1988 cookbook Fare to Remember *by the Assistance League of St. Louis*

- about 1 cup milk
- about 1 cup packaged dry Italian bread crumbs
- 1 (1-lb) package frozen, precooked ravioli, thawed
- olive oil cooking spray
- ¼ cup grated Parmesan cheese or to taste
- pasta sauce for dipping

Preheat oven to 425 degrees. Pour milk into a small bowl. Pour bread crumbs into a shallow bowl. Dip ravioli into milk for 10 to 15 seconds. Lightly coat ravioli with bread crumbs. If necessary, add more milk and/or bread crumbs to bowls. Place coated ravioli on a sheet of waxed paper or parchment paper. Spray ravioli on both sides with cooking spray. Place on cookie sheet. Bake 14 to 15 minutes, turning halfway through baking time and spraying with more cooking spray if needed. Serve hot, sprinkled with Parmesan cheese. Serve with pasta sauce. Yield: 25 to 30 ravioli.

St. Louis Crab Rangoon

This appetizer is found at all St. Louis area Chinese restaurants. *Recipe and diagram for folding contributed by Aldred Hellmich for the December 28, 1992* St. Louis Post-Dispatch *Recipe Exchange column*

- 1 lb package crab meat (cleaned and cartilage removed)
- 2 (8-ounce) packages cream cheese, room temperature
- 1 egg yolk
- dash steak sauce
- dash garlic powder
- dash ground pepper
- salt, to taste
- dash MSG (optional)
- 80 (3-inch) wonton wrappers
- vegetable oil for deep fat frying

In paper toweling, squeeze crab to remove excess liquid; chop. Using mixer, combine chopped crab, cream cheese, egg yolk, steak sauce, garlic powder, pepper, salt and MSG if using it. Place about ½ tsp crab mixture in a mound in the center of square wonton wrapper. Then fold wrapper diagonally into a triangle, leaving top and bottom edges slightly separated. Dab a bit of filling on each side of the mound; draw midpoints of both legs of the triangle together over the exposed filling; pinch securely. Fold in the bottom corners like wings. Fry in hot oil (350 to 375 degrees) until delicately browned. Drain on paper towels. Serve hot. Yield: 80 squares.

Texas Sheet Cake

This cake is popular because of its flavor and its size, fit for a crowd. *Adapted from the 2001* St. Anthony's Cooks *cookbook*

- 2 cups all-purpose flour
- 2 cups granulated sugar
- ½ tsp salt
- 1 tsp baking soda
- ½ cup (1 stick) butter or margarine
- 1 cup water
- ¼ cup unsweetened cocoa powder
- 1 cup buttermilk
- 1 tsp vanilla
- 2 eggs

Chocolate Icing:

- ½ cup (1 stick) butter or margarine
- 6 Tbsp buttermilk
- 4 Tbsp unsweetened cocoa powder
- 1 (1-pound) box powdered sugar, sifted
- 1 tsp vanilla

Preheat oven to 400 degrees. Grease and flour an 11-by 17-inch jelly-roll pan. Sift flour into a large bowl. Add sugar, salt and baking soda. Stir together. In a saucepan, bring butter or margarine, water and cocoa powder to a boil. Add the hot liquid to the dry ingredients. Add the buttermilk, then the vanilla, then the eggs, beating after each addition. Pour into the pan; bake for 20 minutes or until done. Frost with chocolate icing while cake is still warm. Yield: 40 servings.

Bring butter or margarine, buttermilk and cocoa powder to a boil; cook for 2 minutes. (Mixture will curdle as it boils.) Add sugar and vanilla. Beat until smooth. Yield: 40 servings. Hints: If you do not have buttermilk on hand, pour 1 tablespoon white vinegar into a measuring cup then fill with milk and let stand for 5 minutes. For transporting without the frosting sticking to plastic wrap or foil, place an unused 11-by-17 inch jelly roll pan over the frosted sheet cake and tape the two pans together.

Rye Bread with Dill Dip

The origin of this appetizer is unknown but it has been popular for decades and appears in various forms in many vintage St. Louis cookbooks. *Recipe adapted from the 2001 St. Anthony's Cooks cookbook with slight modifications*

1 2-lb round rye bread (set aside)
16 oz mayonnaise
16 ounces sour cream
2 Tbsp Beau Monde seasoning
2 tsp dill weed
2 Tbsp dried onion flakes
2 Tbsp parsley flakes
4 ounces cream cheese (optional)

Mix items and chill for three hours before serving. Slice off top of rye bread and scoop out center of bread then pull it apart into bite-size pieces. Place dip in center of hollowed-out bread loaf and place the loaf on a tray. Surround the tray with the bread pieces for dipping. (When the bread pieces are gone, eat the rye "bowl.")

Friday Fish Fry Beer-Battered Fish

The tradition of Friday fish fries has its roots in the Catholic practice that did not allow meat to be eaten on Fridays. Fish fries were once held throughout the year and were popular for both restaurants and community groups such as the Veterans of Foreign Wars and Knights of Columbus as well as local parishes. Today, the fish fries are generally popular during the Lent season and are a tradition that keeps parishioners bonding while raising money for the local church. *Recipe from the 1984 Food Editors' Hometown Favorites Cookbook, contributed by then-St. Louis Globe-Democrat Food Editor Diane Wiggins*

1 cup buttermilk baking mix
1 cup beer (your favorite brand)
• garlic salt, salt and pepper, to taste
2 to 3 lbs of cleaned fish fillets (the catch of the day, cleaned and filleted)
• vegetable oil for frying

Combine baking mix, beer, garlic salt, salt and pepper in a bowl. Dip cleaned fish fillets in batter. Fry in hot oil in a deep fryer or skillet until golden brown. Drain on absorbent towels. Serve hot. Yield: 4 servings.

Potato Candy

This recipe is a regional favorite using mashed potatoes. Similar to an uncooked fondant, it can be made into different types of candies such as stuffed or formed with dates or cherries or dipped in chocolate. *Recipe shared by Marian Altschuh in 1993 for the St. Louis Post-Dispatch Recipe Exchange column*

1 teaspoon vanilla
¼ teaspoon salt
¼ cup mashed potatoes, unseasoned
4 cups powdered sugar
1 cup smooth peanut butter

Add vanilla and salt to potatoes. Chill. Slowly add powdered sugar to potato mixture until mixture is stiff and dry. Divide into 3 parts. Roll out each part ¼-inch thick on waxed paper to form a 4-by 12-inch rectangle. Spread with a thin layer of peanut butter. Roll up lengthwise as for a jelly roll. Repeat with remaining dough. Let chill several hours. Slice each roll into 24 pieces. Store in refrigerator. Yield: 72 pieces.

Some Family Favorites

Easy Fruit Cobbler

Mama Tina's Butter Pecan Cookies

Old-Fashioned Sugar Cookies (Cut-out)

Mom's Corn Fritters

Mom's Candied Sweet Potatoes

Mom's Homemade Flour Tortillas

Easy Fruit Cobbler

This is a recipe from my hometown, McAllen, Texas. *Adapted from the 1996 Hidalgo County Historical Museum's Mesquite Country cookbook with modifications*

1	stick butter or margarine
1¾	cups sugar, divided
¾	cup all-purpose flour
1½	tsp baking powder
¼	tsp salt
½	cup milk
3	cups fresh fruit of choice
•	cinnamon or nutmeg to taste (optional)

In microwave oven, melt butter in an 8 X 12-inch glass baking pan. In separate bowl, sift together ¾ cup sugar, flour, baking powder and salt. Add milk and mix well. Pour over melted butter; do not stir. Add fruit in layers. Sprinkle remaining 1 cup sugar over fruit. Dust with cinnamon or nutmeg. Bake at 350 degrees for 45 to 60 minutes or until top browns. Serve with vanilla ice cream. Note: this recipe is on the sweet side so cut back on the sugar a bit if you don't like your cobbler really sweet. If you use canned fruit, decrease sugar sprinkled over fruit to ¾ cup. Yield: 8 servings.

Mama Tina's Butter Pecan Cookies

My mother's recipe and a family favorite. The original source is unknown but a similar cookie is sold at Lubeley's Bakery.

1	cup butter or margarine
¾	cup granulated sugar
2	eggs
1	tsp vanilla
2¼	cups all-purpose flour, sifted
1	tsp baking soda
½	tsp salt
1	cup chopped pecans
•	additional pecan halves or pieces for top of cookies

Cream butter and sugar until light and fluffy. Beat in eggs and vanilla. Sift together dry ingredients; blend into creamed mixture. Stir in chopped pecans. Roll into small balls and place on ungreased cookie sheet (recommend parchment paper). Top each cookie with a pecan half before baking. Bake at 375 degrees for 8 to 10 minutes. Yield: 4 dozen.

Old-Fashioned Sugar Cookies (Cut-out)

This recipe has never failed me. The cookies are delicious and also smell great. The cookie stands alone without icing. *Adapted from the 1983 cookbook Cookies by Natalie Hartanov Haughton*

1	cup butter, room temperature
1½	cups granulated sugar
1	tsp vanilla extract
1	tsp orange extract
3	eggs
3¾	cups all-purpose flour
•	pinch of salt
2	tsp baking powder
¾	tsp baking soda
•	sugar crystals, optional

In a large bowl, beat together butter, sugar, extracts, and eggs until light and fluffy. Beat in flour, salt, baking powder and baking soda until thoroughly blended. Divide dough into two equal portions. Wrap (or place in freezer bags) and refrigerate until firm, several hours or overnight. To bake cookies, preheat oven to 350 degrees. Line cookie sheets with parchment paper. Keep dough you aren't working with in the refrigerator. On a floured surface, roll dough 3/16 to ¼ inch thick. With lightly floured cookie cutters, cut into desired shapes. Place 1½ inches apart on baking sheets. Bake 7 to 9 minutes or until pale in color. Baking time varies depending on thickness and size of cookies. Watch carefully. Remove cookies and cool on racks. Yield: 80 cookies, depending on size of cutter. (Note: If using sugar crystals, sprinkle on cookies prior to baking.)

Mom's Corn Fritters

This is another longtime family favorite with unknown origins. My mother always piled these corn fritters (which resemble petite golden pancakes) high on a platter. My family ate these with lemon instead of powdered sugar. I always make a double batch as any extras can be easily reheated in the microwave.

¾ cup unsifted all-purpose flour
2 tsp baking powder
1 tsp granulated sugar
½ tsp salt
1 large egg, slightly beaten
⅓ to ½ cup milk
1 16-ounce can corn (drained)
• vegeatable oil for frying

Combine flour, baking powder, sugar and salt. Stir in egg and milk, and then add corn. Prepare electric skillet by placing ¼ inch vegetable oil and heating it to 375 degrees. Drop batter by tablespoons being careful not to let the fritters run into each other in the skillet. Note: If you make them too large (more than 3 inches around) they will be hard to turn over. Skillet fry 3 to 4 minutes until golden then flip with a spatula and fry the other side. Drain on plate lined with paper towels to absorb oil. Serve with lemon slices if desired.

Mom's Candied Sweet Potatoes

8 to 10 large sweet potatoes
1 cup firmly packed brown sugar
1 tsp salt
2 Tbsp grated orange rind
1 cup orange juice
¼ to ½ lb butter (one to two sticks)
• optional pecan pieces and miniature marshmallows, to taste

In a large saucepan, cook sweet potatoes in salted boiling water until tender. Cool then peel and slice lengthwise. Combine sugar and salt in a small bowl. Arrange potatoes in two layers in a 13-by 9-by 2-inch baking pan. Pour orange juice and rind over potatoes. Sprinkle with sugar mixture. Dot with butter. Cover with foil. Bake for 30 minutes at 325 degrees then uncover Add marshmallows and pecan pieces if you like. Continue to bake until potatoes are browned and glazed and marshmallow start to brown. Yield: 14 servings.

Mom's Homemade Flour Tortillas

6 cups flour
4 tsp baking powder
1 cup shortening (or use butter or half butter and half shortening)
3 tsp salt
2¼ cups hot boiling water

Mix all items except water until mixture is crumbly. Add boiling water. Be careful. Knead very well. Let stand in bowl with tea towel over it for 10 minutes. Form the dough into small flat balls, tucking the dough under with your fingers as you move the dough in a circular motion. Once all dough is formed into flat 3-inch or so "patties" and is completely cooled, use a rolling pin and roll the dough out into a 6-inch or so round shape. Turn dough as you go to get to the round shape. Cook by placing on a flat griddle. Brown one side then use a spatula to flip over and do the other side. Watch carefully to avoid burning. Serve warm with butter. Store extras in refrigerator.

Route 66 Party

Route 66 can be a part of many different party themes or it can stand alone as its own theme. Some themes that can be easily combined with Route 66 are a road trip, Disney Pixar's *Cars* movie, racing, 50s rock and roll, go west or cowboy, or a back in time party. The possibilities are limited only by your imagination. If you live near the old road, try to incorporate getting out on the highway as part of the party experience by using a drive-by scavenger hunt. (Two examples follow.) If you don't live near the path, use maps to familiarize guests with the 8-state path.

How to Throw a Route 66 Party

Here are some ideas that can be incorporated into any party featuring Route 66.

SETTING: Decorate the main wall (if indoors) or the outdoor area with a representation of the 8-state path. My son's party was in the dead of winter so it was indoors. I used 2 rolls of brown wrapping/craft paper to make a 2-lane highway and yellow construction paper to make the dividing line. I used Route 66 shield-shaped signs for each state (from a book and blown up on a copier) and then decorated each state's area. I didn't have much room so I used wall decorations and added a few props that were used for games and activities such as a saddle (mounted between two chairs), a tepee and a large palm tree with lights on it.

Our official starting line was Illinois so I had Route 66 Illinois helium balloons and I put a Route 66 Illinois temporary tattoo on each child for check in. (I got these from the Illinois Route 66 Association). You can use travel posters if you can find them (Chicago, etc.) or blow up images from books or postcards that the guests will like. Sample decorations include Missouri: Arch; Kansas: sunflowers; Oklahoma: Will Rogers or cowboy; Texas: Lone Star flag, cowboy or oil; New Mexico: Southwestern/ Native American; Arizona: cactus; and California: beach setting with palm tree and the large Hollywood letters. You can fill in gaps with sign such as See Meramec Caverns, Here it Is, Tucumcari Tonite, Wigwam Village, Tepee Curios, etc. and use some of the game items as props.

Announce the location of the party outside by making up a sequential Burma Shave sign using red poster board and white painted letters. I couldn't come up with anything clever so mine just read, "Too young to shave, Too young to drive, Still able to party, 'Cause we're alive! Happy 8th Birthday. The last one read, "Burma Shave." Incorporate any other theme as you wish.

INVITATION: (My son really challenged me because he wanted the *Cars* movie, NASCAR, and western themes woven in with Route 66.) Using a fun "Greetings from Route 66" postcard, I made an invitation that also had clip art. Continuing with this combo idea, it could read "The *Cars* Radiator Springs gang is teaching Lightning McQueen about Route 66 by having a leisurely race across the 8-state path. You are invited to join ____ as he/ she celebrates his/her __ birthday on ____ at _____ from _____ to _____. We will gear up for our trip by eating lunch then we'll head out on the highway from Illinois to California, stopping along the way to play games, make crafts, and see the sights. We are heading west so please wear any western attire you may have. Come join us and see for yourself that you can still get your kicks on Route 66. Confirm your spot by calling reservation agents (parents) _____ and ___ at ____ no later than ____. (If you live near the highway's path you can add: In order for you to experience the highway firsthand, we have included a Drive-By Family Scavenger Hunt for you to do before the party.) I placed a big Ted Drewes Mother Road sticker on the outside of the envelope.

FOOD: Plan an 8-state menu. If you don't have to serve kid-friendly food, I encourage you to use authentic recipes from restaurants along the Route 66 path. You can make this formal (Fred Harvey style) or informal. I served a Blue Plate Special and decorated like Steak 'n Shake and racing using black and white checkered tablecloths and paper goods with red flatware and red balloons. Drinks were served in Big Texan-style boots (bought from Oriental Trading), which the kids took home with them. All the girls got Milk Duds a la Lou Mitchell's in Chicago. (You have to explain these things or they won't be worth the effort.)

A SAMPLE KID'S MENU: Illinoi- Cozy Dogs (use frozen corn dogs or get ingredients from them); Missouri- Wagon Wheel Motel macaroni and cheese (wagon wheel-shaped pasta); Kansas- sunflower-shaped grill cheese sandwiches; Oklahoma- Chicken in the Rough (chicken nuggets); Texas- U Drop Inn potatoes (frozen mashed potatoes or fries); New Mexico- Fat Man Sourdough Biscuits (use refrigerated biscuits); Arizona- rattlesnake eggs (deviled eggs); California- Bono Orange juice, McDonald's shakes or fruit skewers. Later, after games and craft were completed, I served a Route 66 cake made at Lubeley's Bakery and a mini Ted Drewes cup. Vary the menu by filling in with any restaurant that was on the path.

PHOTO OPPORTUNITY: As kids arrived, I had them pose individually in front of the tepee. I sent the photo home with the thank you note.

GAME AND CRAFT IDEAS: Keep the crafts and games in order by state and stick to your agenda as the guests make their way to the finish line in California. I had a separate craft table at the other end of the room to keep the dining table for food and drink only and games in the center. I also did a few crafts at one time so the kids wouldn't have to keep rotating then did a few games in a row. For each activity, announce the name and explain the significance.

ILLINOIS: Make a neon sign for your mom and pop business. (Explain that the small businesses needed to attract customers from the road so they used colorful and oversized signs to get them in their door.) Use Magic Color Scratch postcards from www.handsonfun. com. To help, I gave the kids western stencils and they came up with great ideas. Game-We played Cozy Dogs vs. Muffler Man. (Explain that the corn dog was invented in Springfield, Illinois on 66 and was actually called the Cozy Dog. Muffler Men were huge fiberglass sculptures, which also helped attract business or draw attention.) I bought the stuffed Cozy Dog couple from Bob Waldmire and used a large Rescue Hero for the Muffler Man. The kids were divided into two teams, one with the Muffler

Man and the other with the Cozy Dogs. They had to pass them to the end of the line and back in a variety of ways including through their legs and over their shoulder. Trade items and do again.

MISSOURI: Make a bumper sticker. (Explain how Meramec Caverns invented the bumper sticker and placed it on all visitors' cars. Originally they tied them on to the bumpers then they stuck them on.) You can pass out some famous Route 66 attractions such as the Blue Whale, Meteor Crater, the Devil's Rope Museum, etc. and have them come up with something to fit the place or if they are too young, just let them make up their own place. Some asked to use the western stencils again. I gave them peel off magnets for them to attach to the back. Game-Village of Marlborough Speed Trap Relay Race. (Explain that some small towns along Route 66 depended heavily on the revenue they earned from speeders and how some places gave tickets for even minor infractions.) You can use a variety of vehicles if you have more space. I was severely limited so I could not use Power Wheels vehicles. I used a Little Tikes Cozy Coupe for the speeders and a Little Tikes Police Car. The kids were too big to fit in them so they had to push them to the end spot and turn around then the next team member took over. The police officer also had to wear a police helmet. After they completed one round, they switched teams.

KANSAS: Decorate a Route 66 road sign. (Explain that in the early days of the highway, the roads were rough, directional signs were few and far between, and maps were in early stages. Mapquest, GPS and even AAA Trip-Tiks came way later. Road signs today use reflective paint but at one time signs were hard to see. To help visibility, glass was added to some road signs.) Blow up and photocopy a Route 66 road sign on cardstock. (We did Missouri but you can use Kansas or any of the eight states). Attach a large craft stick to the back with glue or glue dots. Buy shiny flat beads and have them glue these around the sign. Game: We played Drive Down Main Street (Red Light, Green Light). (Explain that Route 66 crossed different types of terrain including large cities like Chicago and St. Louis, was the main street for some small towns, and also crossed the desert and mountains, ending near the Pacific Ocean.) The kids all lined up side by side and tried to be the first to reach me--they could only move forward at the green light command.

OKLAHOMA: Attraction: For Oklahoma, we stopped at the Will Rogers Memorial Museum. (Explain that Will Rogers was a beloved humorist who was more popular in his day than even the President. He grew up near Route

66 in Oklahoma. After he died in an airplane crash, the highway was named the Will Rogers Highway.) I let the kids sit on a (borrowed) saddle placed between two chairs. Surprisingly they all wanted to participate. I also passed around authentic cowboy and horse items such as a bit and bridle, real stirrups, etc. Many of the kids had never seen these before. Game: (Explain that Will Rogers was also an expert roper.) The kids got down on the ground and pretended to be cows. One person was Will Rogers who, with an authentic lasso, tried to rope the cows. Give all the kids a chance to be Will.

TEXAS: Game: (I explained that we were now getting to the Wild West.) We had a stick pony relay race around cones. You can have the kids hold a cowboy hat in one hand and the pony in the other. Keepsake: (Explain that there is a place in Texas called the Cadillac Ranch where old Cadillacs with fins are buried in a row.) Buy a plastic Cadillac and have all of the kids sign it for the birthday child.

NEW MEXICO: Quick Shop Game: We stopped at Tepee Curios. I purchased Route 66-related items at the dollar store such as western, transportation/travel, rubber snakes, dinosaurs, horse calendars and stickers, etc. then placed them all inside the tepee. The kids drew numbers for their turn in line. The child had 10 seconds to decide on something in the shop and come out or they would go away empty handed. The rest of the kids counted to 10 and were (unexpectedly) very strict about the time rule. It was a huge hit. Of course, they kept that item. Craft: We also did a Mexican tile rubbing (www.handsonfun.com).

ARIZONA: While at the craft table we decorated individual tepees (also from Oriental Trading). (Explain that Route 66 brought out creativity and fun and that one motel chain rented rooms in tepees. It is called Wigwam Village.) Game: Snake Pit Stop (Explain that there were many attractions on the road trying to compete for the tourists' dollars. Some were genuine and some were pure money grabs.) I got them all excited about stopping at a great snake pit attraction. (Get them pumped up.) When it was time to show them, I brought out a bunch of rubber snakes in various sizes. They booed but still took a snake home. Then I brought out a real snake--a pet snake owned by a teenage neighbor. She held it and let everyone touch it, showed them the skin it shed, etc. Their favorite part was when the snake accidentally crawled into her clothing and she had to get it out through her sleeve.

CALIFORNIA: We played one last game-Cross Sitgreaves Pass. (Explain that before getting to California, the last part of Arizona was a very difficult mountain pass that

was narrow, steep and had sharp hairpin turns.) Using a Little Tikes Race Mountain each child was given a race car. They lined up their car even with another racer then let their car go, hopefully arriving in California. They got to keep their race car.

In celebration of completing our journey, we had a Route 66 cake and Ted Drewes frozen custard. Everyone wore a Steak'n Shake paper cap as the birthday hat. (When I taught a Route 66 class at school, I gave each student a California orange when we completed our journey.) Depending on your party, you could also go Hollywood, hit the beach, or get stuck on an L.A. freeway, etc. The main idea is to also celebrate the completion of the Route 66 journey at the conclusion of the party.

There are many other activities you can substitute including tire relays, catch the (inflatable) tires, make a Native American craft or jewelry, create a Burma Shave ad, design a door hanger, make a hubcap rubbing, give an architecture lesson, etc.

MUSIC: As an additional activity, explain that the *Route 66* song by Bobby Troup was a huge hit with its jingle "Get your Kicks on Route 66." Have the guests come up with a different jingle, assuming that the highway had ended up being Route 60 (as the leaders had originally hoped for), such as "Your trip will be nifty if it's on Route 60." Then try to do Route 62, 64, and 68. This can be done as a group or teams. You can have everyone come up with songs that include Route 66 states or towns or you can even do this Encore-style where they have to sing part of the songs. Example: Amarillo by morning, standing on a corner in Winslow, Arizona, etc. You can add a round of songs with cars such as T-Birds, Cadillacs, etc. You can also do karaoke and vote for whose version of *Route 66* is the best. Don't forget about the *Cars* CD. It has two versions of *Route 66* (one by St. Louisan Chuck Berry and the other by John Mayer) and lots of other great songs.

MOVIE: If you have a sleepover or a party that goes into the evening, you can incorporate a drive-in movie experience, complete with outdoor screen and popcorn. (Explain that the drive-in is part of Route 66 because they were in the same era of increased mobility thanks to the automobile.) The *Cars* movie, with its setting in a bypassed Route 66 town, is an obvious choice here. Glow in the Dark necklaces could also be incorporated as wear your own neon or placed in the loot bag if you have a daytime party.

LOOT BAGS: I used bags from Donut Drive-In. To try to get the kids excited about Route 66, I collected brochures and gave everyone a Missouri and Illinois map. I also included an Airstream trailer soap, a western-themed tissue pack, a sample size Funks Grove maple sirup bottle, Abraham Lincoln penny chocolates, and a natural rock. I made a small book for each child with the story of Route 66 and some coloring pages. I made each child a personalized Route 66-shield shaped cookie. They also took home their crafts, race car, curio shop selection, and Big Texan boot. A local Valvoline Oil shop gave me some leftover *Cars* movie posters and each child got to take one home.

THE ROUTE 66 PARTY WAS A HUGE HIT!

The birthday boy who started me on my Route 66 journey

Route 66 Cake

Muffler Man vs. Cozy Dogs

Burrma Shave signs announce the party

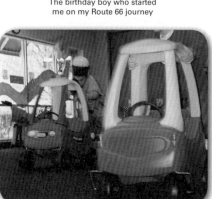

Village of Marlborough SpeedTrap Game

Big Brother as Steak 'n Shake server

Snake Pit Stop

Bumper Sticker Craft

Reflective Road Sign Craft

[Note: The detailed information in the following scavenger hunts is taken from the book, *Route 66 St. Louis: From the Bridges to the Diamonds*. The information is accurate as of the printing of this book but be prepared for changes as the road continues to constantly evolve.]

This is a short version that can be used for parties, church activities, school and scout activities, visitors to the area, etc. It can be done by couples, teams, parent and child groups or even an entire bus load of people. It can easily be incorporated into a Trivia Night. You can have a prize(s) or just do it for fun. You can add a requirement that participants take a photograph at certain spots to ensure there is no cheating. If you have more time you can add the second one (Times Beach to Twin Bridges) as well. Of course, feel free to make up your own! I used it as an educational/family-bonding opportunity and sent it with the invitation to my son's Route 66 birthday party. Think creatively and the opportunities are endless.

Start at 7th and Chouteau at the Eat-Rite Diner
1. What is the price of 6 Hamburgers? _____

Look across the street and see the Municipal Free Bridge later renamed the MacArthur Bridge. Look for the Nestlé Purina building.
2. How many red segments are in the Nestlé Purina Checkerboard sign on the tower building? _____

Drive down Chouteau to Tucker/12th Street. Make a left onto Tucker and take Tucker south until it becomes Gravois. You will be following Gravois to Chippewa to Watson Road.

Look for St. Michael's Orthodox Church on right.
3. What color are its domes? _____

Note the use of curves and glass block on many buildings. Other buildings will also have round porthole windows. Keep an eye out for these as you drive on.

Find St. Francis De Sales Church at corner of Gravois and Ohio. This church has the highest steeple in St. Louis.
4. Below the steeple there is a clock. Below it, how many window panels are there? _____

Find Hodak's Restaurant at 2100 Gravois on left side of road.
5. What color are its awnings? _____

Find Kutis Funeral Home located at Gravois and Nebraska.
6. What is located above the door that faces Gravois? _____

Find the car dealership at 3181 Gravois, on the site of once famous seafood restaurant Edmonds. (corner of Gravois and Compton)
7. What is the phone number painted on the building next door? _____

Find F. W. Clemens at 3357 Gravois at corner of Gravois and Cherokee. This is the oldest continually-operating business on St. Louis' Historic Route 66 that I could find, in operation since 1878. (Ralston Purina was founded in 1894.) F. W. Clemens used to sell feed.
8. What do they sell now? _____

Continue on Gravois. At Grand and Gravois, observe South Side National Bank. Follow the curve past the White Castle. (Don't turn right onto Grand.)

Find Gravois Auto Top and Seat Covers at 4017 Gravois. Note the cool sign. At one time there was neon across the roof and the arrow was animated.
9. What colors are in the sign? _____

Quick detour off Route 66. Instead of turning right at Chippewa, continue on Gravois passing Meramec and the long Missouri Pacific viaduct with pedestrian walkways. As you exit the tunnel, look for the windmill. This is the Bevo Mill Restaurant built in 1916 by August A. Busch Sr. to promote low alcohol and non-alcoholic beer.
10. What color is its bell-shaped base? _____

Return to Chippewa/Route 66

At the SE corner of Morganford and Chippewa, 4298 Chippewa, was the 2nd oldest Steak 'n Shake in St. Louis, opening in January 1949.

Find Keller Apothecary at 5201 Chippewa since 1933. (corner of Brannon and Chippewa)
11. Where the 2 corners of the building meet and above the door, there is something round and shiny sticking out of the building. What color is it? _____

12. The Famous Bar, on Route 66 since the 1930s, is just west of Keller Apothecary. Describe its awning. _____

Find Walter Knoll Florist's former site at 5501 Chippewa (corner of Chippewa and Regal Place). The Knolls are the oldest rose growers west of the Mississippi, in business since before 1883. They were at this building from 1949 until 2008.

Look back to the east and see a building standing high above the rest. This is the psychiatric hospital formerly called State Hospital. It is on the Hill, at the highest point of the city of St. Louis.

Find 5805 Chippewa. Now Tekwani Vision Center, it was once The Ranch House.
13. The building is what color with what color shutters? _____
_____

See Hampton Village on left, one of the oldest shopping centers in St. Louis, partially built in 1939 by Harold Brinkop. It started off as 20 stalls leased to merchants and farmers and Bettendorf's, one of the city's first supermarkets, was on site by 1941.

Continue on Chippewa to Donut Drive-In at 6525 Chippewa.
14. Counting one side of the sign, how many doughnuts are on the sign? _____

Historically, the old Watson Road came south from Hampton, went by today's Pietro's, then continued past today's Donut Drive-In as Watson Road, maintaining that name past the River Des Peres, through Shrewsbury, Marlborough, Webster Groves, Crestwood, and Sunset Hills. In 1950, the small section of the old Watson Road from the Donut Drive-In to the city limits was renamed Chippewa.

Find Garavelli's at 6600 Chippewa. This has been various restaurants including the Club Shangri-la, Parente's Italian Village, Saro's Sunny Italy, Hagiparis' then Garavelli's.
15. What's their phone number according to the sign? _____
_____

The Starbuck's was the site of the very first Steak 'n Shake in St. Louis, opening in December 1948.

Just before you get to Ted Drewes, on the right at Chippewa and Plainview, was one of 3 Route 66 locations of the famous Parkmoor restaurants. (currently Eagle Bank)

Find Ted Drewes Frozen Custard at 6726 Chippewa. Family business since 1929 and at this location since 1941.
16. What hangs from the roofline? _____

Cross over River Des Peres. Observe the Laclede Gas gasometer in the background. On the right is Rosebrough Monuments, in business since 1845 and at this location since the 1960s. Hi-Land Miniature Golf was just behind it.

Detour off Route 66. Get in the left turn lane and make a left onto McKenzie (strip mall and fast food restaurants on right)

Follow McKenzie south down to Weber Road. Make a right on Weber Road to Mesnier School at 6930 Weber Road. Take a photo with the Velvet Freeze cone.

17. How many scoops and what colors are they? _____
_____

Get back on Weber Road turning right as you come out of school. Cross over McKenzie to Gravois Road. Make a left on Gravois heading east and find Phil's Bar B Que at 9205 Gravois (north side of street)
18. The famous neon sign was recently destroyed due to a car accident. What replaced it? _____

Continue east on Gravois and find Federhofer's Bakery at 9005 Gravois.
19. How many candles are on the cake? _____

Continue to 8411 Gravois Road to the Wonder Bread Thrift Store, formerly a Chuck-A-Burger. Note that this stretch of Gravois Road was the first paved road in the entire state of Missouri, paid half by the State and half by August Busch. Get back on Gravois heading west and turn right at McKenzie. Notice the old Dairy Queen at the corner. Right on McKenzie to Chippewa. Just before Chippewa/ Watson Road make a left in the last entrance for Resurrection Cemetery and follow the road around to Section 11. Look for the pedestrian tunnel (now sealed) that once went under Highway 66. **End of Detour.**

Make a left on Chippewa/Watson Road and back on Route 66.
20. Go under the train tracks. What does the train trestle say?
_____

Immediately after crossing, look to your right. This is the area where people slept to escape the city heat.

This area was remote when Route 66 started. It filled in to have many mom and pop motels and restaurants. Most were razed for retail developments or new restaurants.

Pass Rothman Furniture (once Spartan Department store). Look left for Provider Plus, which was the site of the Crystal Court owned by the Rischbieter's. Rischbieter's car repair shop (since 1941) also had gas pumps at one time.

Coral Court Motel, famous for its architecture and as a place for lovers, was on the right immediately after Rothman's.
21. It is now _____subdivision.

Directly across the street is the Wayside Motel, one of 4 remaining motels in this stretch built in the 1930s/early 1940s for Route 66. The carports used to have garage doors but these were removed. Otherwise, the motel looks very similar to its original likeness.
22. What color are its doors?_____

Find the Chippewa Motel and the Duplex Motel, two of the oldest motels in this strip. This area has several long-running Route 66 businesses including Sunset Lanes Bowling Center, Wolfsburg Automotive, Happy Joe's and Lubeley's Bakery. The buildings for Cruisin' Route 66 (once Johnny Garavaglia's), and Watson Bar and

Grill (once part of Marty's Watermelon Stand) are just a couple of the buildings in Marlborough with roots to the Route 66 era. Tower Tee Golf is just behind the south part of 66, extending from the train trestle to Laclede Station Road.

Continue past Laclede Station Road. At the long light, observe Yorkshire Village, an early shopping center built by Adrian Koch, and the Quik Trip and General Grant apartments, once the site of the Rest-Wel Motel. The Missouri Motel was just to the west. [Note: The area on the left from here to Elm/Rock Hill and extending south to Gravois was once all owned by Ulysses S. Grant.]

Find 8208 Watson Road (near Edgar Road). This was the La Casa Grande Motel, which once had a beautiful red neon sign that read "La Casa Grande Like A Fine Hotel." A neon clock was over the office door.
23. The old motel recently got a fresh coat of paint. What color is it today? _____

Find the Sappington Farmer's Market (originally Rapp's) and take a photo with Farmer Fred and his son Clyde.

At the west end of the shopping center, look for 8500 Watson Road-Fishin' Hole/Tracker Boat Center. The old entrance wall to the Cordia Court/later Motel U.S. Grant still remains.

At the corner of Elm and Watson Road, the Walgreens was Gus Keehn's Market and later Katz Drug. The Steak 'n Shake was originally a Howard Johnson's. Elicia's Pizza was the Catalina gas station with the Catalina Motel to the east, followed by the Alma Motel at 8544 (currently a vacant Taco Bell building).

Find the Watson Auto Plaza and Malone's, once the 66 Auto Court site. The apartment complex across the street, currently Webster Pines, was once the Evergreen Motel.

Find Sappington Cemetery at 9121. Look for the Daughters of the American Revolution marker.
24. Soldiers buried in this cemetery fought in how many different wars? _____

Next, observe the shopping center where the Aldi's is. This entire area was the Motel Royal at 9282 Highway 66. The Oaks Motel (approximately the Montgomery Bank area) and Kennedy's Happy Landing (Firestone store now) were across Highway 66.

Look for the Schnucks Shopping Center. This was once the site of the 66 Park-In Theatre. Look for local pizza chain, Imo's where you can get pizza made with Provel cheese and cut into squares. (This was originally Tobey's and later a Steak 'n Shake Jr.) The Barnes and Noble Bookstore just west was the site of the last trailer park in Crestwood.

Pass Crestwood Mall, once the only shopping mall in the area. President John F. Kennedy campaigned here in 1960. The mall is currently being redeveloped.

25. What is at the northwest corner of Sappington and Watson Road? _____
[This was originally the Korn home and a very early Phillips 66 gas station. Later, the Crestwood Bank Building was on the site and then a small shopping center came in behind the Wuellner Gulf Station that included a Schnucks, Flaming Pit and Crestwood Shoe Repair.]

Find Walnut Park Auto Body. This place was on Route 66 starting in 1947. Look across the road for the cupola above the Watson Plaza Shopping Center. It was once on the Colonial Hotel. Jack in the Box was the site of the Bel-Air Motel and the Bally's (east of Walnut Park Auto Body) was the site of the Lone Star Motel.

26. Find the Crestwood Bowl. Describe its neon sign._____
_____

Find the medical buildings at 10000 Watson Road, once the Blue Haven Motel site. Look for Rich & Charlie's, once Krabbe's Grill and later il Vesuvio. Look across the street to Truman Bank for the site of one of Roland Sander's gas stations.

Observe the McDonald's site, the first McDonald's in Missouri and the KFC site, once the site of the Highway 66 Chuck-A-Burger. Find Johnny Mac's, originally the Blue Bonnet Motel site and then Jim Keehn's dealership.

Find the restaurant building that was most recently the Que Pasa Cantina. This was once the Vi-Don Motel site. Find Bank of America, once the Twin Six Motel site. Don De Foe's Flowers has been a long-term tenant in the shopping center just to the east of the old Twin Six. Don helped me reconstruct this end of Watson Road.

Look for the Rain Tunnel car wash at 10215. This was the site of another one of Roland Sander's gas stations.

Continue to the junction of Watson Road and Lindbergh Blvd. This is where the Bypass and Historic 66 routes joined at the cloverleaf bridge. The Westward Motel was where the Hampton Inn is today. The northwest corner was once the Park Plaza Motel with the adjoining Nelson's Café.
27. What is there today? _____
_____

28. Bonus: Find Emmenegger Park by taking Geyer Road to Powder Valley then continue west over 270 and left into the park. Look for the steps that once led from the Sylvan Beach Restaurant down to the pool area and the Meramec River. How many steps? _____

You have completed the Route 66 St. Louis Drive-By Scavenger Hunt. Congratulations on your new Route 66 knowledge. Tell others and preserve what remains!

Start at the Route 66 State Park in Eureka, formerly Times Beach. (Take I-44 to the 266 exit)

1. Inside the Visitor Center, there is a fireplace. What is it made of/ what color is it? _____

2. Find the Sylvan Beach Restaurant sign. What color is the neon? _____

3. Explore the park site. Look for the mound where the buildings and the Times Beach water tower are buried. What is the closest intersection/roads? _____

Go to the south end of the park where the boat launch is located. This area was where the Times Beach swimming hole was located. Look across the river to the top of the bluff for where the Famous-Barr Outing Ranch was located.

Get on I-44 west and take the 109 exit. Turn right into the shopping center and follow the road around past Byerly's RV. When you get to the barricades, observe this area. In front of you, in between the railroad tracks, was the Rock City complex consisting of 2 motels, 2 gas stations, 2 restaurants and 2 taverns. There was even an ice cream shop.

Continue west down Fifth Street. This area before Central had the bulk of Eureka's Route 66 businesses including the White Squirrel, Radforth's Café, Gerwe's Log House Café/ Bob Klinger's Shell Station, Smoke Gudermuth's station, and Gudermuth family property.
4. The two-story Brown Mug/Dr. Beckmeyer building (NE corner) still stands. What is its current status/business? _____ _____

5. After Central, there is a Quonset hut that was originally Howald's Feed Store. What is there today and what color is the building? _____

6. Look for the Dairy Queen. There is a home next to it. What is the street address for it? _____ _____

This was Earl Cahoon's home. He was an early (possibly original) owner of the Times Beach Café. The Double Diamond Tourist Camp and Phillips 66 station (owned by Cahoon) were directly across his home on Highway 66. Wetzel's Café was just west of the Dairy Queen on the south side of Highway 66. All three sites are now I-44.

Continue past Six Flags.

7. Stop at the Holiday Inn Six Flags. Make your way to the Haymarket Restaurant to see the historic barn and exhibits on how the Eckelkamp family preserved the barn. Go to the rear of the property to see other ruins. What else remains from the old site? _____

Head south on Six Flags Road/Allenton Road. Note: Devine's Tavern (by Long Ford) and the Sites Café were to the left/east. The CCC Bus Stop was straight ahead on SE Corner. Turn right.

8. Find the KOA campground, once the Allen family home and later Peck's motel and pool. What train component is on the premises? _____

Pass one of John Darling's gas stations, now Platinum Motors at 18505.

9. Make your way to what remains of the Al-Pac Motel. (It is to the right of the metal Darrah Contracting building.) There is an old building out back that was once owned by Fred and Jean Miller. What color is its door? _____

Look for Hyndrich Bros. Towing at 18593 Highway 66, immediately west of Darrah Contracting. This was the site of the Beacon Motel. Some cabins remain in the rear and the office unit is near the highway.

10. The building at 18601 was Sifford Auto Repair. What color is the striping? _____

Pass Select Motors and the prison.

Proceed to the Red Cedar Inn.
11. What does the sign say above the marquee section? _____ _____

12. If you make it to the top of Jensen Point (wear tick repellent!), look for some interesting openings in the limestone. What do you think they were for in light of the late 1930s date of construction? _____ _____

Pass the silica mines to the Beacon Car Wash. The Beacon motel sign was rescued and relocated here.
13. Describe the Beacon sign. _____ _____

14. The white building (at 611) with teal and pink striping was once a Zephyr station. How many garage doors does it have? _____

15. Look for 428 E. Osage. This was once Whitlock's Sinclair and later Jerry and Edith Miller's sandwich shop. What do you notice about the front door? _____

16. The Quonset hut (originally Miller's Laundromat) is currently _____

17. Find 422 E. Osage. This was Jerry and Edith Miller's home on Route 66 for the duration. What color is it and what color is the roof? _____

18. Find Bud's Market and Big G Tire. This was originally the Cities Service Station. What color is the mansard roof? _____

19. Find Frank Brocato's old home at 66 and North Olive. Is there a chimney? _____

20. Look for the Bay's complex. What color is the trim that stands out? _____

21. Find the Buzzard's Roost, the oldest building in Pacific, east of and across from Sand Mountain. What direction does the house face? _____

Bonus: Find and photograph the Henry Shaw Gardenway sign at Blackburn Park.

22. Find the former Cave Café at Third and West Osage. (rock building at 302/304) What businesses are there today? _____

Look for the dental office at Fifth and Osage for the site of Parrett's Restaurant. Proceed down the road to the Chinese restaurant that was once Baker's gas station. Next door, the A-frame building was the Frost Top Custard Shop. Look for the McDonald's, Taco Bell area. This was the Cottrell family businesses. Look for the Movie Gallery. This was once the Cleveland's Market site.

23. Find the Alan Pritchett Tavern, which became Pemberton's. (white building at 1806) How many front doors does the building have? _____

Next, look for the KFC and the area just west of it. This was Pardon's restaurant and later Lazy Larry's. Find the Mobil station across the road. This was the approximate site of the OK Motel.

24. Find the Pacific Bowling Center at 2009 W. Osage. What is painted on the east wall? _____

Look for LaMar Parkway. At the southwest corner was the Lone Pine Motel.

25. Locate Engelhart Road. Immediately west is the Engelhart farm. What old structure do you see? _____

Look for the JB Industrial building at 2960. This was once part of the Butler's Grill tavern and behind it was the family home. Find 3132 W. Osage. This building was George's Apple Orchard. Across the highway, 3133 was once Bob Church's filling station.

26. East of the Car Quest and Today's Country Garden there are some white buildings with green roofs. This was the Normandy Motel. What color are the shutters? _____

On the north side and just west was the Crest restaurant site, currently a vacant building owned by M & M Auto Sales.

27. Find the building at 3220 W. Osage. This was the first location for the Mule Trading Post. What color is the building? _____

28. Look for the dying Trail's End Motel. How many cars are parked out front? _____ Which letter(s) is missing from the MOTEL sign? _____

29. Find Opal's Tavern at 3257 W. Osage. What color is the trim on this building currently? _____

Look for the storage sheds that were once the OK Motel. (south side of the road just east of M & M Auto Sales) Proceed to Highway 100 where the Original route crossed here in Gray Summit near the Shaw Nature Reserve. Observe the area. This is where the Mabel Miles home and Miles Modern Motel were as well as the Weight Station. The new Diamonds was located where the commuter parking lot is today, east of the Diamond Inn Motel.

30. Find Robertsville Road. Look for the apartment building at 2928 that once had the Gardenway sign on top of it. How many windows are on the side facing east? _____

31. Find the Mabel Miles home just behind on Robertsville Road. How many windows are on the front part of this 2-story white building? _____

32. The Gardenway Motel is next. Are all of the letters on the roof intact? _____

Find Brush Creek Cemetery where Spencer and Ursula Groff are buried. Just east of the cemetery is the 33 Mile Post building and a few outbuildings.

33. Find the Wayside Farmer's Market. (There for the duration and still going strong!) What kind of gas is being sold and what's the current price of regular unleaded? _____

34. The building next door was the Mingle Inn. How many dormers does this building have in front? _____

35. Find the old (second/brick) Diamonds building. What remains of the name on the rooftop? _____

Optional stretch past the Diamonds to the Twin Bridges

36. Find the Sunset Motel sign. How many rays project from the sun? _____

37. Find 600 Highway AT, once the American Inn. What is the current status/business? _____

38. Find the old Zephyr station, once a thriving business on this stretch. How many wing-like lights does it have? _____ _____

Find the Pin Oak Creek RV Park and Hill Top Road. The Hill Top Grill and gas station with its huge Stop Save sign was located just before Hill Top Road on Highway 66. Just before Highway O and the Twin Bridges, the existing building on the right was George's Tavern and Bait Shop. Look across the road for Key's.

39. Noble and Edna Key, who got their start at the Diamonds, went out on their own and opened Key's Twin Bridge Café. It also had a gas station. Which end was the gas station building? _____

40. Are there still Twin Bridges over the Bourbeuse River? __ _____

You have completed the Route 66 Times Beach to Villa Ridge Drive-By Scavenger Hunt. Congratulations on your new Route 66 knowledge. Tell others and preserve what remains!

Photo Credits

Unless otherwise indicated, all modern photos are taken by the author who owns the copyright. All postcards and ads are from the author's collection unless otherwise indicated. Menus are from the 1976 *Gateway Gourmet* book, courtesy Russell Kruetzman, unless otherwise indicated. Matchcovers are largely from the collection of George S. Lux and the late Gene Kitson and those from author's collection are not distinguished. Vintage photographs are from many sources and are credited here to the extent possible.

Front Cover: all modern photos by author unless they also appear in the book and are separately credited below. (Note: Some front cover images were lost in the design process but appear on the website.)Photos by or from others that appear only on the cover: photo of Missouri Route 66 Chevy (also on downtown divider and back cover) © Joe Sonderman, courtesy Joe Sonderman; Big Chief billboard courtesy Wildwood Historical Society; plane pulling Spencer's Grill banner photo by Francis Scheidegger, courtesy Kirkwood Historical Society archives; Galley West photo, Lazy Larry fan, Steiny's Inn postcard and Times Beach Water Tower photo courtesy Route 66 State Park Museum/Missouri Dept. of Natural Resources; Checkerboard Square sign courtesy Nestlé Purina PetCare Company; Butler's Grill courtesy Ron Butler; Danny Donuts courtesy city of Crestwood; Keller Drugs sign courtesy Keller Apothecary; 66 Park-In Theatre photo courtesy Mike Keehn; Croft Cowboy muffler man © and courtesy Patricia Fitzgerald; AAA landmark thermometer courtesy AAA Missouri; George's Apple Orchard photo courtesy Janet and Jim Daniel; Photo of St. Louis statue © and courtesy Patricia Fitzgerald; and Forest Park Highlands poster courtesy St. Louis County Parks Department. Other images are cropped from ads and matchcovers.

Title Page: Wetzel's Café photo courtesy Joy Drewel.

Foreword: photo of Johnny Rabbitt © Suzy Gorman, courtesy Ron Elz.

Introduction: Greetings from St. Louis postcard, author's colletion, courtesy Curt Teich Archives.

Downtown Divider: Greetings from St. Louis postcard, author's collection, courtesy Curt Teich Archives; aerial view of downtown courtesy Museum of Transportation; and Ralston Purina Complex courtesy Nestlé Purina PetCare Company.

Original Alignment Divider: Motor Inn postcard courtesy Meramec Valley Historical Society.

Gaslight Square: Three Fountains postcard, author's collection © and courtesy Art Grossmann.

Blueberry Hill: Chuck Berry photo © and courtesy Patricia Fitzgerald.

Engelhard's: 1937 greeting card courtesy Brentwood Historical Society.

Buckingham's: author's collection, courtesy Curt Teich Archives.

Big Chief: menu courtesy Wildwood Historical Society.

Purina Farm: Ads courtesy Nestlé Purina PetCare.

Historic Route 66 to 270 Divider: Bauer's Ranch House postcard courtesy Joe Sonderman collection; Marty's Watermelon Stand photo courtesy Mike Keehn; 66 Park-In photo courtesy Wehrenberg Theatres; Cloverleaf Bridge photo courtesy Missouri State Archives.

Bevo Mill: postcard author's collection, courtesy Curt Teich Archives.

Southtown Famous-Barr: photo courtesy Museum of Transportation.

Garavelli's: vintage menu author's collection.

Ted Drewes: vintage building photo courtesy Ted Drewes.

Shop 'n Save: Hi-Land Golf Big Boy © and courtesy Shellee Graham.

Original McDonald's: photo courtesy city of Crestwood.

Chuck-A-Burger on 66: courtesy Stille family.

Rich & Charlie's: Krabbe's Grill courtesy Krabbe family; il Vesuvio courtesy city of Crestwood.

Chain of Rocks City 66 "Connector" Divider: Fun Fair Park aerial promo card and Swooper photo courtesy Greg Thone.

Vess Soda: Santa promo courtesy Don Schneeberger; restored Vess rotating bottle courtesy Jackie Treesh.

Brooks Tangy Catsup: Vintage water tower photo courtesy www.catsupbottle.com.

Chain of Rocks Path Around St. Louis/Bypass Route Divider: Airway Drive-In courtesy Wehrenberg Theatres; Chuck-A-Burger at St. Charles Rock Road courtesy Stille family; Downtown Kirkwood courtesy Kirkwood Historical Society.

Yacovelli's: Café photo courtesy John and Jan Yacovelli.

Sunset 44: photo © and courtesy Evelyn Maurath Clapp.

Spencer's Grill: building photo courtesy Irene Spencer and menu from Kirkwood Historical Society archives.

Green Parrot Inn: photo courtesy Toothman family.

Continuation of Historic Route Divider: Valley Mount Ranch courtesy Kraus family; Lone Elk Park photo © and courtesy Patricia Fitzgerald; Times Beach flood photo courtesy St. Louis County Police Dept.; Devine's Tavern courtesy Eureka Historical Society and Meramec Valley Historical Society; Cave Café, the Crest, Farmer's Wayside Market, old Diamonds, and American Inn postcards all courtesy Meramec Valley Historical Society.

Fenton, Times Beach, Rock City and Eureka: Bridgehead Inn courtesy Route 66 State Park/Missouri Dept. of Natural Resources; Chicken Coop photo courtesy Betty Campbell Cunningham/Route 66 State Park Museum/Missouri Dept. of Natural Resources; Kessler's courtesy Marlene Hedrick and Meramec Station Historical Society; Times Beach Café courtesy Bob and Linda Kovis; Sylvan Beach Restaurant courtesy Frank and Vivian Sagehorn; Steiny's Inn menu courtesy Eureka Historical Society; Lou Gerwe's Log House Café, Deke Keeton's Rock City, and Wetzel's Café all courtesy Joy Drewel; Al-Pac postcard courtesy Joe Sonderman collection; Ed LaMar at Ozark Café courtesy Bud LaMar.

White Squirrel: photo courtesy Joy Drewel.

Sites Café: courtesy Donald Poertner and Barbara Johnson.

Haymarket: courtesy Eureka Historical Society.

Red Cedar Inn: Red Cedar Tavern photo courtesy Ginger Smith Gallagher.

Henry Shaw Gardenway, Jensen Point, and Shaw Nature Reserve: Jensen Point postcard courtesy Meramec Valley Historical Society.

Parrett's: photo courtesy Mike and Fay Parrett.

The Diamonds: Diamonds photos courtesy Meramec Valley Historical Society.

Additional St. Louis Institutions Divider: Busch's Grove photos courtesy St. Louis County Parks and Recreation; Wright City Big Boy's postcard author's collection, © and courtesy Art Grossmann; Noah's Ark postcard author's collection, © and courtesy Art Grossmann.

Definitely Worth Driving to in Missouri Divider: Zeno's photo courtesy Michael and Tracy Sheffer; Alberta Ellis' Hotel photo courtesy Ora Logan; Bradbury-Bishop Deli courtesy Bruce and Peggy Richardson.

Scavenger Hunt #2: Hill Top Grill photo courtesy Meramec Valley Historical Society.

Back Cover: Times Beach Café sign courtesy Bob and Linda Kovis; Green Parrot Inn postcard from author's collection, courtesy Curt Teich Archives.

Selected Bibliography

Anheuser-Busch. *Great Food, Great Beer: The Anheuser-Busch Cookbook,*
   Sunset, 2007.
Assistance League of St. Louis. *Fare to Remember,* 1988.
Clark, Marian. *The Route 66 Cookbook,* Tulsa: Council Oak Books, 1993.
De Smet Jesuit High School Mother's Club. *Pierre's Secrets,*
   St. Louis: 1980.
Haughton, Natalie Hartanov. *Cookies,* Tulsa: HP Books, Inc., 1983.
Hidalgo County Historical Society. *Mesquite Country, Tastes and Traditions
   from the Tip of Texas,* Memphis: Wimmer Companies, 1996.
Hines, Duncan. *Adventures in Good Eating,* Bowling Green, 1952.
Ingle, Paul. "End of the Road," *Illinois Times,* September 25, 2003.
Junior League of St. Louis. *St. Louis Days, St. Louis Nights,*
   St. Louis: 1994-95.
McGinley, Lou Ellen. *Honk For Service,* Tray Days Publishing, 2004.
Meramec Valley Senior Citizens. *Favorite Recipes of Meramec Valley Senior
   Citizens,* Eureka, Missouri: undated.
Missouri Botanical Garden Historical Committee and Women's Association.
*The Shaw House Cookbook, A Collection of Choice Receipts from
   a Golden Era of St. Louis Living,* St. Louis: 1963.
Miss Hulling's. *Miss Hullling's Own Cook Book,* St. Louis: 1962.
Miss Hulling's. *Miss Hulling's Favorite Recipes,* St. Louis: 1969.
Miss Hulling's. *Miss Hulling's 50th 1928-1978 Anniversary Cookbook,*
   St. Louis: 1978.
Ostmann, Barbara Gibbs and Jane Baker, eds. *Food Editors' Hometown
   Favorites Cookbook,* Maplewood, New Jersey: Hammond, Incorporated, 1984.
Pet, Inc. *A Celebration of Cooking In America, Timeless Recipes From the
   Kitchens of Pet,* Elmsford, New York: The Benjamin Company, 1984.
Pope's Cafeterias. *No Experience Necessary: Original Recipes From the Pope's
   Cafeterias in St. Louis,* St. Louis: 1979.
Repertory Theatre of St. Louis Backers. *Cooking For Applause,* St. Louis: 1981.
Salvation Army Women's Auxiliary of St. Louis. *"Clowning Around"
   with Cookery* St. Louis: Western Printing and Lithograph Company 1965.
Sappington House Foundation. *A Book of Favorite Recipes,* Circulation
   Services, Inc. 1968-69.
St. Anthony's Medical Center. *St. Anthony's Cooks,* Lenexa, Kansas:
   Cookbook Publishers, Inc., 2001.
St. Louis Art Museum. *The Artist in the Kitchen,* St. Louis: Garlich
   Printing Co., 1977.
St. Louis Globe-Democrat, St. Louis, Missouri.
St. Louis Post-Dispatch, St. Louis, Missouri. Feature Stories, Special Request
   column and Recipe Exchange column.
St. Louis Symphony Women's Association. *Symphony of Cooking,* St. Louis:
   Western Printing and Lithograph Company, 1954.
St. Louis Symphony Women's Association. *The New Saint Louis Symphony
   of Cooking Bicentennial Issue,* St. Louis: Western Printing and Lithograph
   Company, 1964.
St. Louis University High School. *Billiken Gourmet,* St. Louis: 1976.

Additional Resources

www.explorestlouis.com

www.visitmo.com

www.familyattractionscard.com

Route 66 Associations with many additional links

www.missouri66.org (Missouri)

www.ilassoc.org (Illinois)

www.carrollsweb.com (Kansas)

www.oklahomaroute66.com (Oklahoma)

www.barbwiremuseum.com (Texas)

www.rt66nm.org (New Mexico)

www.azrt66.com (Arizona)

www.route66ca.org (California)

www.national66.com (national preservation group)

www.route66magazine.com (magazine covering all 8 states)

www.legendsofamerica.com (detailed travel site)

www.66postcards.com (Joe Sonderman's vast collection)

www.kidson66.com (free Route 66 coloring pages)

www.homeschooling.about.com (free printable Route 66 activity sheets)

www.orientaltrading.com (inexpensive novelties and crafts)

www.handsonfun.com (craft items)

About the Author

Norma Maret Bolin grew up in McAllen, Texas. After graduating from McAllen High School, she moved to Houston where she received her undergraduate degree in Hotel and Restaurant Management from the University of Houston's Hilton School of Hotel and Restaurant Management. In the hospitality industry, she served as a food and beverage manager and specialized in event planning. In 1986, she moved to St. Louis. Completely unaware of Route 66 and its routing in the St. Louis area, she worked briefly at the Breckenridge Frontenac on the former Bypass route and worked as a health inspector for the City of Crestwood where she inspected all of the Crestwood restaurants, most on the former Route 66. Norma left the food service industry for the legal and corporate world, graduating from St. Louis University School of Law in 1992. More recently in 2006, Norma took her son to see the *Cars* movie. Her son's interest in Route 66 led to her own discovery of Route 66 and, in turn, her in-depth research of Route 66 in the St. Louis area. She lives with her family in Webster Groves, Missouri, just blocks from the Mother Road.

The Route 66 St. Louis Cookbook

The Mother Lode of Recipes
from the Mother Road

St. Louis Transitions • P.O. Box 191401 • St. Louis, Missouri 63119 • www.route66stlouis.com

Visit www.route66stlouis.com for a listing of Norma Bolin's personal appearances and signings and to order additional copies of the *Route 66 St. Louis Cookbook: The Mother Lode of Recipes from the Mother Road*. If you are in the United States and prefer to send payment through the mail, use the order form below. For international orders, please contact the website. You can also visit the website to get information on and to order the upcoming book, *Route 66 St. Louis: From the Bridges to the Diamonds*.

Please send me ___ books @ $19.95 _____

Missouri residents add $1.51 sales tax for each book _____

Add $5.00 for postage & handling for the 1st book _____

Additional books shipped to same address, add $3.00 _____

Additional books to different address, add $5.00 _____

Total _____

Make check or money order payable to: St. Louis Transitions

Ordered by: (please print)

Name _____

Address _____

City _____ State _____ Zip _____

Ship to: (if different address)

Name _____

Address _____

City _____ State _____ Zip _____